Drawing *the* Portrait

Step-by-Step Lessons

for Mastering Classic Techniques

for Beginners

Braden Messer

Drawing *the* Portrait

Step-by-Step Lessons for Mastering Classic Techniques for Beginners

Braden Messer

Editor: Kelly Reed
Project manager: Lisa Brazieal
Marketing coordinator: Katie Walker
Copyeditor: Linda Laflamme
Cover design: Aren Straiger
Composition: Anthony Paular Design
Cover Illustration: Braden Messer

ISBN: 979-8-88814-140-3
1st Edition (1st printing, June 2024)
© 2024 Braden Messer
All images © Braden Messer unless otherwise noted. Image on cover and throughout the book based on photograph by Ollyy/Shutterstock.com. Pages 22-23 images from first vector trend/Shutterstock.com. Image of man on page 33 and throughout from photo by Evilicio inc. Image of woman on page 33 bottom right and throughout from photo by Ben Iwara.

Rocky Nook Inc.
1010 B Street, Suite 350
San Rafael, CA 94901
USA

www.rockynook.com

Distributed in the UK and Europe by Publishers Group UK
Distributed in the U.S. and all other territories by Ingram Publisher Services

Library of Congress Control Number: 2023944083

This book is printed on acid-free paper.
Printed in China.

Drawing *the* Portrait

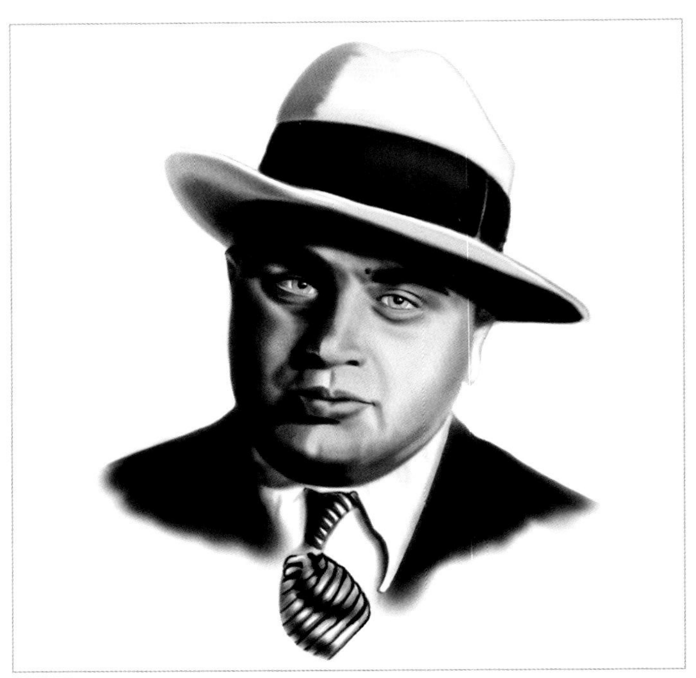

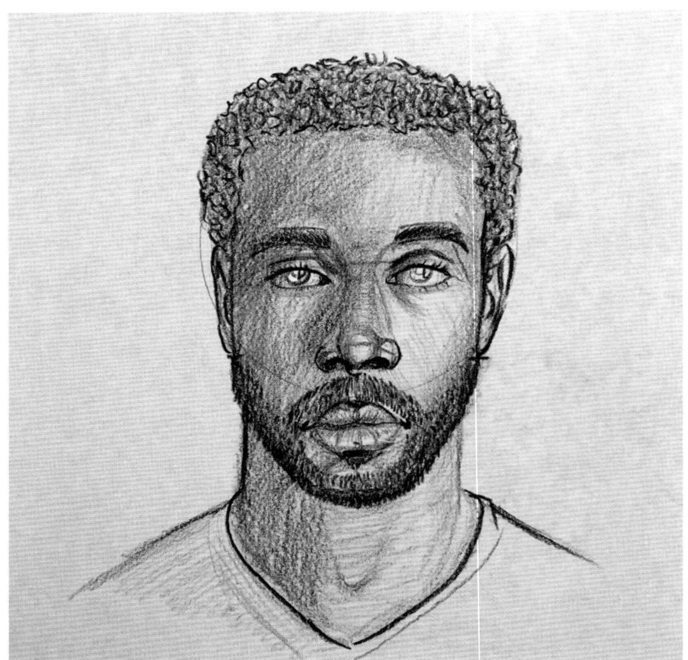

Examples of portraits by the author. Top image drawn digitally using Procreate, bottom image drawn by hand. The lessons in this book apply to all mediums of drawing.

TABLE OF CONTENTS

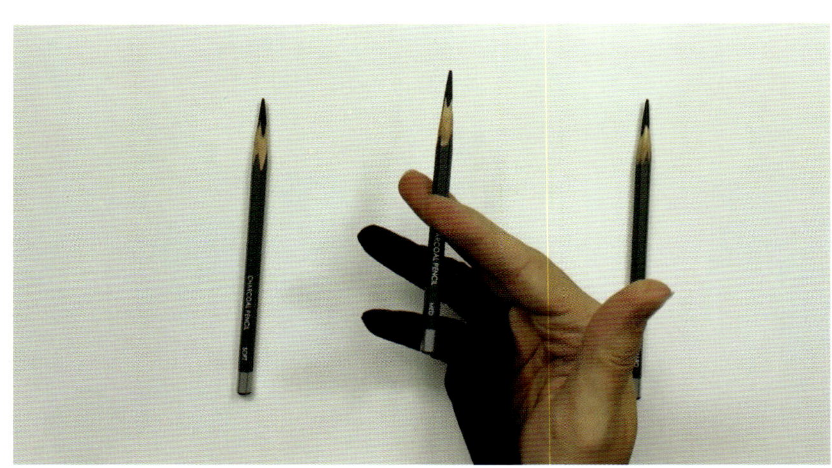

Orientation *and* Materials

"Creativity takes courage."
—*Henri Matisse*

Congratulations on making a sound investment in yourself. Drawing is something that is as innate to the human condition as breathing. We started communicating through "art" on cave walls thousands of years before the first recorded languages were written. One could say that we are all artists to some capacity. The only question is whether we want to manifest that power within ourselves.

You bought this book for a reason, and if I had to guess it's because you feel lost and are looking for guidance on how to draw a portrait accurately. This book has been meticulously constructed to guide you through the flow for drawing most portraits. Before we get too deep into that, I want to tell you a story about perfection and the creative process.

Perfection Is a Myth

Once there was an art class, and in this art class there were a lot of students. Some were more artistically inclined, while others struggled with creation. The professor walked into the class and said, "Okay listen up, today we are going to be covering the art of ceramics." He split the class right down the middle and explained, "All you on the left side of the room will be judged solely on the quality of your work, while the rest of you will be judged on the quantity."

Now here was the kicker: The side of the class that would be judged on quality could make *only one* pot. That pot had to be perfect; there could be no imperfections. The quantity side of the class had to make pot after pot—as many as they could possibly produce.

What do you think the professor received? When all was said and done, the students who made a quantity of pots ended up producing a more perfect pot than the students who made only one. The moral? We need to immerse ourselves in our art repeatedly to become better and closer to the ideal of perfection.

Keep this story with you on your journey through creating. When you grow frustrated, it will remind you that you are right where you need to be. Perfection is something to strive for but that, hopefully, you never actually achieve. Remember what Michelangelo said, "The greatest danger for most of us is not that our aim is too high and we miss it, but that it is too low and we reach it."

How to Use This Book

Drawing portraits is not an easy task, and it has a handful of unique challenges. To help you, this book is project based and each chapter covers a specific facet of the process. After you read a chapter's principles and techniques, you will have the opportunity to practice them with a project designed to increase your comprehension. Resist the urge to skip ahead. Taking the book in order—one chapter and one project at a time—will help you to fully understand the entire process from beginning to end. Each chapter flows into the next in a linear progression: Chapter 1 covers such basic techniques as how to properly wield your pencil when drawing, then Chapter 2 introduces some basic construction principles. From there, each chapter focuses on a single aspect of a portrait drawing—the eyes, the nose, the lips, hair, and so on— offering plenty of opportunities to practice techniques along the way. Chapter 10 ties together all you've learned throughout the book in three final portrait projects, allowing you to apply the new skills that you've developed.

Basic Drawing Concepts

Before we jump into the actual drawing, I want to make sure that you understand the fundamentals and some terms you'll encounter in the chapters ahead. Let's start with the most basic: Whenever you put pencil to paper what you end up with is a line.

What is a line?

A *line* is a moving dot. When you place your pencil on the paper the head creates a dot on the paper, and then by either pushing or pulling that dot across the paper you create a line.

What do you mean by "pushing" or "pulling?"

That's a great question, because they are two different techniques. When you *push* a line, you move the head of the pencil across the paper in a direction away from your hand. When you *pull* a line, you drag the head of the pencil behind your hand. Both techniques will give you the same desired result: a line. Depending on exactly what you are drawing and personal preference, however, you may want to use one technique over the other.

Drawings at their most basic are a massive conglomerate of all sorts of lines with varying pressure controls, qualities, and weights. Some lines are defined, others are implied, but no drawing could exist if it wasn't for contour lines.

What are contour lines?

Contour lines are lines that show you where an object ends. By themselves they convey an object's basic two-dimensional shape only. Whenever you begin to draw a portrait, you first will draw contour lines to get a sense of where the boundaries are. Once these are implemented, you can start to focus on the different line qualities throughout the drawing.

What are line qualities?

A line's *quality* is its thickness or thinness. By varying line quality you can start to bring out the illusion of three-dimensional form. Now varying a line's quality from, say, a super-thin quality to a thick quality also tends to influence the line's weight.

What are line weights?

A line's *weight* is the strength of the line. Think of it as how dark or light the line appears on paper. The darker the line, the heavier the weight; the lighter the line, the lighter the weight. There tends to be a correlation between a line's weight and its quality, but this is not always the case.

Now that you understand the basics of line definition in drawing, let's take it one step further and consider implied versus defined lines.

What are implied lines?

Implied lines are lines that are suggested by a change in color, tone, or texture or by the edges of shapes. If that definition slightly confuses you don't worry. Most of the time when drawing, you will convey implied lines by varying your values and showcasing them through contrast via the value scale. If you create a tonal break between the eye socket and the bridge of the nose, for example, the contrast between your high and low values will bring out an implied line.

What are defined lines?

Defined lines are continued without any break. Typically, they will have a mid to heavy line weight. Defined lines are the opposite of implied, because they are lines that have a constant quality and weight of some kind throughout their span.

As you progress through this book, you will see these two line types pop up repeatedly, so it is very important that you know and understand each of these definitions in their entirety. As I mentioned previously, a drawing is simply a conglomerate of all sorts of lines that suggest shape and form.

What is shape in drawing?

At its most basic, *shape* is the outside edge of a drawing. The shape of your portrait will be conveyed via your contour lines. It is important to remember that shape has very little to do with the form of your drawing. A drawing's shape is two dimensional and so has no volume or form. It is not until you introduce shading to your shape that you start to bring out different values and, subsequently, volume. The more values you have in a drawing the more dimension you will convey. More dimension is tied closely to accentuating the value scale to its fullest potential. This will help you transform your drawing from a basic shape to a shape that has form.

What is form in drawing?

Form is an element of art that is three dimensional and enclosed. Form has volume that includes height, width, and depth (as in a cube, a sphere, a pyramid, or a cylinder). Form may also be free flowing. Fundamentally, varying your values throughout an artwork will convey form. The more you accentuate the value scale as you draw your portrait, the more volume you will convey and the more realistic it will become.

What is the value scale?

In essence, the *value scale* is a gradual gradation effect between complete white and complete black. The tones that are in between these two opposites vary in lightness as you trend higher towards white and become darker as you trend lower towards black. The principle of the value scale is also present when you move beyond the monochromatic scale into color, as long as you vary your pressure control. If you press harder on the paper while you draw with a red pencil, for example, the result will darken and its value will lower. If you use a lighter pressure in another area, the value there will be higher. This is true regardless of whether you use charcoal, graphite, or colored pencil.

Drawing Materials

This book is formulated for a charcoal approach to drawing portraits. Although you can use these principles with whatever medium you like, you will get the most out of the book if you follow the three-layered method.

What is the three-layered method?

The *three-layered method* is how I draw with charcoal, and it uses three grades of charcoal: soft, medium, and hard. The difference between these three ratings is the amount of binder agent that has been infused into the charcoal during the manufacturing process. Charcoal with a soft rating has little to no binder, a medium-rated charcoal has a 50-50 split, and charcoal rated hard has the most binder infused. Different grades are better for different aspects of your portrait, so it is important to understand how each grade reacts to the paper.

When should I use soft charcoal?

After you are satisfied that you have your contour lines in their proper place, use *soft charcoal* for your base layers. Because soft charcoal is pure charcoal without any binder agent, it spreads across the paper evenly. When it comes time to start using heavier pressure controls and pushing that charcoal down into the paper, you will get an even distribution of charcoal across the drawing.

When should I use medium charcoal?

Medium charcoal is the Goldilocks of the three-layered method. It has the perfect balance of binder agent, so it holds together but also spreads nicely for value building. A *medium charcoal* lends itself well to line work as well as lowering values in certain areas of your portrait such as the eye sockets, bottom plane of the nose, the upper lip, and bottom of the chin.

When should I use hard charcoal?

Because hard charcoal contains the highest amount of binder agent, it does not blend well and is not suited for value building (like medium charcoal) or foundational layering (like soft charcoal). Think of *hard charcoal* as your detail charcoal. This is the one you will use to bring out strands of hair, skin blemishes, and detail work such as reflections in your subjects' eyes, cracks in the lips, and so on.

When adding those details, things may not always go as planned. The ability to erase, and eraser choice, is just as important as charcoal choice. I tend to use multiple types of erasers because different areas of the drawing will call for different types of eraser work. The two main approaches to erasing are retrieving high values and saving high values.

What does "retrieving high values" mean?

When you *retrieve* your high values, you are erasing line work or shade work that you previously placed upon the paper. In other words, you are lightening up the value conveyed in that specific area to retrieve or bring back the higher value.

What does "saving high values" mean?

When you *save high values* in areas, you simply are not lowering the values in those specific areas at all. Rather than use an eraser, you draw around those high value areas. You have no value to retrieve, so you have essentially saved the values.

Now, I will be the first to tell you that you will retrieve values much more frequently than you will save them. Not to mention retrieving is much more flexible than saving. When you retrieve your high values, you allow yourself to adjust and define certain areas of your portrait via eraser work. When you save high values, there is no way to adjust; you are stuck with what you saved or did not save, and that is it.

Which erasers should I use?

At the end of the day, the choice of eraser is up to you. I like to use three types of erasers when I draw: a *medium-tip retractable eraser*, a *battery-operated eraser*, and a *fine-tip eraser*.

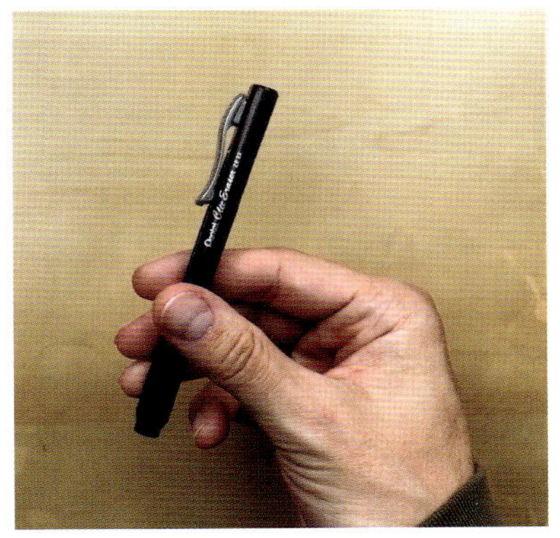

Pentel Clic Eraser

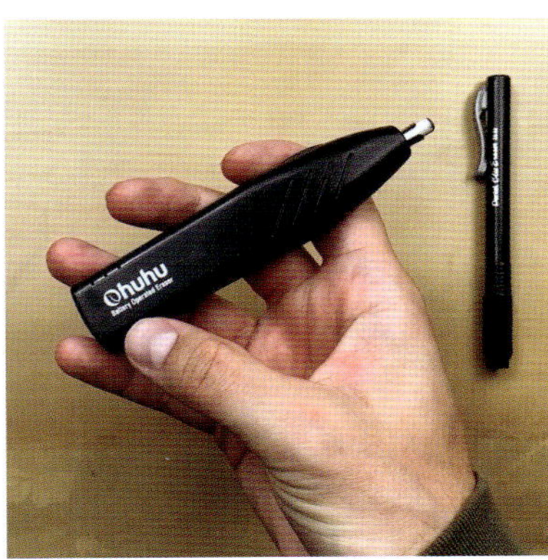

Ohuhu Battery Operated Eraser

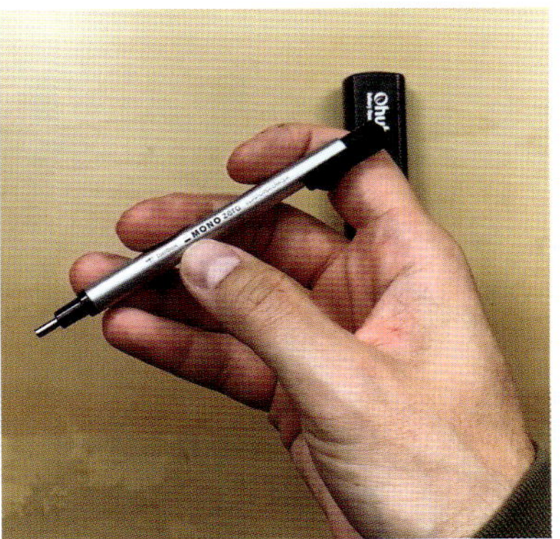

Tombow MONO Zero Eraser

When you combine brushes with your charcoal and erasers, you can work a little bit of magic with the three-layered method.

Why use brushes?

With *brushes*, you can produce gradation with very little effort and take your artwork to the next level. Without gradation, your drawing will look very gritty. The portrait will not have the gradual soft flow between values, and it simply will not be as aesthetically appealing as it could be. Brushes blend all three grades of charcoal and give the drawing a sense of softness that is reminiscent of real-life portraits.

You don't have to spend a bunch of money on a fancy set of brushes. Most any brush will do the job and do it well. For my drawings, I use angled and round tip brushes like those shown here to blend charcoal and help bring out smooth gradation.

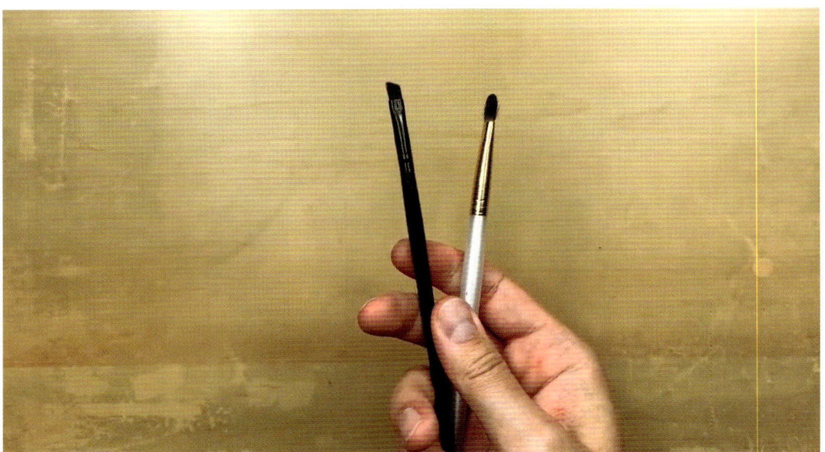

Why use smudgers?

For blending your charcoal, you can also use *smudgers*. They are available in all sorts of sizes, so it is good to make sure you have a set that gives you a wide range from small to large.

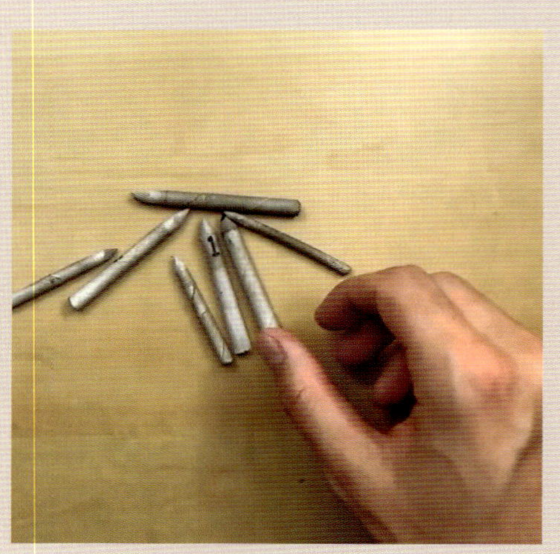

Although smudgers do not allow for the same smooth gradation as brushes, they do allow more control over exactly where you need to place that blend within your drawing. Suppose, for example, you need to blend the charcoal on an eye lid, but you don't want to accidentally blend into the eye. A small smudger would be the ideal choice in this situation, because it would enable you to blend that small area without straying into the eye.

As with brushes, you can spend as little or as much as you want for smudgers, but I always use the most basic ones I can find.

Scan the QR code for a list of the exact materials that I use in my portrait drawings.

Drawing Hacks

When it comes to charcoal, working smarter not harder will save you from frustration. Here are a few tricks I've discovered that will help any project go more smoothly.

Drawing hack 1: Prep charcoal

Here's a trick you can use to prepare some soft charcoal for building up your base layers or blending areas of your portrait: Use a sandpaper strip to grind soft charcoal into a container (I use a simple candle lid). Make sure to use soft charcoal, because you don't want any binder agent in charcoal used for base layering and initial blending.

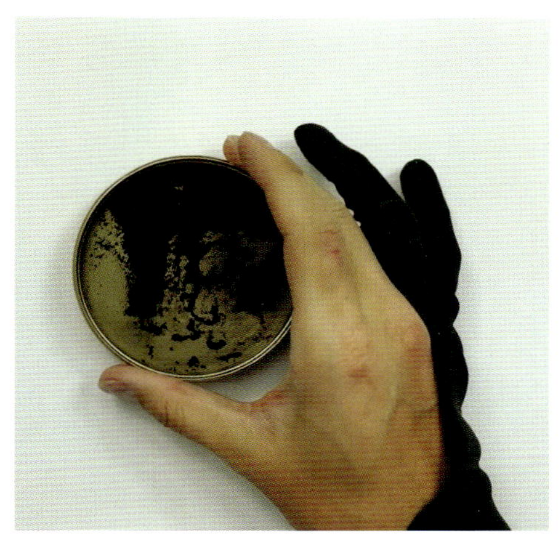

Drawing hack 2: Check tone

To save your drawing from unnecessary adjustments, keep a piece of scratch paper handy. Now you can dip your brushes and your smudgers in the ground soft charcoal, and then check your tone on your scratch paper before you take either tool to your drawing. This hack will help you throughout the creative process.

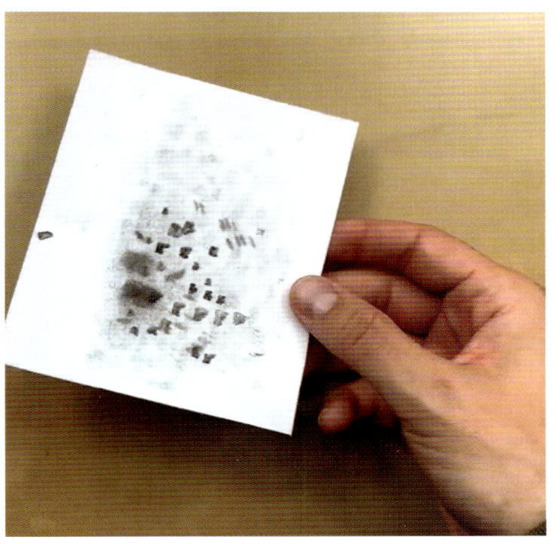

Drawing hack 3: Sharpen stronger

When it comes to sharpening your pencil, you may think that any sharpening tool or technique will do. Maybe, but if you really want to give yourself the edge, sharpen your charcoal pencils into what I call "quad tips." I sharpen my pencil tips on four sides, which helps them hold up better to accidental breakage. They also perform exceedingly well when detailing eyes, hair strands, skin blemishes, and similar parts of a portrait.

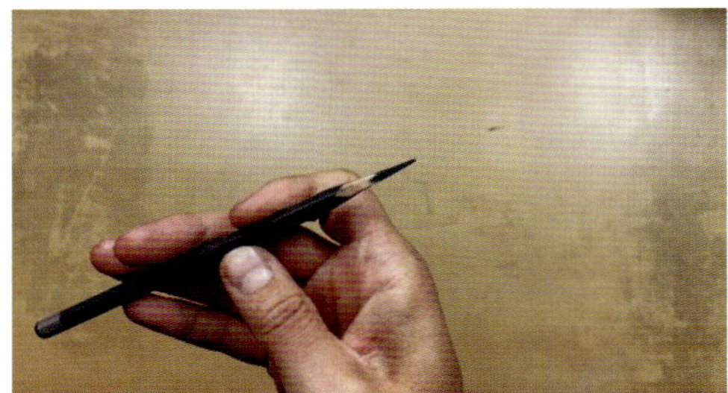 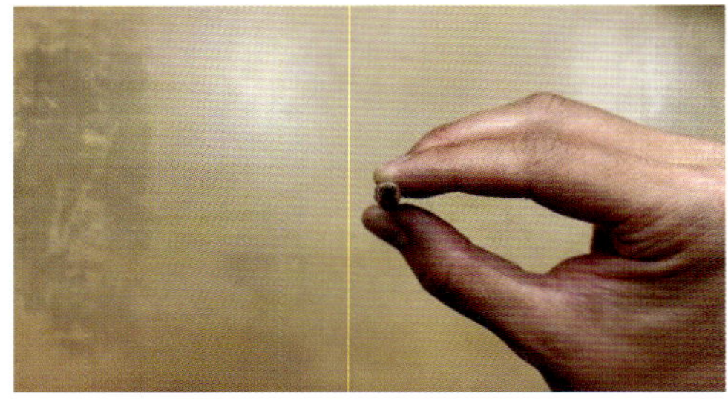

Drawing hack 4: Avoid smears

If you have ever drawn with graphite or charcoal (or watched someone do so), you know how easy it is to accidentally smear the drawing. The biggest culprit is the artist's own skin, because skin oil is an excellent absorber of both graphite and charcoal. Keep your skin off the paper you're drawing on, and you'll minimize smearing. But how? You can use a second piece of paper as a protective layer to prevent your drawing hand 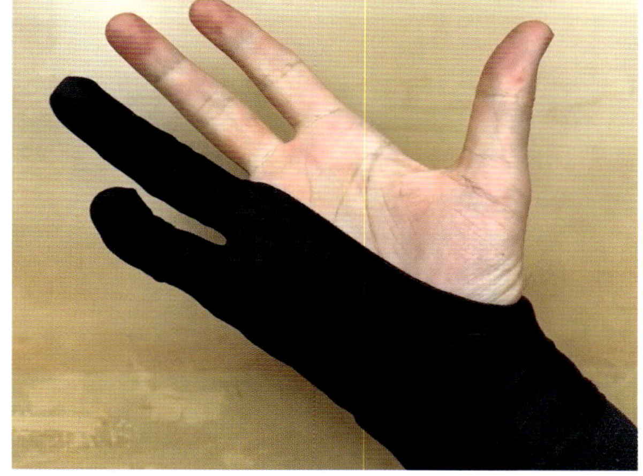 from resting on the drawing paper, or you can be fancy and stylish like me and wear a drawing glove. A drawing glove allows you to draw without your skin touching the paper and thus is the perfect solution to the problem of accidental smudging. Bear in mind, however, that a glove will still smear if you drag it across swaths of charcoal or graphite. Its main purpose is to keep the oil from your hand from touching the paper and then subsequently absorbing whichever medium you are using.

CHAPTER 1

Basic Drawing Techniques

"Practice is the best of all instructors."
—*Publilius Syrus*

For any new venture you pursue, you first need to practice basic form and techniques. The time you invest in mastering the fundamentals will make things easier in the long run. Drawing is no different, and certain approaches work better than others.

Who hasn't looked at a drawing in progress and been discouraged by the results of their efforts? Maybe you've even crinkled some up and tossed them in the trash. The trouble isn't a lack of desire, fortitude, or talent to succeed. You are simply struggling to execute the proper form and techniques necessary to convey your desired effect on paper. Practicing the basics will ease your difficulties, and this chapter will help you.

So, what is the first thing that you need to understand when drawing a portrait?

Pressure Control

Pressure control is simply a matter of regulating how hard or lightly you press on your paper as you push or pull your pencil across it. It is paramount that when you first start drawing you use a very light pressure. You want to caress the paper, feel the paper, tell the paper that everything is going to be okay because you care about it that much. That is how light you should be drawing your initial linework when you start a drawing.

When do I use different pressure?

Remembering when to use the correct pressure is simple. When you start, when you are the most uncertain, use very light pressure. Once you are confident with your basic shape and proportions, then you can start to solidify your line work (depending on what you are drawing) by upping the pressure and lowering the value.

Where do I use different pressure?

You should fluctuate from light pressure to heavier pressure only where you are trying to cement a basic shape by thickening specific line qualities and darkening specific line weights or where you are lowering the overall value in a specific area of the drawing. (More on these techniques later.)

Why use different pressures?

Odds are that at some point you will need to make an adjustment of some kind, and good pressure control will help. Using extremely light pressure in your initial outline, for example, makes erasing undesirable line work easier. Or maybe you want to bring out contrast somewhere by using a heavier pressure, which effectively lowers values. Remember you can always use heavier pressure as you progress through your piece. Start off light, and slowly use heavier pressure as you become confident that your line work is where you want it to be.

Now that you understand the theory of pressure control, try **Project 1**: Take a piece of paper out of your sketchbook, grab your charcoal, and practice using different pressures. Let your childhood spirit freely flow. Have fun with pressure control and try to feel your hand. Watch as you tell it to press harder, press more softly, press extremely hard, press extremely lightly. Perhaps you have never noticed the effect that your pressure has on the paper until now, but then have you ever truly looked at it this closely before?

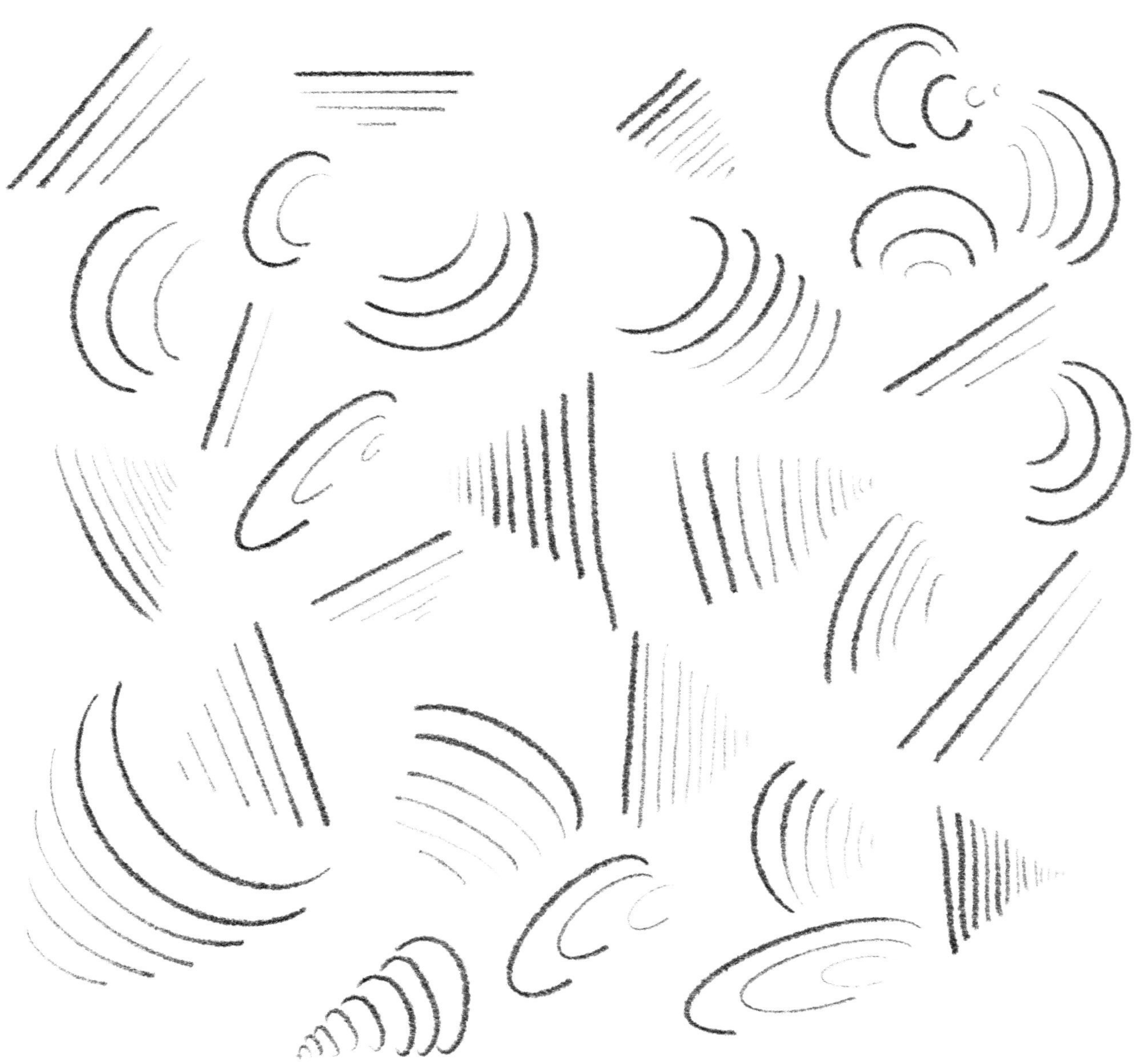

Project 1: Practice pressure control

The Circle

When looking at a subject or reference for your portrait, take a moment to really study the shapes that comprise the face. Notice that a circle makes up most of the basic shape of the cranium. Being able to see this circle is important, because drawing it is the necessary first step to constructing a solid foundation for your portrait.

What is it?

A circle is a closed two-dimensional figure in which the set of all points of the plane is equidistant from a given point called the center—at least that's the dictionary's definition of it.

When do I use the circle?

Drawing out your circle, regardless of angle, will always be the very first step in the process of drawing a portrait. Bear in mind that the circle does not need to be perfectly symmetrical, so long as it's height is relative to its width.

Where do I use the circle?

Because it is the first thing that you draw on paper, you can place your circle almost anywhere. Typically, you should aim for the center roughly one third of the way down from the top of the paper. This placement lends itself well to the overall composition of a portrait.

Why use the circle?

When drawing complex subjects such as the human face, it is important to approach the task in the simplest way possible. Geometric shapes help us to make sense of what we are drawing, because they lend themselves well to understanding basic shape. Every drawing exists in a two-dimensional space. Yes, it is true that the paper itself is technically three dimensional, but because the drawing lives on only one side of the paper it is only two dimensional. So, using circles, ovals, even lines, helps in the initial phase of drawing portraits.

You can draw a circle in two main ways. You can use a compass, which will give you a perfect circle every time without much effort, or you can draw freehand. Drawing freehand is harder because success depends entirely on your ability. But, you can do a few things to help yourself. The first is to hold your pencil in the *overhand grip* as opposed to the *three-point grip*, which is how most of us learned to write in school. The overhand grip forces you to use a lighter pressure naturally. From there, it's important to straighten your back as well as your wrist. Now, kick your drawing pinky finger out slightly and start to go around and around in a circle, keeping the movement in your elbow, rather than your wrist or forearm.

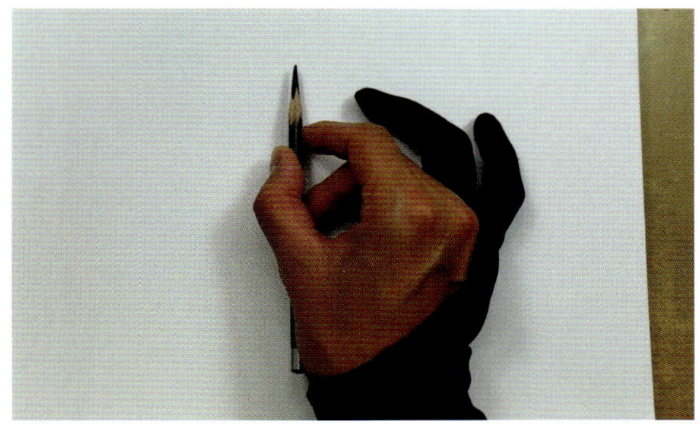

Overhand grip

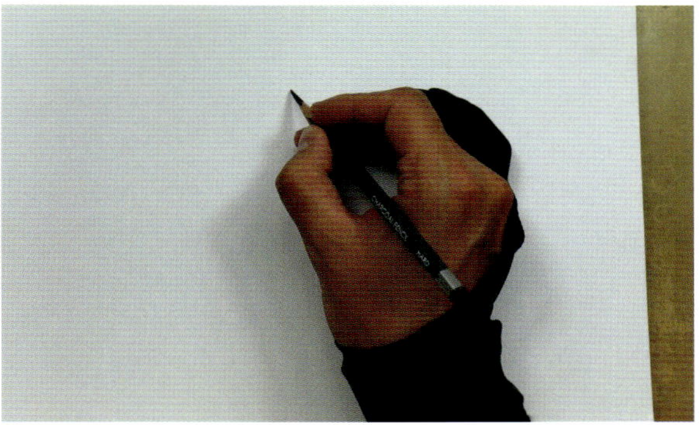

Three-point grip

So now that you understand how important the circle is for your portraits, try **Project 2**: Fill up two pages in your sketchbook practicing circles. Try both drawing methods to see which you prefer.

Project 2: Practice circles

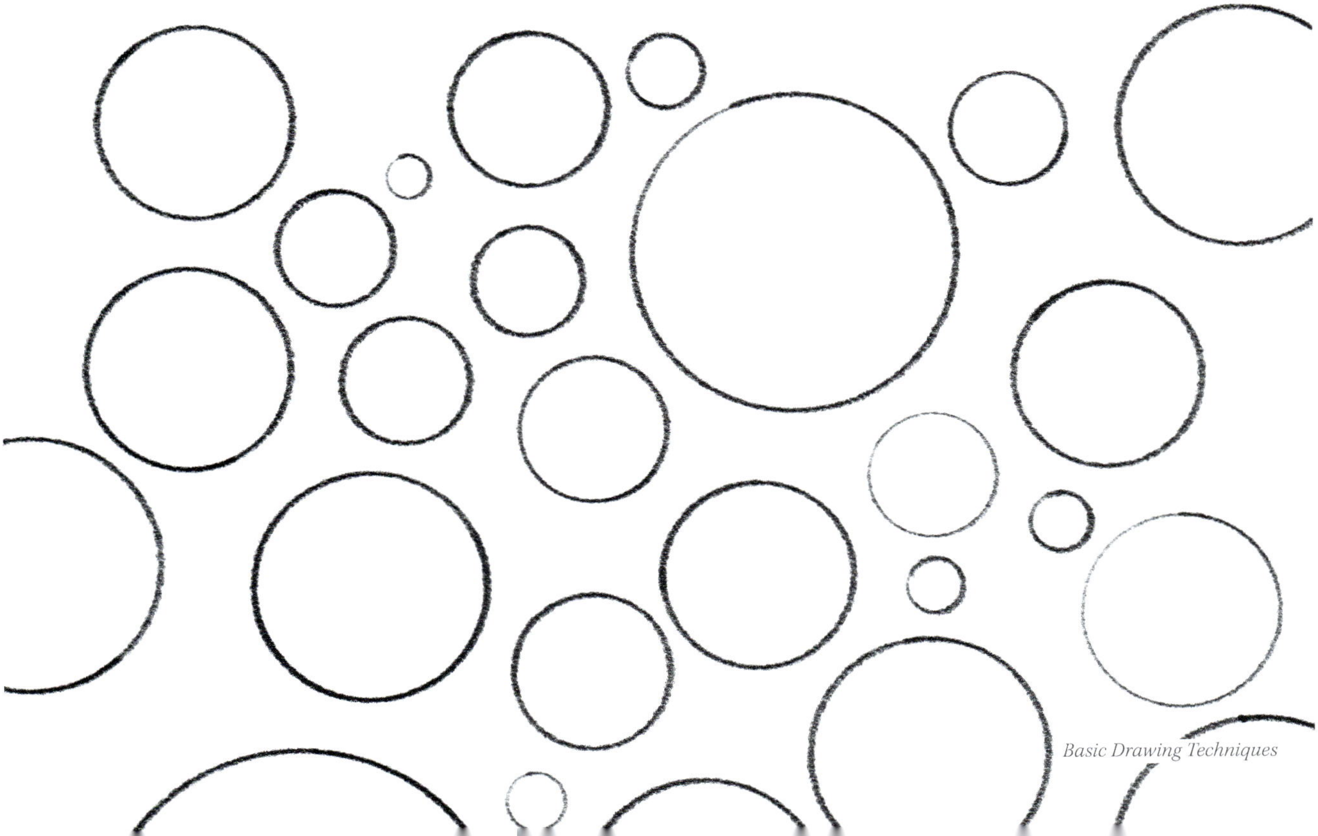

The Oval

After you draw the initial circle of your portrait, you will then need to draw an oval to signify the side plane of your subject's head. It is important to note that the angle of your reference will affect how this oval will look. Given the nature of optics and optical illusion, when you start to turn a circle on a set axis, the shape that you get is an elongated circle or oval.

What is it?

An oval is a curve representing a squashed circle, but unlike the ellipse, without a precise mathematical definition. That's how the dictionary describes an oval, but I prefer to call it a squished circle.

When do I use the oval?

After you are happy with the placement and dimension of your circle, draw your oval to effectively elongate the cranium and give your head a side plane.

Where do I use the oval?

Depending on the angle of the subject, place the oval on the right, the left, or both sides of the initial circle. The height and the width of the oval are not absolute so don't over think it.

Why use the oval?

The initial circle and oval provide a basic structure to help you accurately place the features of your subject. Geometric shapes, such as circles and ovals, help us start to make sense of the shape. The oval helps us to see that the circle's sides have been chopped off, which gives us the beginnings of an elongated cranium.

Time for **Project 3**: Fill at least one maybe even two pages in your sketchbook with ovals. Use the overhand grip to fill in the first page, then use the three-point grip to fill in the second page. Feel what each grip does and does not do for you. Every one of us is different, and some of you may discover that the three-point grip works better for you. Who's to judge? Remember Jimi Hendrix played the guitar backwards and upside down, and he was an incredible guitarist. The most important thing is that you are comfortable with the results on paper.

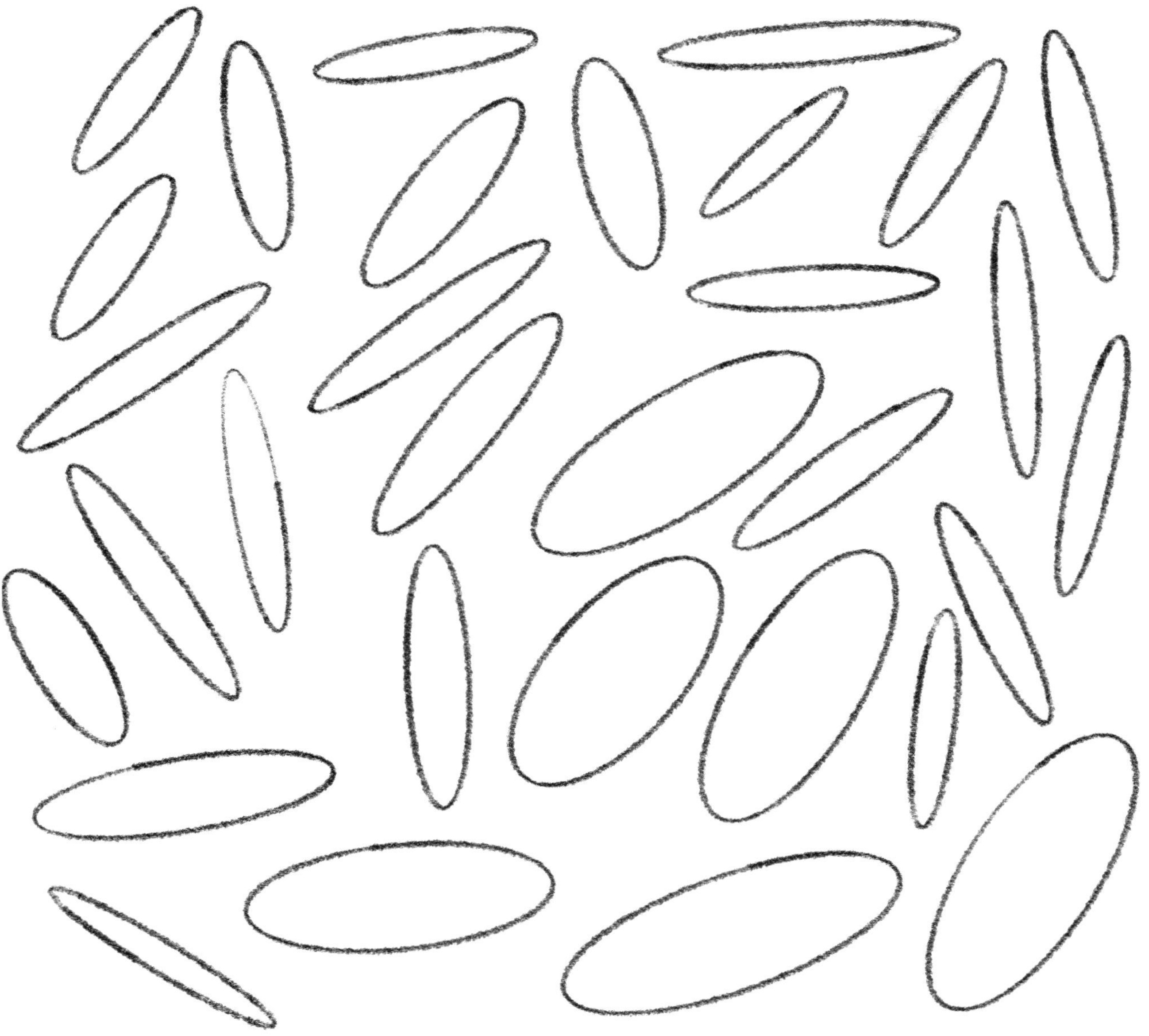

Project 3: Practice ovals

The Straight Line

After you have successfully drawn your circle and placed your oval to identify the side plane of your subject's head, the next step is to draw your vertical axis and your horizontal axis. To draw these, use straight lines.

What is it?

In geometry, a line is an infinitely long object with no width, depth, or curvature. Because of this, lines are one-dimensional objects. However, they may exist embedded in two, three, or higher dimensional space. Or, if you want a more simplistic answer, "a line is simply a dot that went for a walk" according to artist Paul Klee.

When do I use straight lines?

Use straight lines when you are solidifying the angle at which you want your subject's head to be placed. For example, if you want the head to be looking up at a 45-degree angle, then draw your horizontal axis angled by 45 degrees. The subject's eyes will follow that axis line.

Where do I use straight lines?

Use straight lines where you are laying out the vertical axis and horizontal axis on your side plane. Depending on the angle of your subject, you may use straight lines for carving out the eye planes and the nose planes, as well. Make sure you are comfortable drawing straight lines so that you can use them to your advantage when creating the foundation of most any portrait.

Why use straight lines?

This is an honest question, because organic things like us humans clearly do *not* have straight lines anywhere on our heads. When you are constructing the foundation of your portrait, however, think of yourself as a civil engineer of sorts. At this preliminary point in the creative process, you are relying heavily upon geometric shapes to lay down a solid foundation for the layers to come. Straight lines are a crucial component of this drawing formula.

Straight lines are important to draw, but they are not the easiest things in the world to get right. Much like for the circle you have two options: Use a straight edge, or draw them manually. I am a big fan of using tools when needed, but at the same time, there is no substitute for experience. I highly encourage you to challenge yourself to draw these straight lines manually. Depending on the portrait, sometimes it is more advantageous to use the overhand grip than the three-point grip and vice versa.

For **Project 4**, draw one whole page of straight lines in your sketchbook using the overhand grip to push and pull straight lines of various lengths. Then, on a second page, do the same thing using the three-point grip. Remember, *pushing* a line means that your pencil is leading your hand as you move your pencil across the paper. When you *pull* a line, your pencil tip follows your hand across the paper. Be sure to be proactive, both pushing and pulling in your straight-line project as this will help you build good muscle memory not only for line work but for everything. Eventually you will understand the form that you are trying to frame in your portraits, and you will be able to bend your lines slightly like me. Until then, just focus on making your lines as straight as you can.

Project 4: Push and pull straight lines

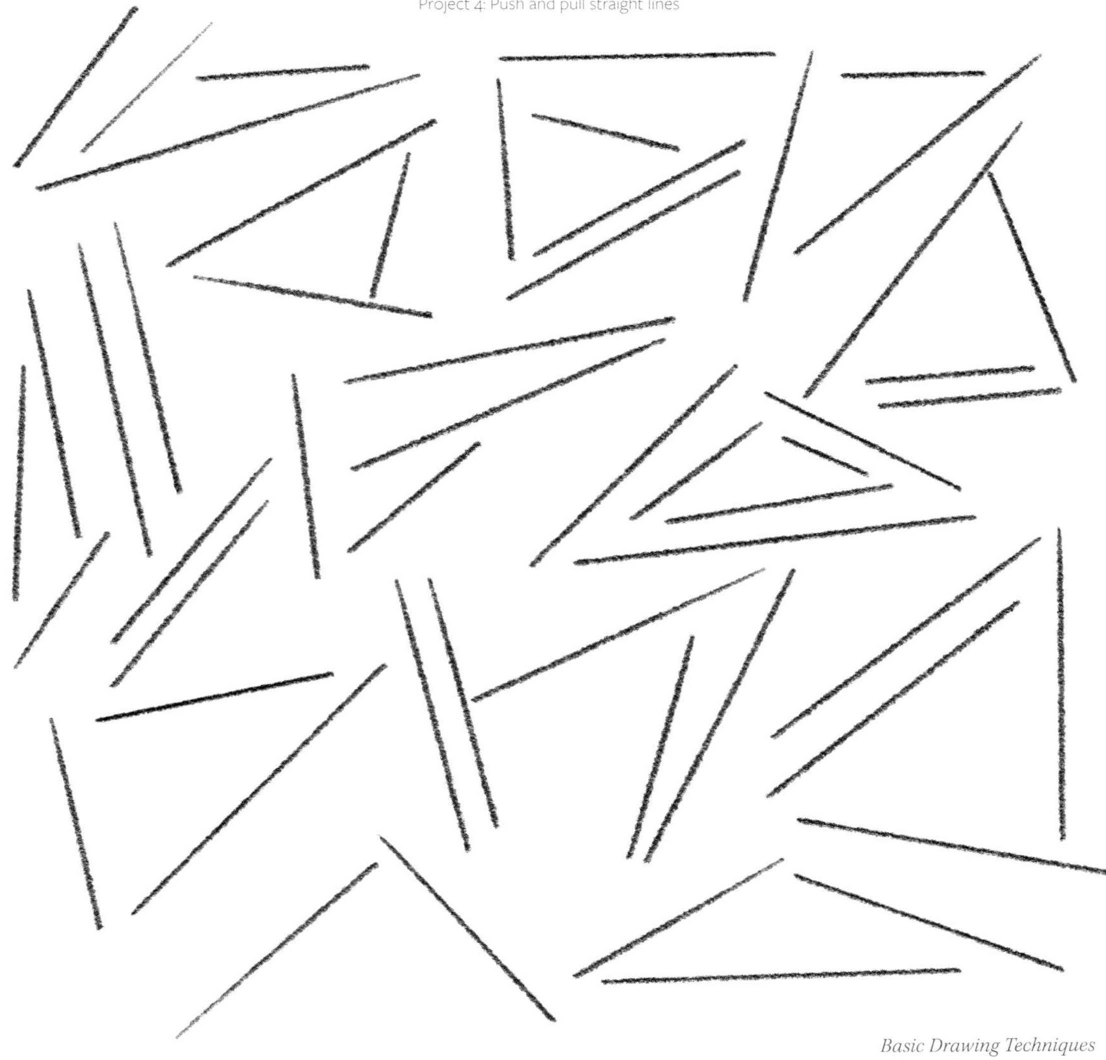

Putting Them All Together

Now that you've practiced your pressure control, circles, ovals, and straight lines, you have the basic knowledge to draw Loomis and Asaro heads. Well, what are those?

The *Loomis method* is a portrait-drawing technique developed by artist and cartoonist Andrew Loomis. He originally intended the method to be used for cartoon characters, but it has been adopted by an array of visual artists over the years for portraiture. Of all the possible methods for drawing portraits, I believe that the Loomis method is the simplest to digest for beginners.

The *Asaro method* is a portrait-drawing technique developed by painter John Asaro. Originally meant for painters, the Asaro head model showcases the planes of the face to help artists easily identify how light casts across the face from various angles.

These are the two main methods that you will learn to wield in your portrait drawings. They provide guides to basic structure and how to successfully navigate the arena of perspective and realism while you draw your portraits. As with most anything, the hardest part is the beginning and that is where these methods allow you to shine. So, let's get started drawing a portrait.

Understanding *the* Loomis Method

"No matter how great your talent, talent has to work with knowledge to do anything well."
—Andrew Loomis

William Andrew Loomis was an American illustrator, writer, and art instructor who studied at the Art Students League of New York under George Bridgman and Frank DuMond. Much of his work was featured in magazines and advertising campaigns, but some of his most significant contributions to the arts came in the drawing books he wrote. *Drawing the Head and Hands, Figure Drawing for All It's Worth*, and *Successful Drawing* are a few of his most notable publications. Widely regarded as his *pièce de résistance*, his method for beginning to draw a portrait is addressed in his book *Drawing the Head and Hands*.

Drawing with the Loomis Method

The *Loomis method* is a drawing approach that uses simple forms and measured landmarks to construct the human head in any angle. This method allows you to easily analyze your reference and begin to understand it in three-dimensional space. I'm sure you have already tried many times to draw a portrait before you came across this book, so you probably already understand the struggle that ensues if you do not have a solid, foundational approach from which to start. The Loomis method solves this problem by providing a foundation for the portrait to come. The Loomis method is more rooted in principle construction than aesthetic appeal, so don't worry about how that foundation looks so much as the proportions that it provides. Now I will show you step by step how to draw a *Loomis head* with this method.

Step 1: Draw Your Circle

Start by drawing a circle to represent the beginnings of the cranium. If you are hesitant to draw one manually, you can use a compass to draw a perfect circle with very little effort and even less stress.

If you want to challenge yourself, draw your circle manually. Now there is a proven way to draw manual circles, and it goes like this: Grip your pencil with the overhand grip, straighten your back, stiffen your wrist and drawing arm, and then draw your circle by moving your arm at the elbow. This is how most professional portrait artists draw their circles.

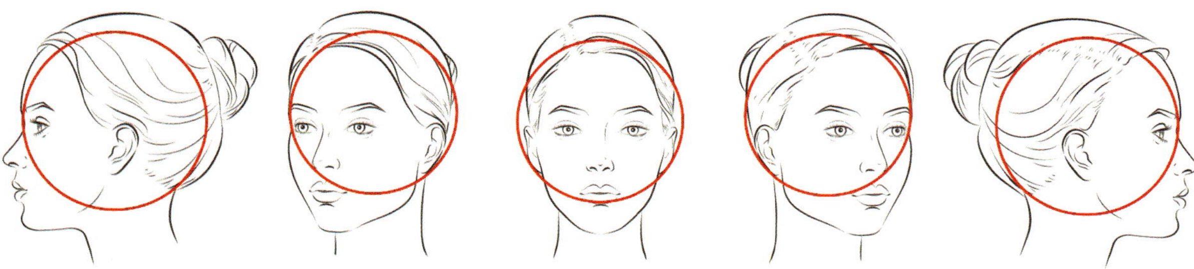

When drawing manually, remember that your circle does not have to be perfect so long as its height is relative to its width.

Step 2: Draw Your Oval

The oval showcases the cranium's side plane, which elongates it. Exactly where you place the oval will depend entirely on the direction that your reference is looking. For example, if you are drawing a profile portrait, then draw the oval as a smaller circle within the larger initial circle due to the nature of the angle. However, virtually any other portrait angle will dictate that you should draw the side plane as an oval of varying degrees.

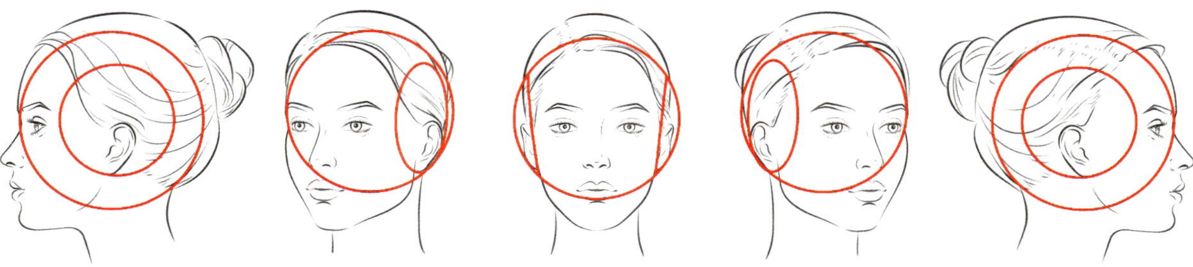

The placement and shape of your oval will depend on the angle your subject is looking.

Step 3: Draw Your Axis Lines

Draw two axis lines inside your side plane (oval). Make the first axis (horizontal) follow the direction that your subject is looking. Place the second axis (vertical) at a perfect 90-degree angle to your horizontal axis. These two lines will help you understand the orientation of your portrait.

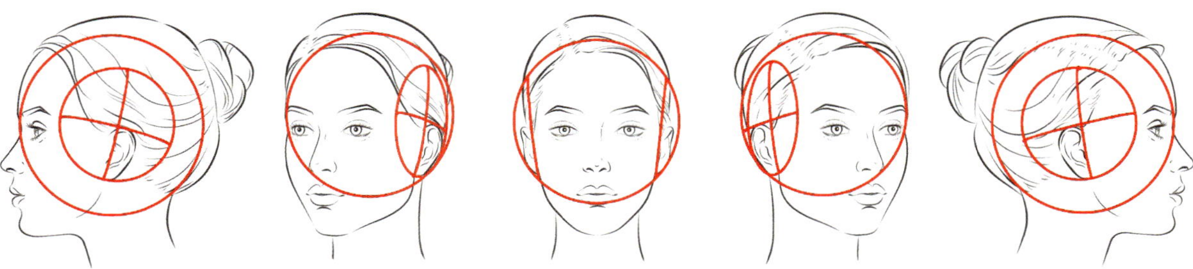

No matter which angles you are working with (even extreme angles), your horizontal axis will always align with the direction of the eyes. Keep this in mind when you begin to draw more complex portraits.

Step 4: Draw Your Guidelines

The four guidelines shown in this step will always be relatively the same no matter the angle that you draw. The Loomis method is extremely simplistic by its very design. These guidelines will help you place the hairline, brow line, nose line, and chin line. We will cover more about specific feature placement in Chapter 9. Our main focus here is for you to get very comfortable with the basic Loomis head. In addition to the main horizontal and vertical axes, the Loomis method includes four guidelines to help you place specific features. You'll learn more about how to use these in Chapter 9. For now, focus on how to draw each.

Hairline

Starting from the top of the side plane and using that as the basis, pull a line across the face. This is your guiding line for the hairline to come.

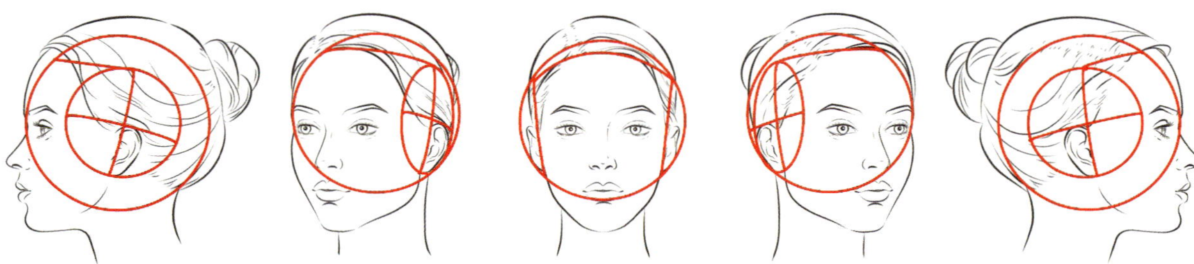

Brow line

Following your horizontal axis line, pull a line across the face. This is your guiding line for the brow line to come.

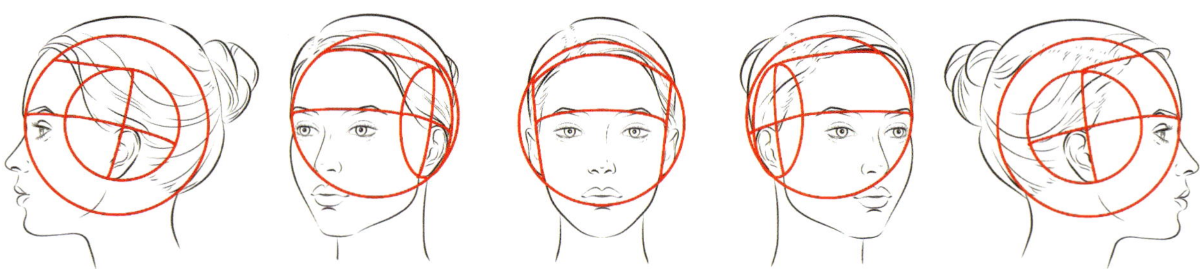

Nose line

Start from the bottom of the side plane and using that as the basis, pull a line across the face. This is your guiding line for the bottom of the nose.

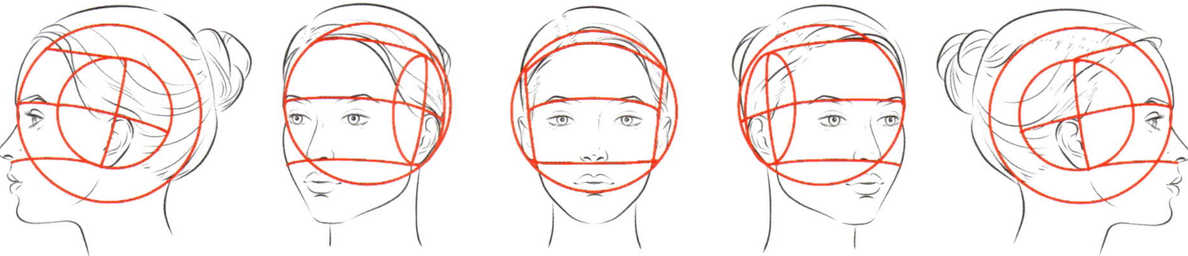

Chin line

Now this is where things get a little tricky. To help you find where to draw the chin line, place your pencil pointing vertically on the face of your Loomis head. Make sure that the pencil tip is in line with the brow line and pinch the pencil where the nose line intersects it. Without moving your pinched fingers, slide the pencil tip down to the nose line. Your pinched fingers now mark roughly where you should draw the line to signify the bottom of the chin.

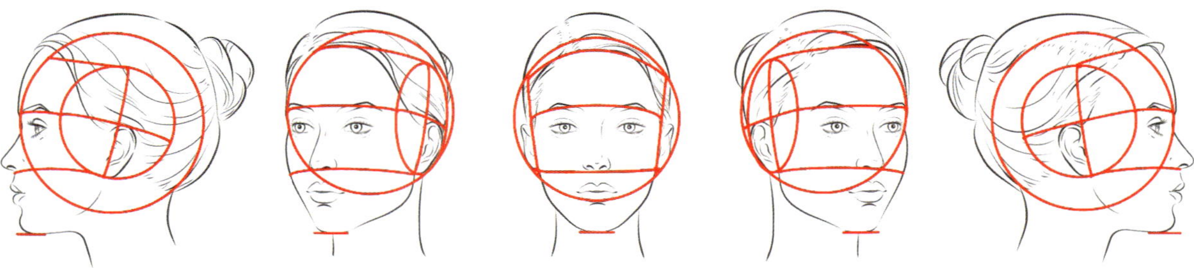

Notice that the face is now divided into three equally spaced sections. To help you understand facial proportions, the Loomis method applies the Rule of Thirds to the subject's face (unlike in photography and videography where the rule applies to the overall composition of the image).

Step 5: Split Your Third Section into Thirds

To help you position the upper and lower lips, add marks to divide the lower third of
your portrait (nose line to chin line) into thirds. These are more anchor points than
lines, and they are adjustable. You can use your pencil to gauge their placement,
similar to how you gauged where to place the bottom of the chin.

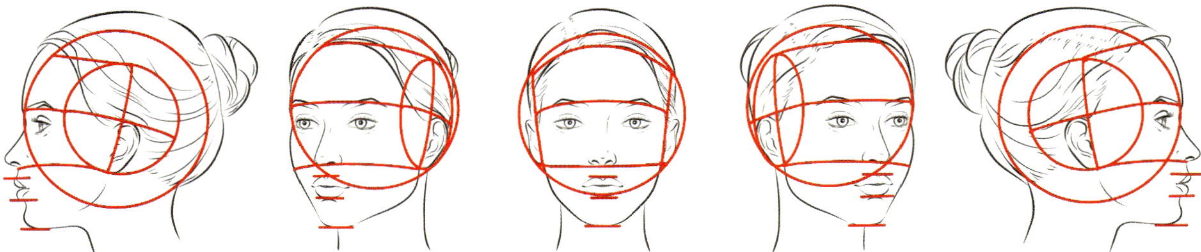

Step 6: Draw Your Jaw Line

To draw the jaw line, start at the bottom of your vertical axis line and pull a line down
then curving across to attach to the chin line.

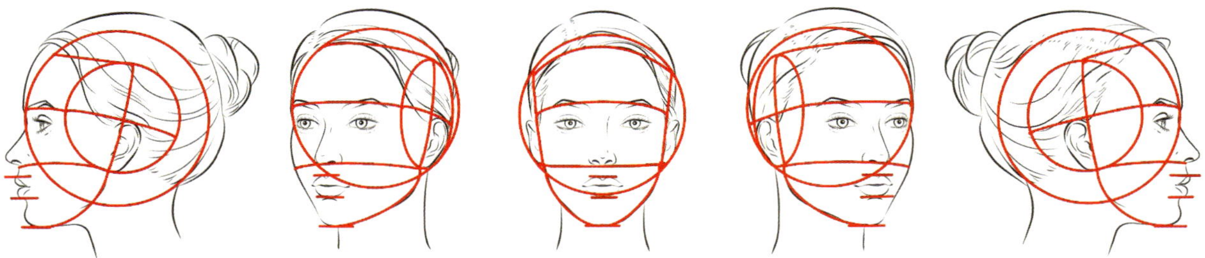

Finally, pull your line up from the bottom of the chin, all the way to the top and
connect it with the initial circle so you have a rough outline of the outside edge of
the entire face.

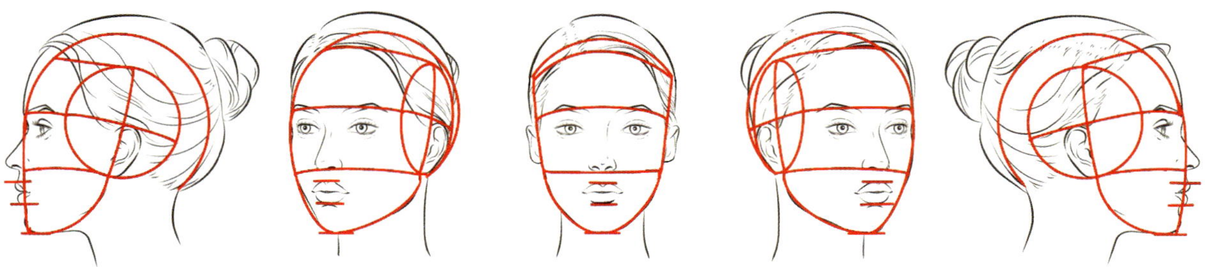

*When you finish this step, you can erase the excessive linework left over from your
initial circle.*

Step 7: Draw Your Cheek Line

Because you have the basic shape of the head established, you can now draw the cheek line. Start from the intersection of your vertical and horizontal axis lines and pull a line over and down in a smooth arcing motion to the jaw line. This line will help you understand where to place the shading for your cheek bones and the corners of the mouth when the time comes.

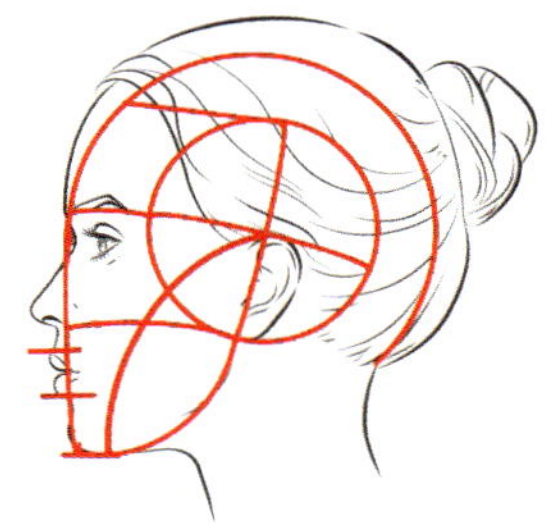
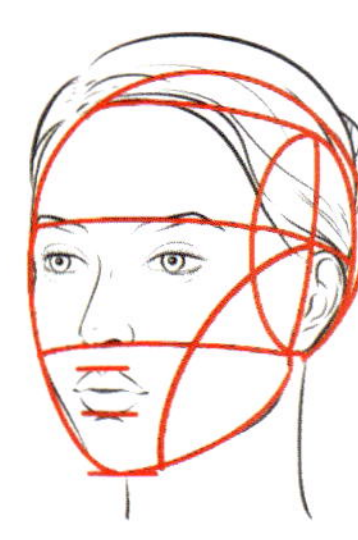
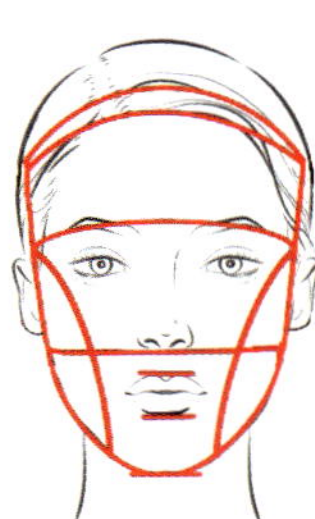
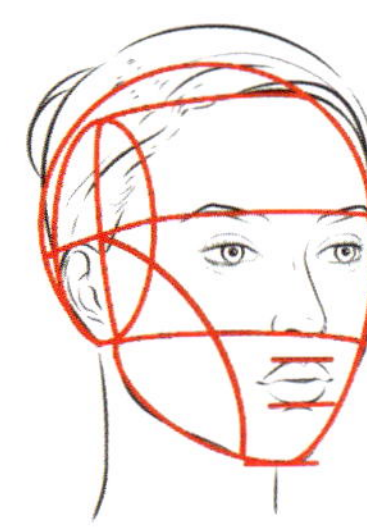
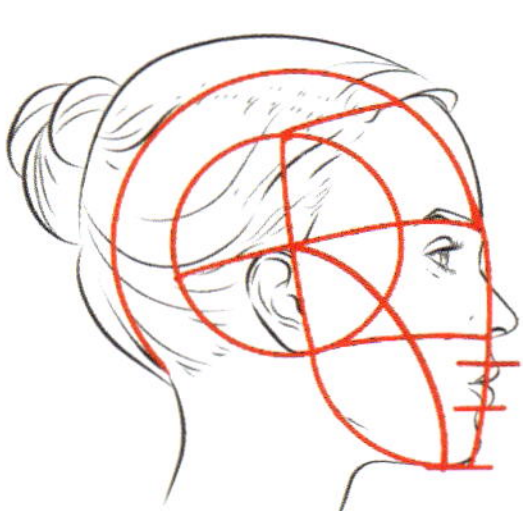

Step 8: Draw Your Neck and Center Line

Your Loomis head is almost finished. All that is left is to draw the neck and center lines. Adding a basic neck shape will prevent your head from looking like it is floating in space by itself. For the back of the neck, start the line following the contour of your initial circle. When you get near the bottom of the circle, pull the line straight down and lift. This will make the cranium bulge out from the back of the neck. Then, to place the front of the neck (the throat), align your neck line with the edge of the initial circle and pull your line down from the jaw line. This will give you a very accurate proportional look for how the neck plugs into your Loomis head.

Lastly, draw a line to mark the exact center of the face on your Loomis head. Notice how this line is applicable only to the straight and three-quarter angles, not the profile angles.

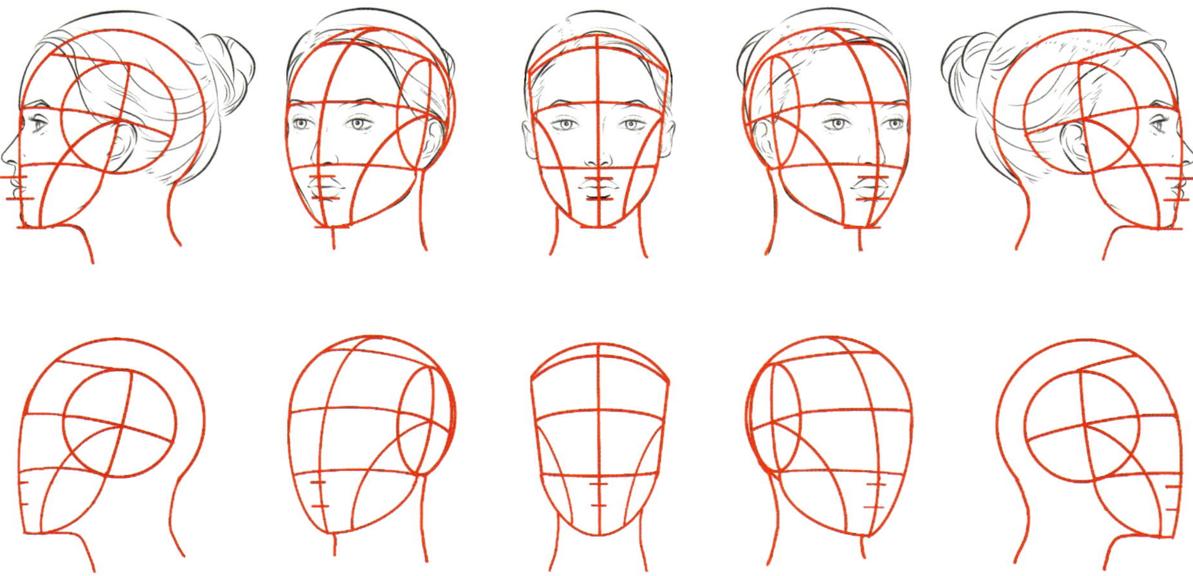

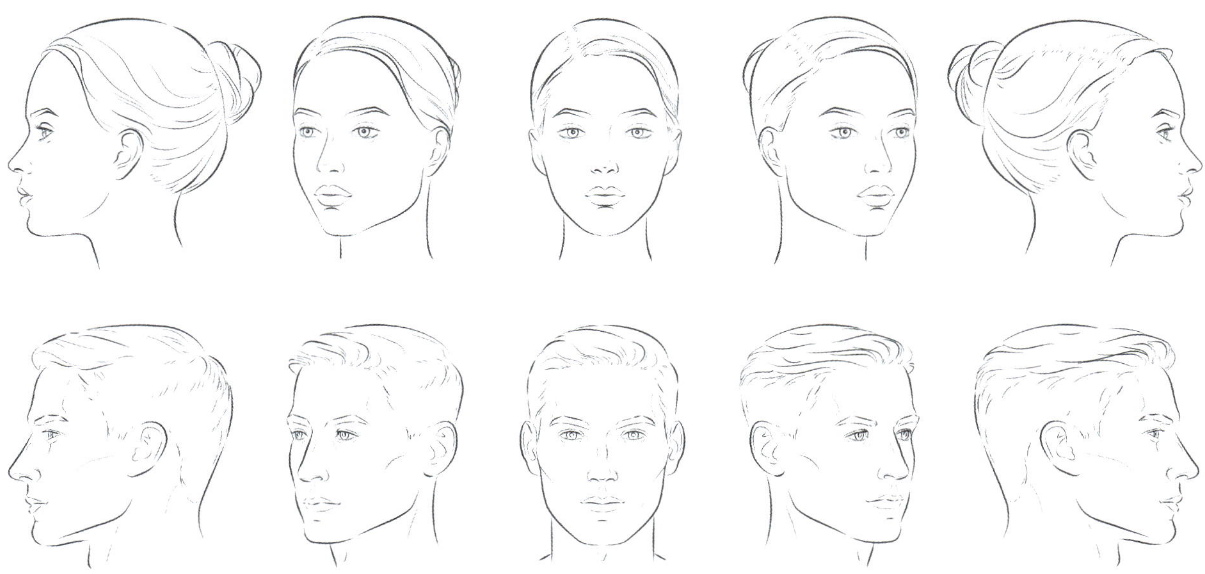

Project 5: Time to Practice

No matter the angle of the portrait you are working on, simply follow the same eight steps to draw your Loomis head. The method works and is a great way to start drawing a portrait. While you're drawing your Loomis heads, remember to use very light pressure so you can make any necessary adjustments without detriment to your final portrait.

Now, for **Project 5**, draw at least 15 Loomis heads in your sketchbook (make sure you have enough pages). Each one should be at a different angle than the previous. Use the reference images below to help you draw your Loomis heads: Draw them over the top of these references to help you develop a solid understanding of exactly how different head angles correlate to the Loomis method and how the Loomis head appears in some of the most common angles that you are likely to draw throughout your art career. Yes, more possible angles exist, but extreme angles aside, this project will give you a solid foundational understanding for how to approach most portrait orientations. For more guidance, scan the QR codes to watch **How to Easily Draw Heads: Understanding the Loomis Method** and **How to Easily Draw the Head from ANY Angle**. These videos demonstrate the Loomis method for 15 portrait angles and include step-by-step tutorials.

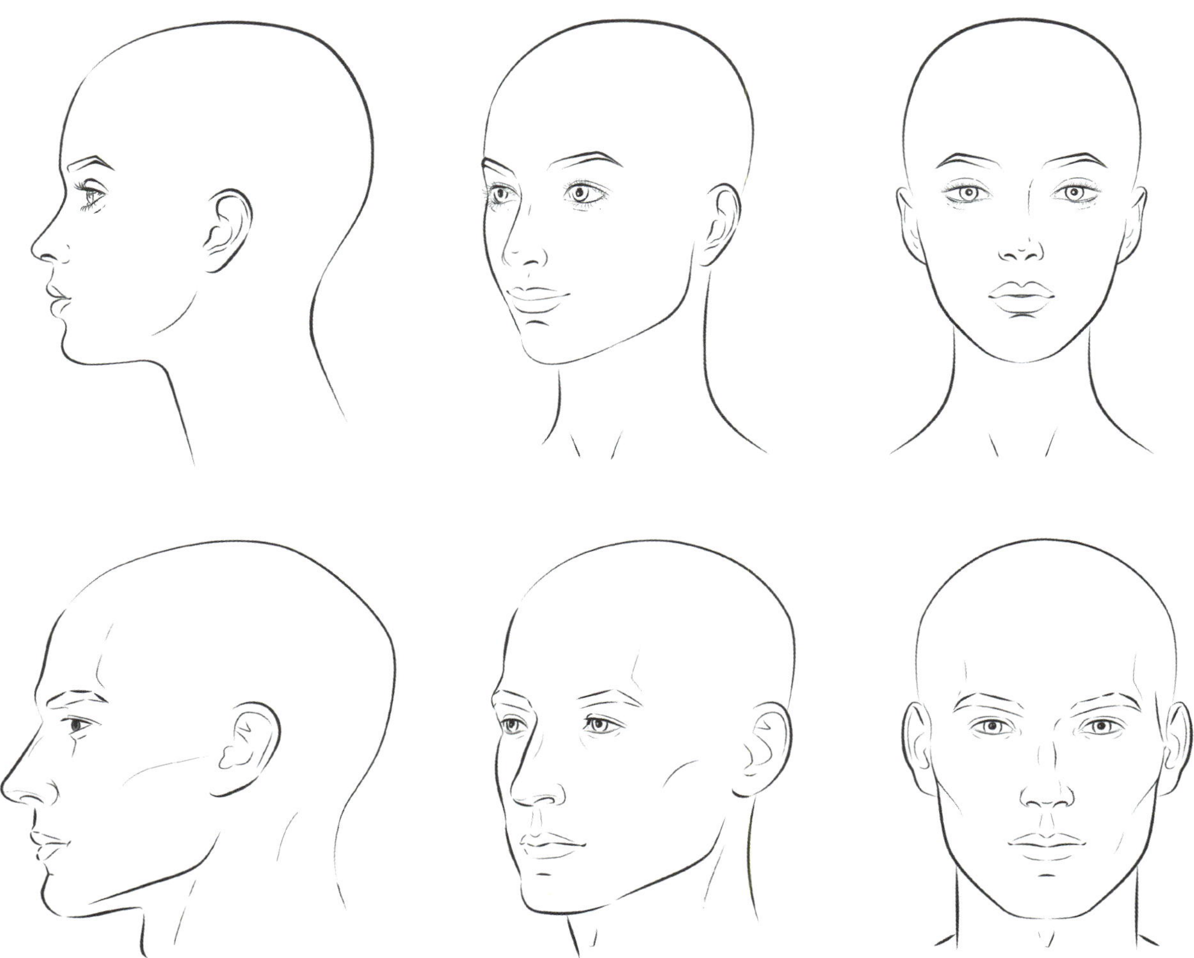

Conclusion: A Melding of Methods

The Loomis method is a tried-and-true approach to drawing the beginnings of a portrait, but it is meant to be a general guide, not an absolute. Most artists find that the struggle with drawing a portrait comes in the initial phase of the process. The Loomis method allows you to follow very simple principal line work so that you can build a foundation before you start placing the features of your portrait. The approach that you will learn in this book is a fusion of both the Loomis method and the Asaro method (more on this one in the next chapter). I believe that each method on its own does not give novice artists enough guidance, but in tandem they provide the perfect balance of shape and form so that you can have the best chance at nailing your proportions from the get-go.

Understanding *the* Asaro Method

> *"This knowledge of the head is only a start.*
> *One must find his or her own path."*
> —*John Asaro*

Artist and educator John Asaro was raised in southern California where he attended the ArtCenter College of Design in Pasadena. Like Andrew Loomis, he also attended the Art Students League of New York (albeit much later). After a 12-year career in commercial art, he moved on to pursue fine art, as well as returned to the ArtCenter College of Design to teach figurative painting. During this time, Asaro developed his concept of "the planes of the head," which later became known as the *Asaro method*. He holds an honorary doctorate from the Academy of Art College in San Francisco and now devotes all his time to painting.

What is the Asaro Method?

Although Asaro no longer teaches, his method continues to educate beginning art-ists about the underlying structure and planes of the face. While teaching at the Art-Center College of Design, Asaro developed the Planes of the Head mannequin, which allowed his students and other artists to see how light reflected off three-dimension-al faces and craniums in different lighting environments. With a better understanding of where areas of light or shadow fell, his students (and others) could better depict the resulting tonal values in their work. As portrait artists, we also benefit: Under-standing and envisioning Asaro's planes will help you not only to more accurately depict the subjects you draw, but also to draw a portrait using no reference.

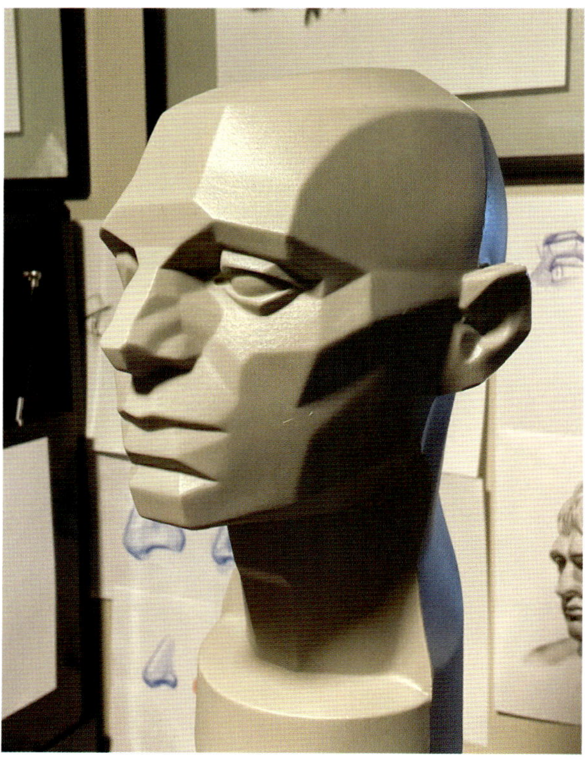

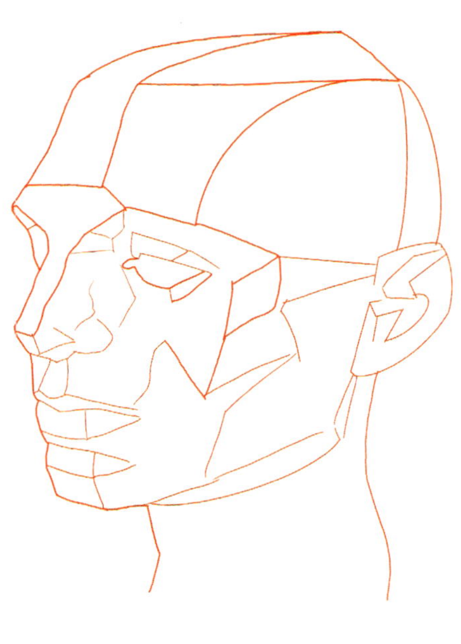

The Asaro method also is useful as a bridge between your initial Loomis head and a full-featured head. You can sketch the planes of individual features, such as the eyes, nose, and mouth, onto a Loomis head. In tandem with the Loomis guidelines, the Asaro planes can help you place facial features. You can also use these planes as rhythm lines to start to add structure to your face, elevating your portrait from a two-dimensional look to a three-dimensional look. Not only that, but the Asaro method can help you to determine exactly where to place your darker tones and build up your lower values, which in turn will start to produce form.

Planes, light, & form

As you can see from the three photos of the Planes of the Head mannequin below, light casts differently across the face depending on the orientation of the Asaro head, revealing the tonal variations across the face.

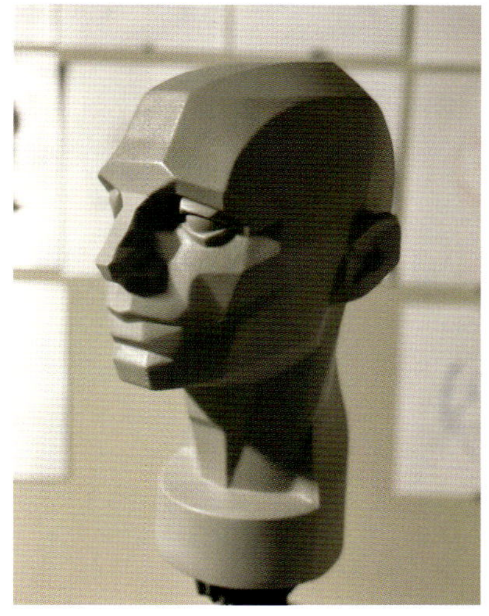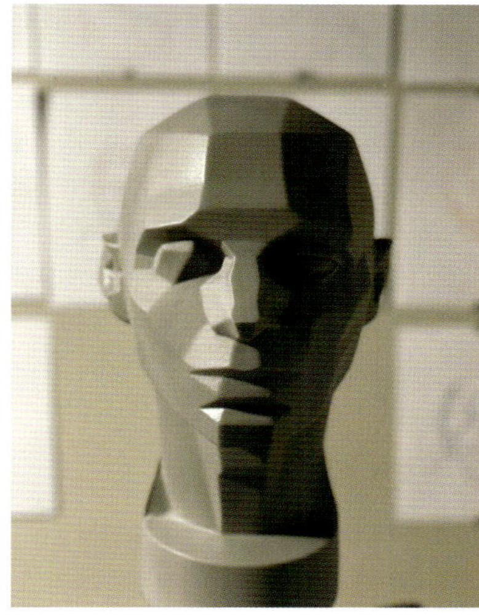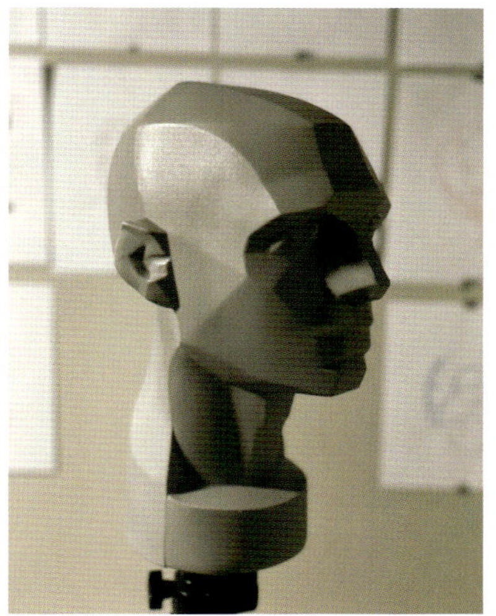

You can use the knowledge of these variations when drawing your portrait. Being able to see the planes with darker tones, for example, will give you the advantage of knowing exactly where to blend between the different planes. This, in turn, will make the whole process of developing your form that much easier.

Study each individual plane. How are they composed? How do they tie into other planes to form a feature such as the nose? Commit to memory the planes that comprise the features, and you'll save yourself so many headaches. In the examples below, notice how I drew different planes for each of the three references.

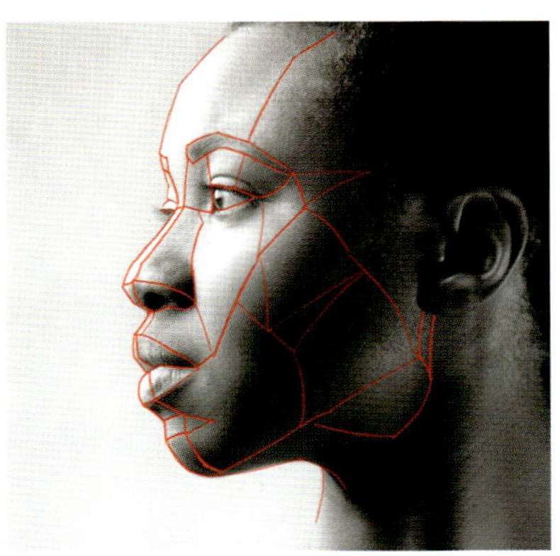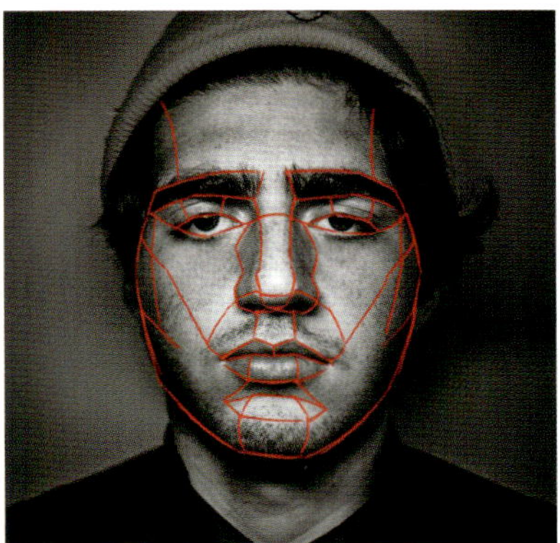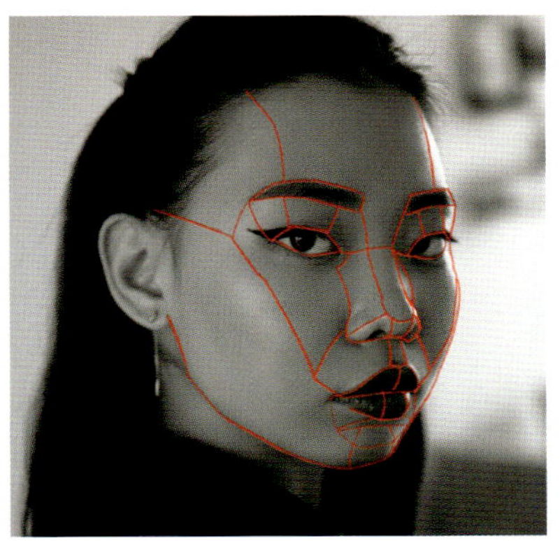

Why? Because not every face you draw will merit the same planes. Sometimes you won't need certain planes drawn in for you to recognize where to shade or not shade. Your approach needs to be founded in the principles of the Asaro planes, but flexible enough that you can accommodate any portrait you draw. No two people look the same—at least not outside identical twins or the occasional doppelgänger.

Draw the planes, not the head

Don't think of using the Asaro method the same way that you use the Loomis method. The planes of the Asaro head are more valuable than the overall head itself. Use the planes to help build the underlying form of your portrait after you have drawn your basic Loomis head. Think of the Asaro method as the next step in the process after you have completed the Loomis phase. You can use as many or as few of these planes as you feel comfortable. Like Asaro himself said, this method is meant to be a guide.

Why is each side slightly different?

That's an excellent question. Subjects of different ages have different bone structures. The right side of the Planes of the Head mannequin represents a younger, less developed bone structure, while the left side models a much older and more developed bone structure. You can use the method to draw almost any face because it is applicable to all ages, sexes, and races with variations only in proportion.

Fusing the Asaro and Loomis Methods

The Loomis and Asaro methods were developed at different times by two different artists. Each brings to the table its own twist on the same concept. In tandem, they're even better. Allow yourself to freely draw portraits, incorporating both methods into your drawing flow. The Loomis method gives you the perfect approach to draw the foundation of your portrait. The Asaro method gives you a solid understanding of the planes that comprise the face and facial features so that you can start to carve out the character of your subject. Let's look at exactly how this approach works using the three most common portrait angles: profile, straight-on, and three-quarter turn.

Step 1: Draw a Loomis Head

The best way to practice the Asaro planes is to draw them on top of a Loomis head. So, first draw a Loomis head.

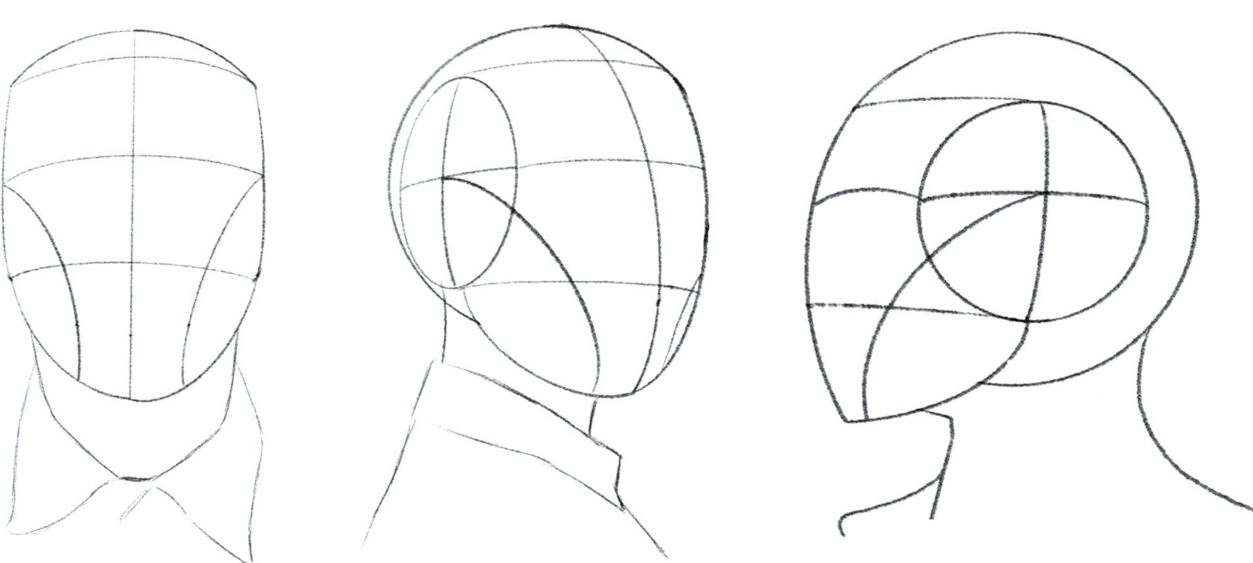

Step 2: Draw the Shoulders and Hair

It is important for you to establish the basic shape of the shoulders and hairline of the portrait. Sketch those in, then start to draw the generic shape of your subject's ears. The hairline on the face side will help you place the nose bridge on the face and ensure it is proportionate to the boundary between the face and the hair.

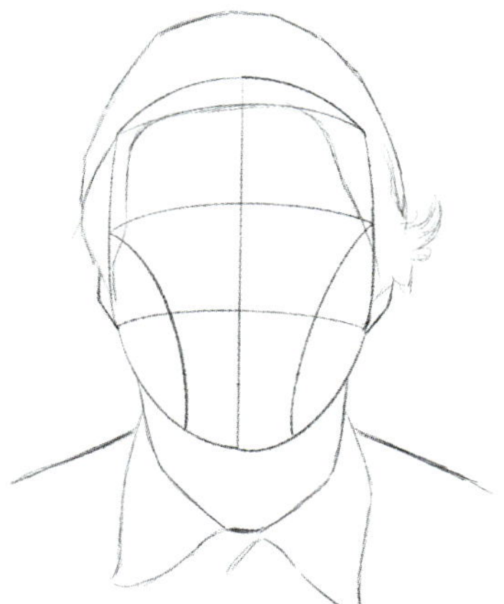
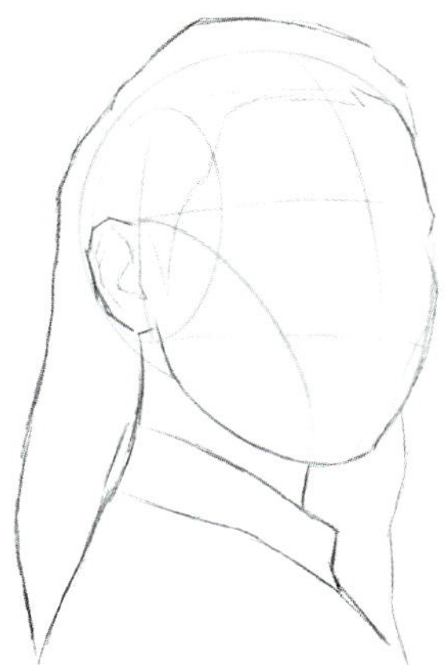
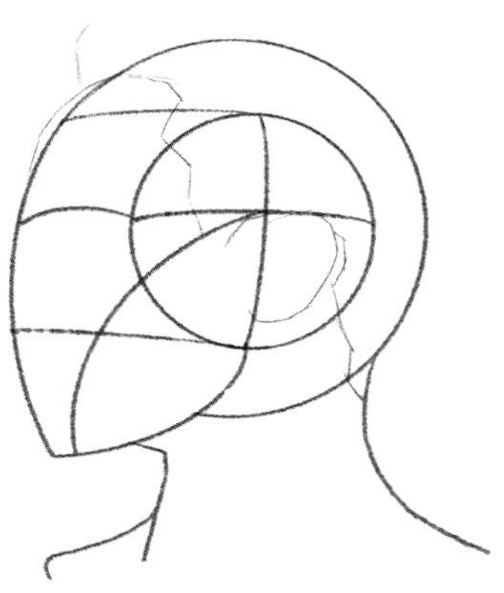

> *Chapters 4 through 8 will break down the planes of each facial feature in detail, so don't get overwhelmed here.*

Step 3: Draw the Eye Planes

Next, draw in the planes of your eyes. The easiest way is to begin by identifying the bridge of the nose. After you have that established, you can draw the remaining planes that showcase the brow line. You can then use the brow line as a guide to extend the three main planes that comprise the eye lid; this will be the same for each side, although the perspective will vary depending on the angle of your reference.

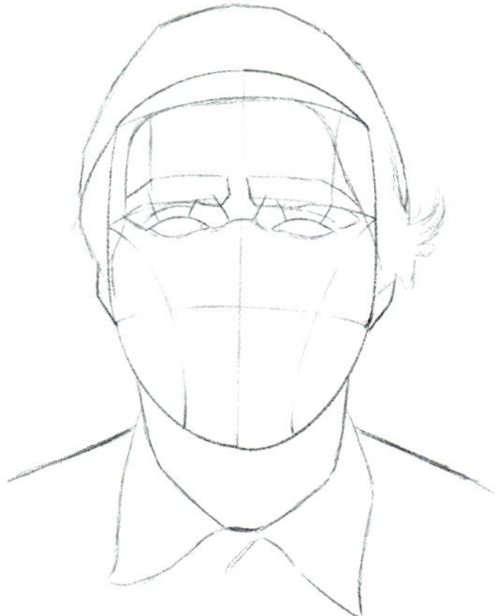
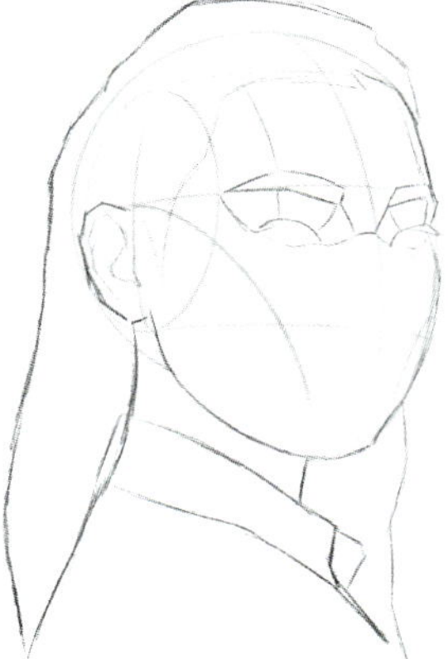
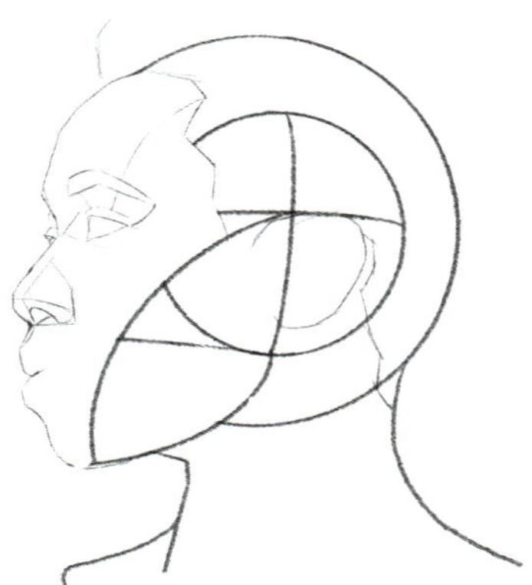

Step 4: Draw the Nose Planes

With the eye planes placed, you can start to draw your nose from the nose bridge. The top plane, which is the nose ridge plane, extends down to the tip of the nose. From here, you can draw the nose slope planes as well as identify exactly where the bottom of the nose ends. Remember that you can use the nose line of the underlying Loomis head to help you nail your proportions for the nose placement. Essentially, the construction flow is from the eyes at the top down to the lips.

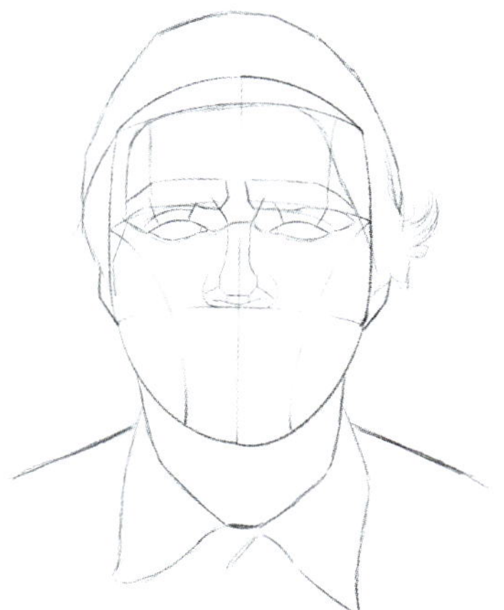 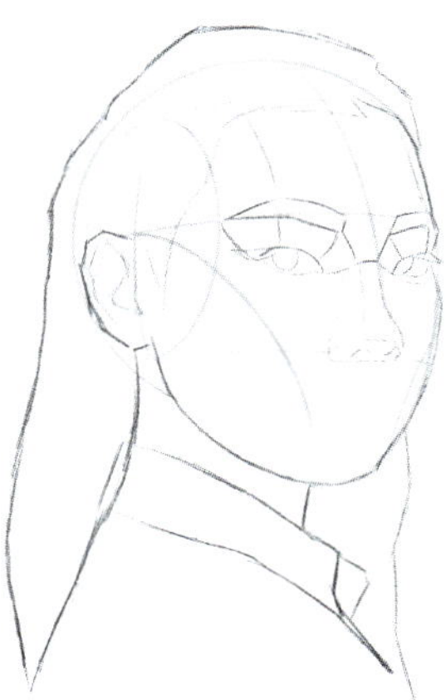 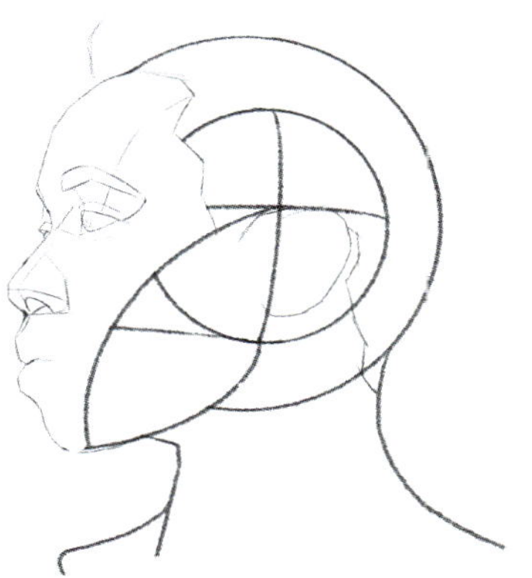

For profile angle portraits, sometimes it's more beneficial to draw the nose before the eyes. Every angle will be different and the construction flow that works well for one angle may not work well for another. Start with the feature that makes you feel the most confident.

According to Asaro, the mouth is comprised of five planes: two for the top lip and three for the bottom lip. A good rule to follow for proper placement of the mouth is to split the third section of the head (between the bottom of the nose and bottom of the chin) into thirds. Place a mark at roughly the top of the upper lip, followed by one at the bottom of the bottom lip. A center mark between these two will align with where the lips come together.

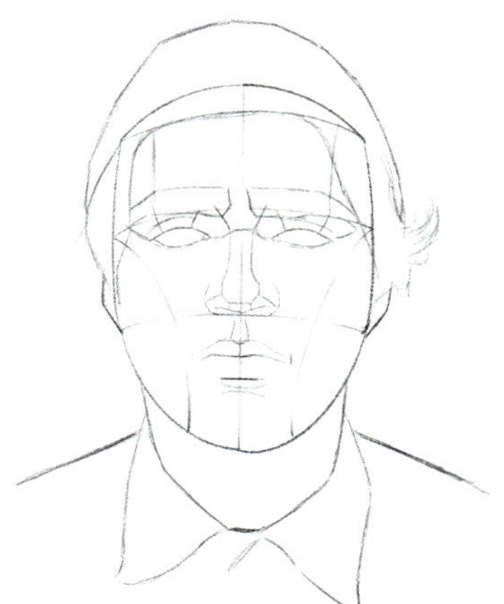 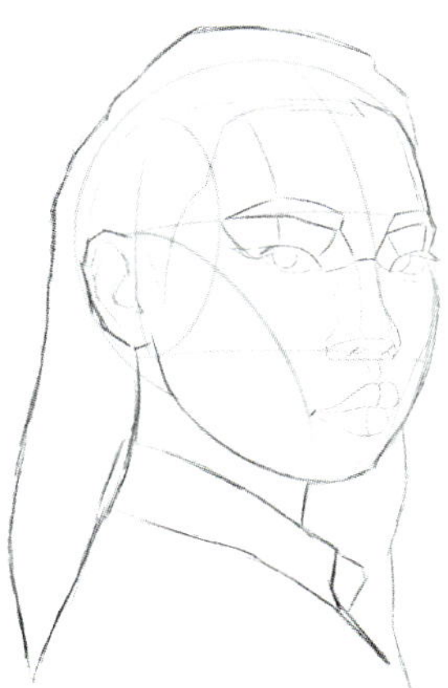 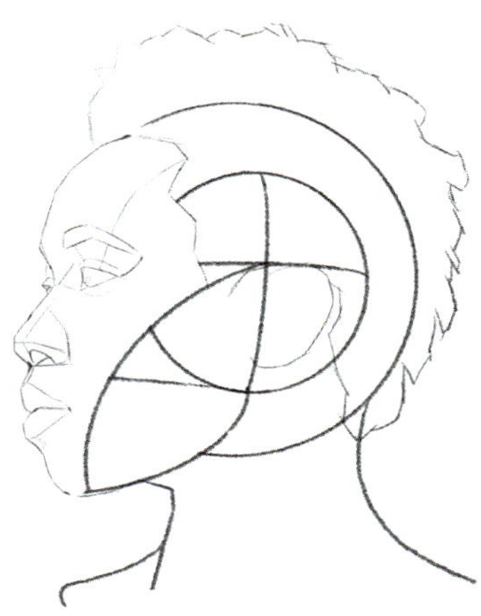

Remember, at this point in the drawing process you are getting familiar with the planes that govern the general underlying form. You should not expect your sketches to look realistic. Instead, focus on understanding how to begin drawing the illusion of three-dimensional form.

Step 6: Add Rhythm Lines

After drawing your basic Loomis head and sketching in the general facial features using the Asaro method as a guide, the rest is simple. All that is left is to sketch in the rhythm lines. Rhythm lines are used in portrait drawings to help bring out the underlying form of a subject. They are best used when trying to showcase a portrait's bone structure and generally help you understand exactly where certain tones need to be placed and shaded. This brings out form by beginning to introduce volume to the drawing.

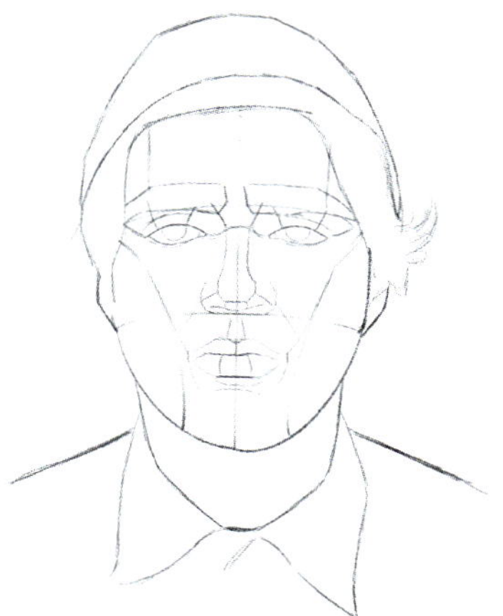
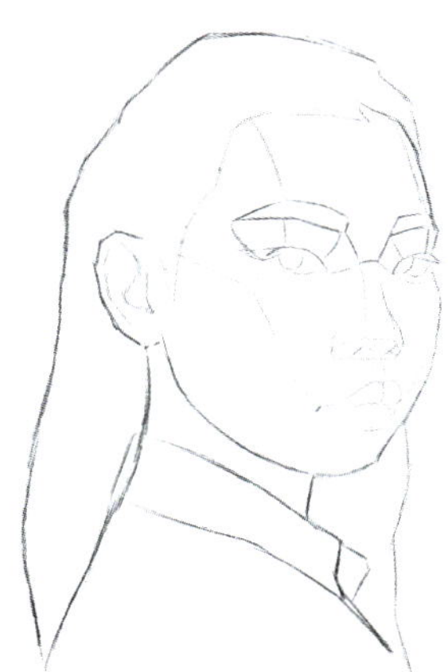
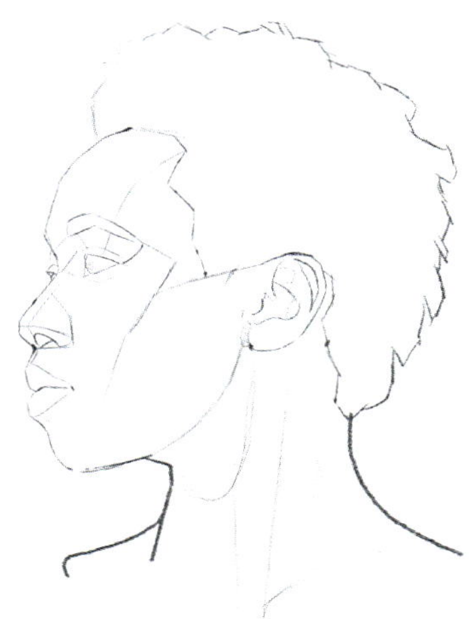

Project 6: Draw a Loomis Head with the Asaro Planes

Now, draw your own Loomis head and add Asaro planes. When drawing in Asaro planes to imply bone structure, you will likely need more in the beginning. That is completely fine! As you progress, you may discover that you require fewer Asaro planes for a successful portrait drawing—so leave a few out. That's completely fine too! If you need a more fluid explanation of the Asaro method and its planes, scan the QR code to watch the video **How to Easily Draw the Asaro Planes | Understanding the Asaro Method**.

Conclusion: Don't Be Afraid to Try

Sometimes tackling something as complex as drawing portraits can be daunting—especially if you have no real fundamental knowledge to lean back on. On their own, the Loomis and Asaro methods have each proven their worth to many, many artists, due to their exceptional simplicity and anatomical accuracy. By fusing them together, we have created something new: a method that hopefully will give you energy and confidence to start drawing any portrait you desire.

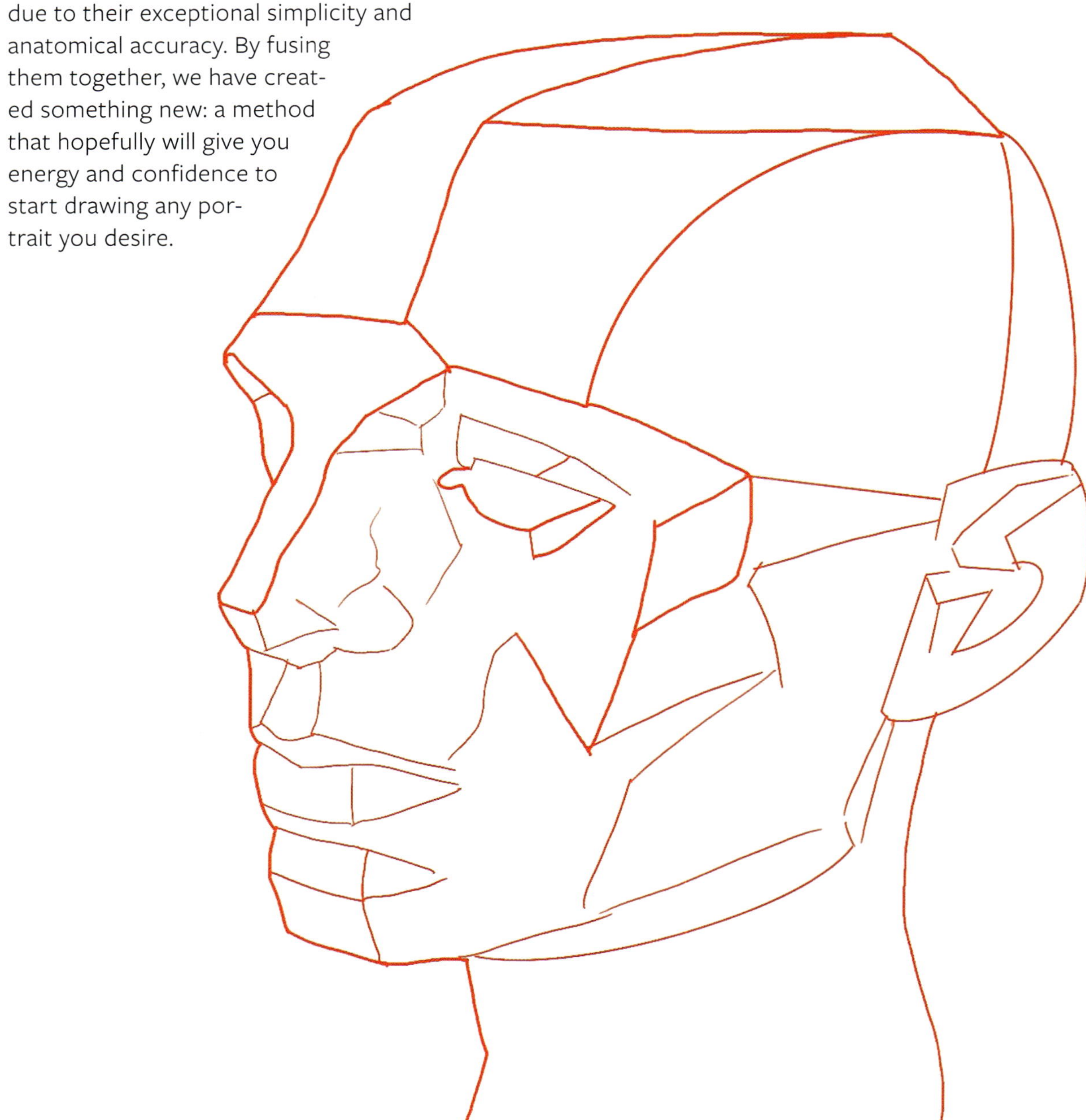

CHAPTER 4

How to Draw *the* Eyes

"The eyes are the window to the soul."
—Unknown

Whether William Shakespeare, Leonardo Da Vinci, Cicero, or someone else was the first to coin the phrase, the eyes do open a view into the person behind a portrait. The problem for most of us, however, is where and how to begin when drawing those all-important eyes. Don't worry, this chapter will give you all the information you need to approach your portrait drawings more confidently and produce more satisfying results. First, we'll walk through how you can use the Asaro method as a basic approach to framing the eyes of your portrait. The structure of the facial planes is the same regardless of your subject— only the proportion changes across different portraits. Then, you'll practice drawing eyes for three common portrait angles.

The Eye Planes

Before you worry about where to place your subject's eyes, I want you to focus on how to draw them. The Loomis method gives you the basic guidelines and structure for eye placement, but it does not provide advice on how to draw them—that's where the Asaro method comes into play. The Asaro method is your guide to constructing eyes, and the Asaro planes (shown below) will help you to construct most any eye.

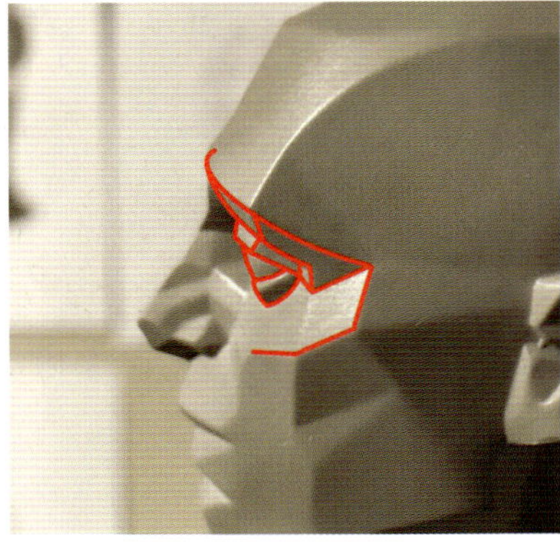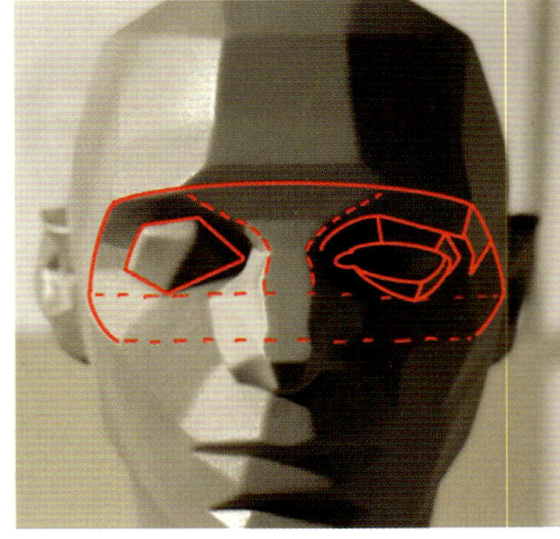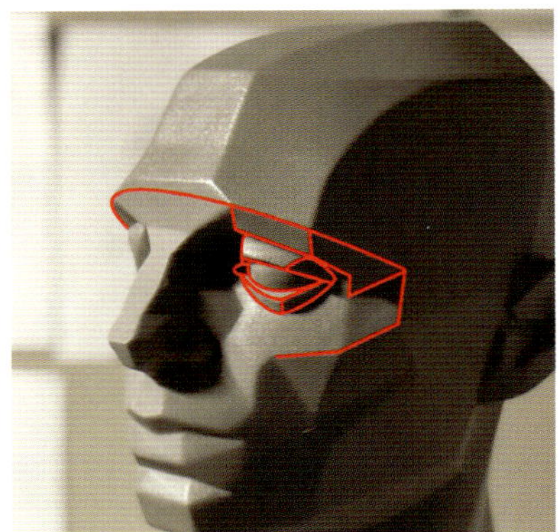

Notice how the line across the top of the planes is the same as the brow line from the Loomis method. This alignment allows you to easily see where you can plug the facial features into your Loomis head. Before you do that though, I want to show you step by step how to draw some eyes.

Step 1: Draw the Nose Bridge

When it comes to the eyes, the portrait angle does not affect how you approach drawing them. In fact, the eyes actually start with the nose: The first step in drawing the framework for the eyes is to establish the nose bridge plane. To do so, pull a line from the inner corner of each eyebrow down to where they are in line with the tear ducts of the subject's eyes. Draw a line that connects the bottoms of the two lines (like a flat-tipped letter "V"), then pull the connecting line over to the inner corner of each eye.

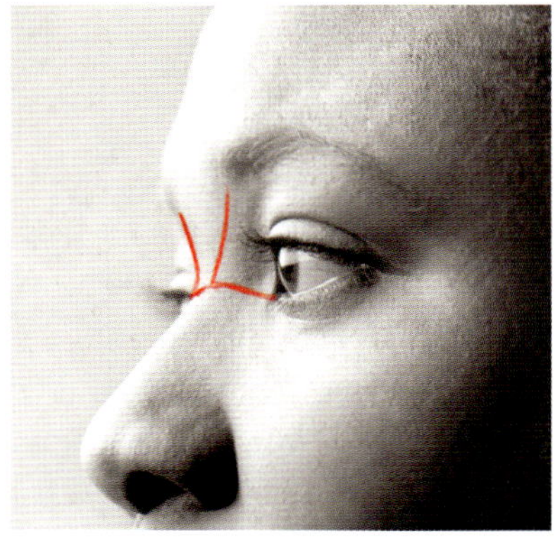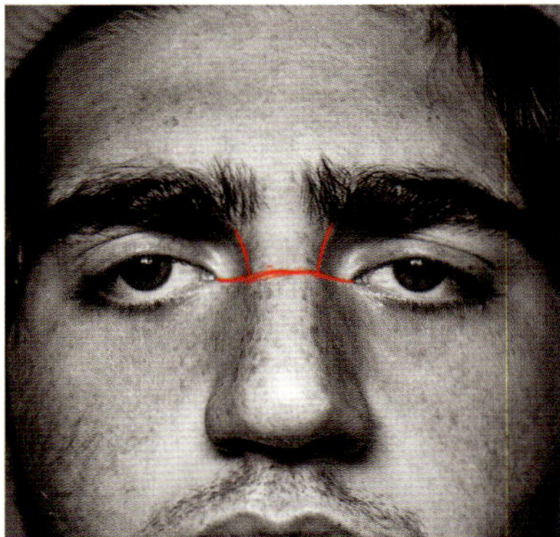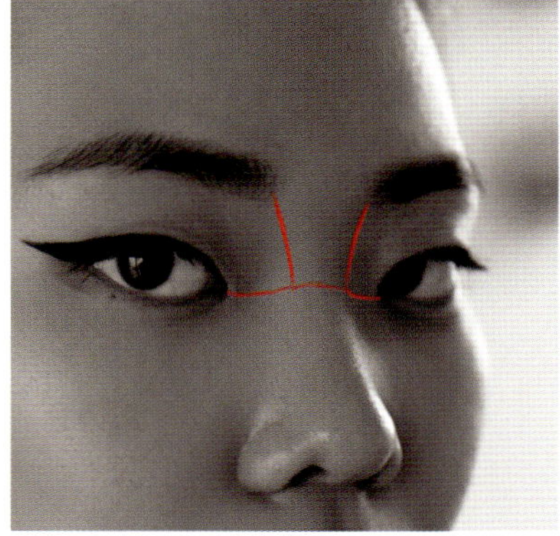

Step 2: Draw the Eyebrows

The eyebrows should extend from the top of the nose bridge plane lines that you drew in Step 1. Draw the basic two-dimensional shape of each eyebrow. Don't worry about detail work at this stage in the drawing process.

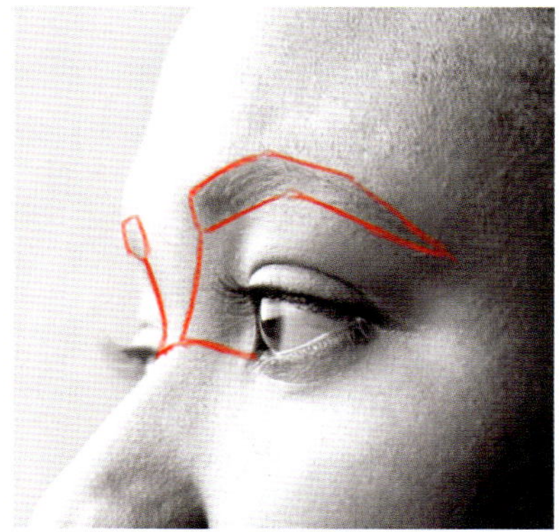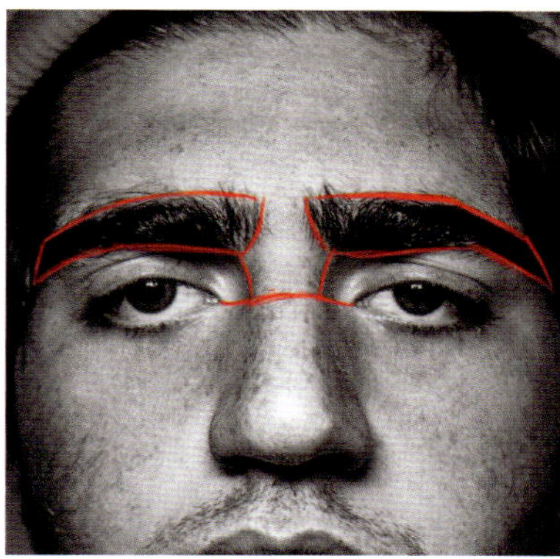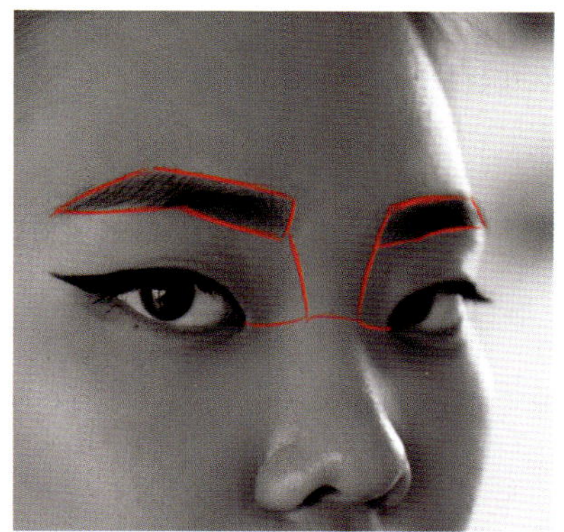

Step 3: Draw the Eye Planes

The eye planes are comprised of three lines called *frame lines*. Pull these down from the eyebrow to end at the edge of the subject's upper eyelid. These lines essentially "frame" the eye and give you necessary structure. Draw the first line one third of the way along the eyebrow from the inside edge of the nose bridge. Draw the second line down from the subject's hairline, flowing it through the eyebrow to the edge of the upper eyelid. This line is an extension of the temple plane line, according to the Asaro method. Extend the third line from the outside corner of the eye to the edge of the eyebrow.

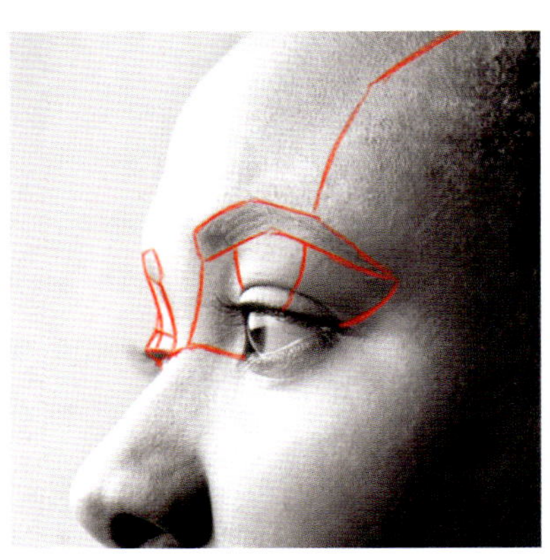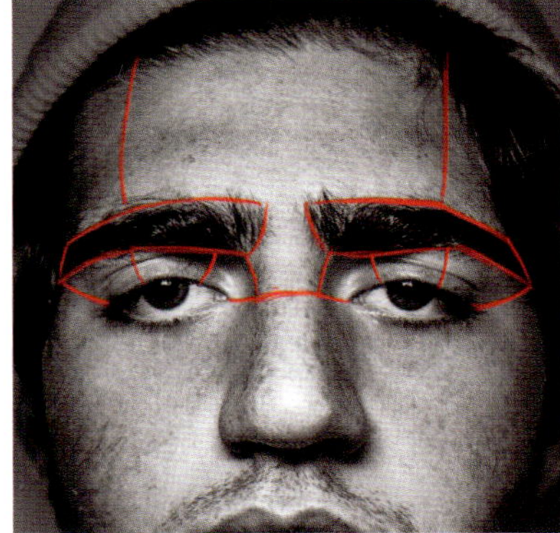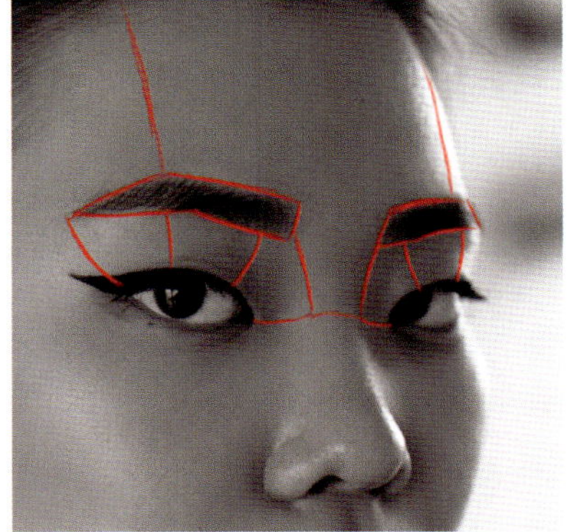

Now that you have the frame lines drawn in, you can connect them together to bring out the basic shape of the eyes and cement the structure needed for the hatching and blending that will come later in the drawing process. Remember, every person's eyes will have a different shape, especially their upper eyelid. In the profile image, notice how we can draw the upper eyelid wholistically, but the three-quarter-turn angle does not merit the same structure. The more you draw different individuals, the more you will become aware of this.

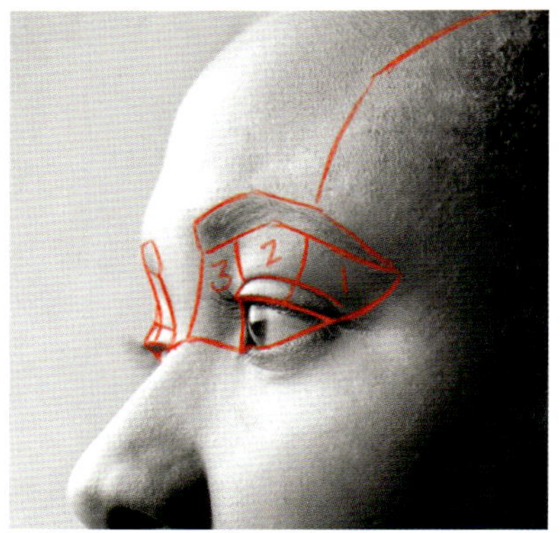
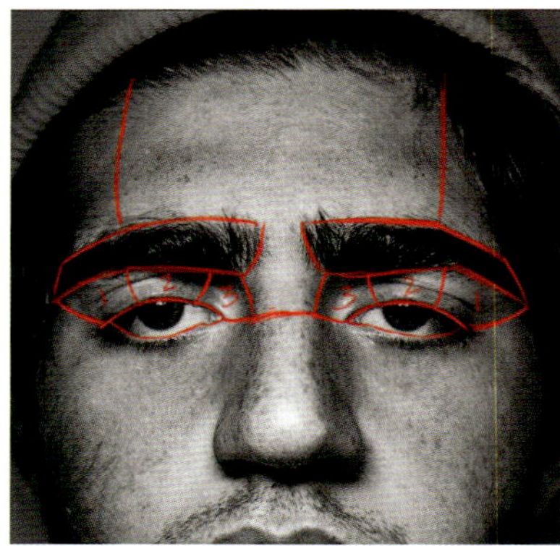
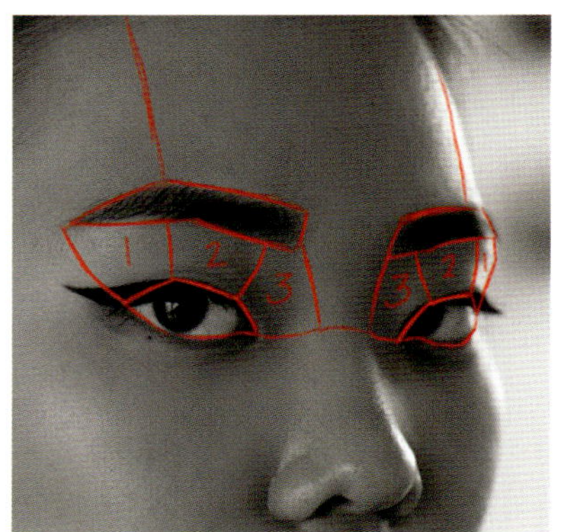

Drawing Eyes Using the Asaro Method

One of the exciting things about this method is once you've done it a few times you will realize that you can use it to draw the eyes from any angle. The versatility of the method allows you to draw everything from realistic eyes to cartoon and anime eyes. Now that you understand the theory of how the method works, get ready to practice.

In the following sections, I'll demonstrate the drawing flow for the eyes for the three main angles—the three pillars in portraiture—that you will run into throughout your art career. We'll use the three references that your final project will be based on in Chapter 10, so you can practice for the final project. Remember to take it slow and enjoy every stroke, smudge, blend, and adjustment.

The Profile Angle

Now in this section I will be showing you the step-by-step drawing process as we draw the eyes at a profile angle.

Draw the nose bridge, which resembles a letter "V" with a flat bottom.

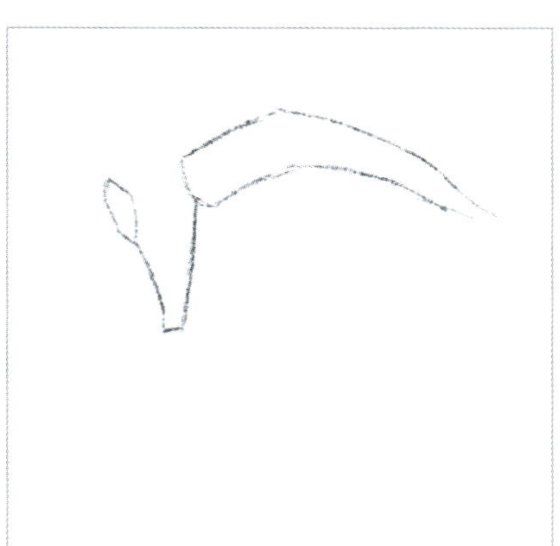

Next, draw the basic shape of your eyebrows. These should extend from the top of your nose bridge.

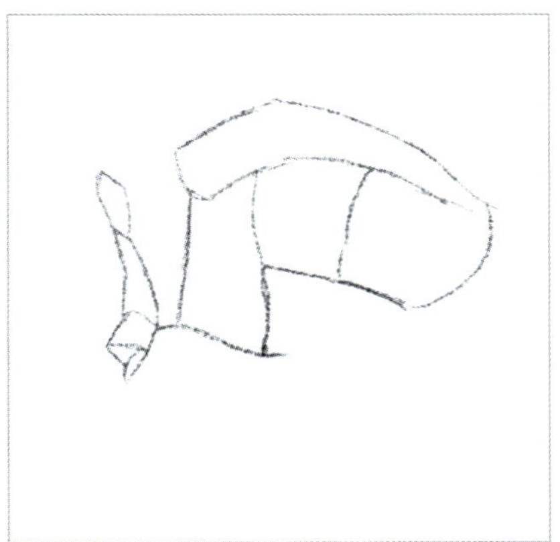

Draw the three eye planes by pulling your frame lines down to the top eyelid.

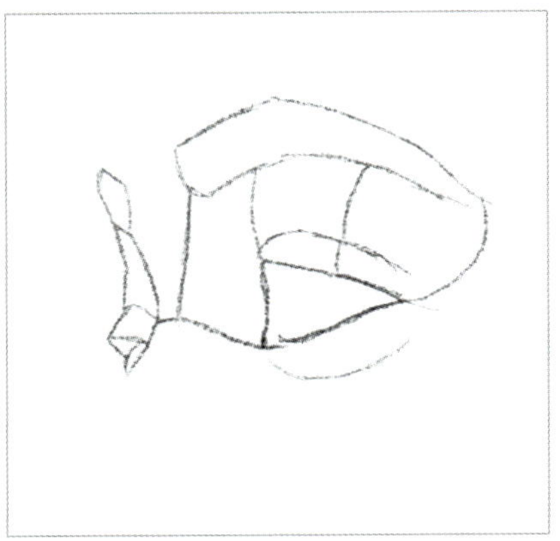

Now you can place the bottom of the eye, as well as solidify the top eyelid fold.

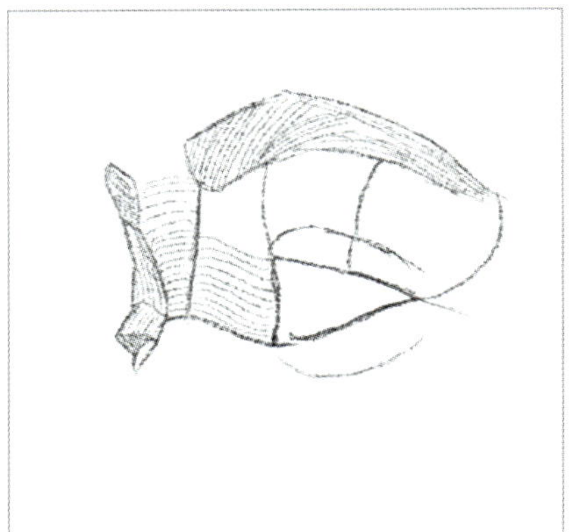

With the basic two-dimensional shape of the eyes framed with Asaro planes, you're ready to begin hatching (pushing or pulling your lines in a single direction) or crosshatching (crossing lines from two directions). As you push and pull your hatch lines, keep in mind the underlying form of the reference.

Best Practice: *Your hatching should flow in the same direction as your underlying form.*

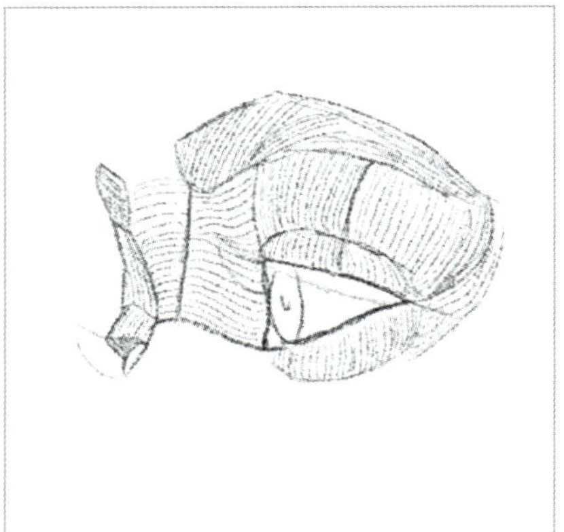

Hatch or crosshatch every plane in your drawing so that it looks like this example.

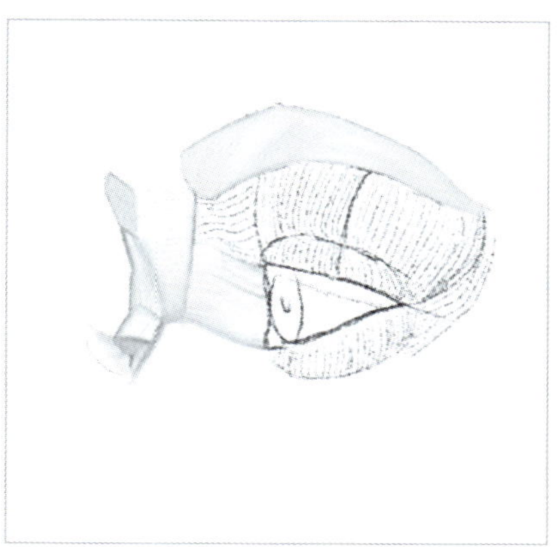

When you're done hatching, use smudgers of varying sizes to blend the hatch marks. While the exact aesthetic conveyed may vary, smudgers will blend both charcoal and graphite. Use the example as a blending guide.

> **Best Practice:** *The shorter your smudger strokes, the softer the blend will be. The longer your smudger strokes, the harsher the blend—to the point where your initial hatch marks will still show through.*

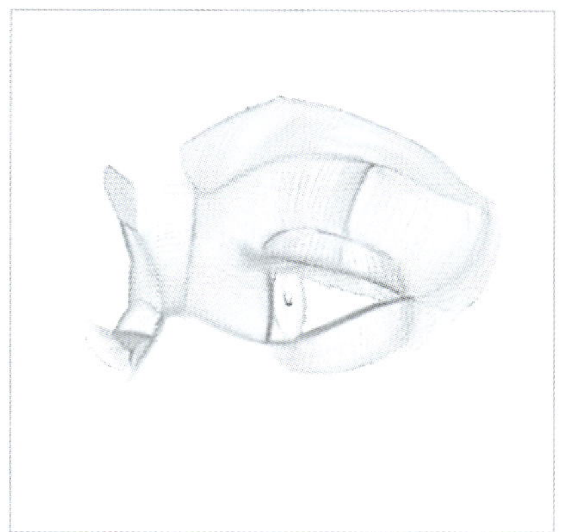

Use your smudger to blend the entire drawing, pushing and pulling in the same direction as your hatch marks. Following the hatching direction ensures you will keep the integrity of the underlying form that you brought out when you initially laid down your hatch marks.

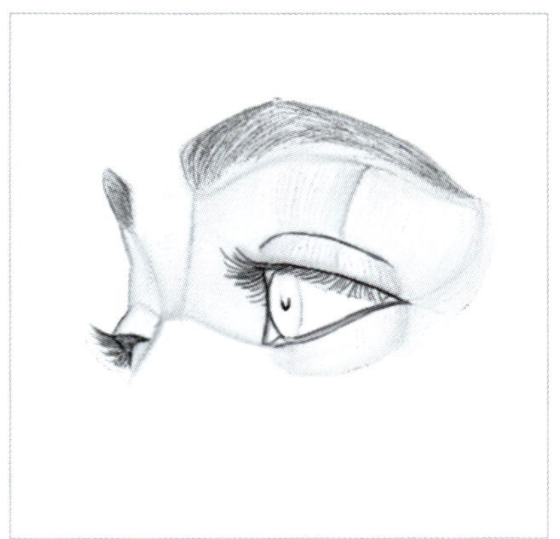

After you blend the base layer, you can start to build up your linework. Begin with the eyebrows and eyelashes. Use a medium charcoal for this step.

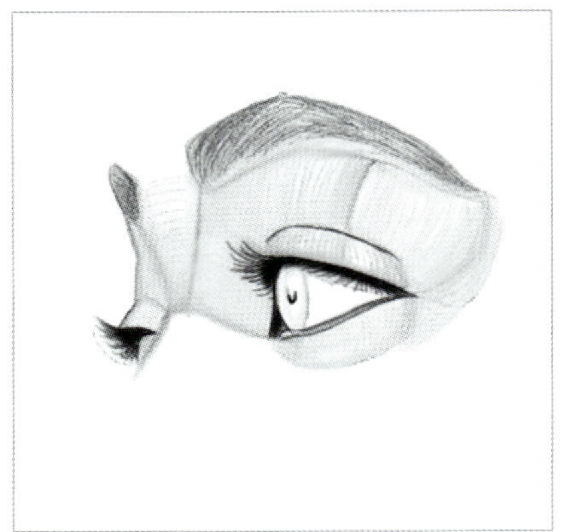

Continue drawing in your eyelashes and eyebrows until you are satisfied. Remember that you can give the bottom of the upper eyelid line a thicker line quality to make the eyelashes look thicker.

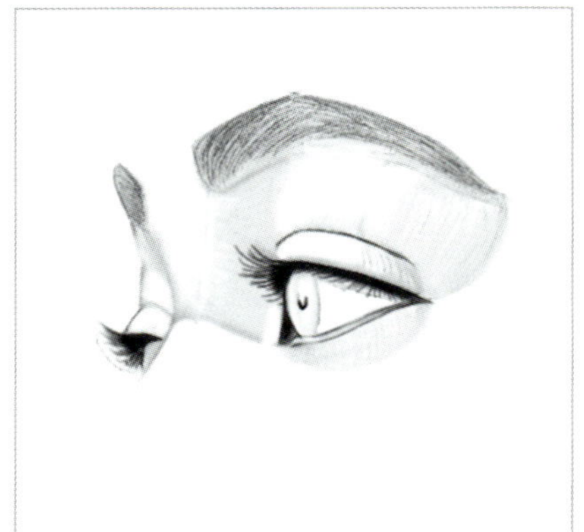

Now you can retrieve some of your high values with your eraser. Make sure you retrieve the highest values in the reference photo, because this will help you accentuate the value scale when we start lowering the surrounding values.

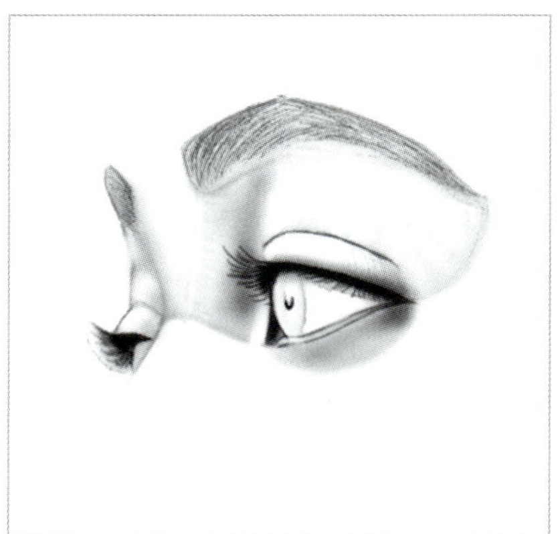

Dip a brush into some ground soft charcoal and test the tone on your scratch paper. (You did follow Drawing Hacks 1 and 2, didn't you?). When you're happy with the tone, start to strategically build up your lower values. (Remember, less is more!)

Best Practice: *If a bunch of charcoal bits fall onto your scratch paper during your tone test, you know that your brush is fully loaded and will convey a lower value.*

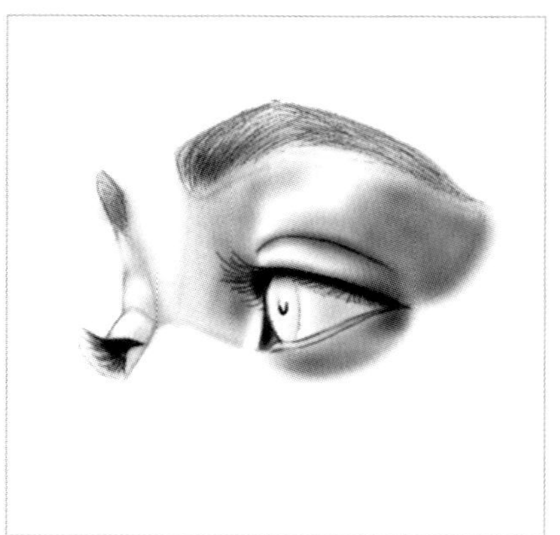

Continue your brushwork to place your low values in the areas that need to be lowered.

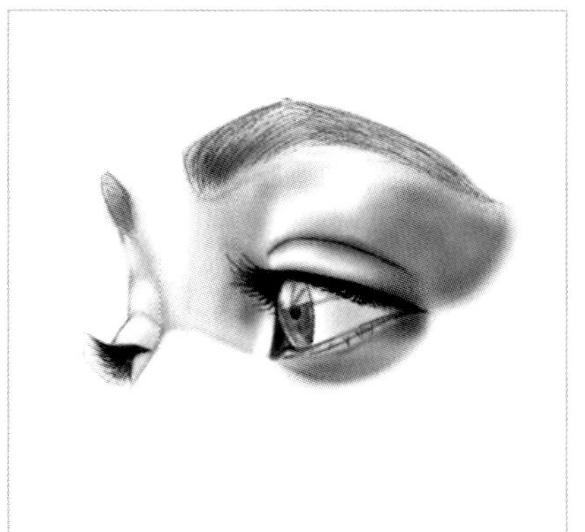

Next, focus on building up the detail in the eye. Use your medium charcoal with light pressure for your base layer, then use a small smudger so that you can place your smudges exactly where you want them. Remember, a smaller smudger gives you more control.

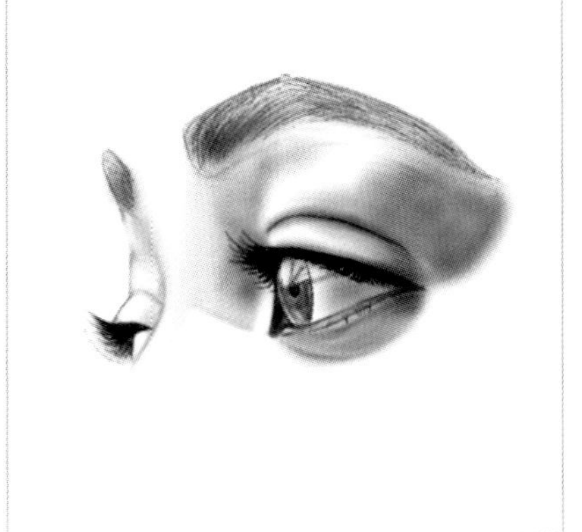

Finally, use a detail eraser, such as a MONO Zero, with very light pressure to bring out detail work. For a soft finish, make sure to go over your blends with an empty brush. This will benefit the drawing by bringing out a soft gradation.

The Straight-On Angle

In this section we will cover the drawing process for constructing the eyes at a straight on angle. Now the straight on angle presents its own challenges in that you have to worry about symmetry. In the other two angles presented in this book you will not have to deal with this, but I will show you how you can begin to tackle this challenge with relative ease.

As with the profile-angle portrait, we'll start with the nose bridge plane.

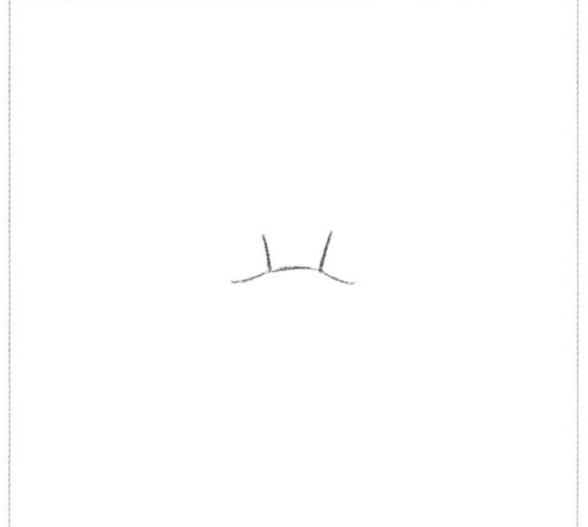

Draw two lines angled slightly towards one another, connect them with a line between their bottom ends, and then extend that line. to roughly where the tear ducts reside on either side.

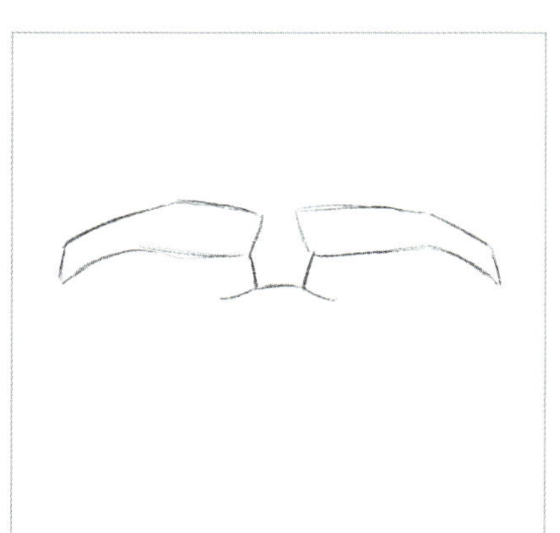

Next, draw in the two-dimensional shape of the eyebrows. I find the overhand grip works well for this, but do what feels the most natural to you.

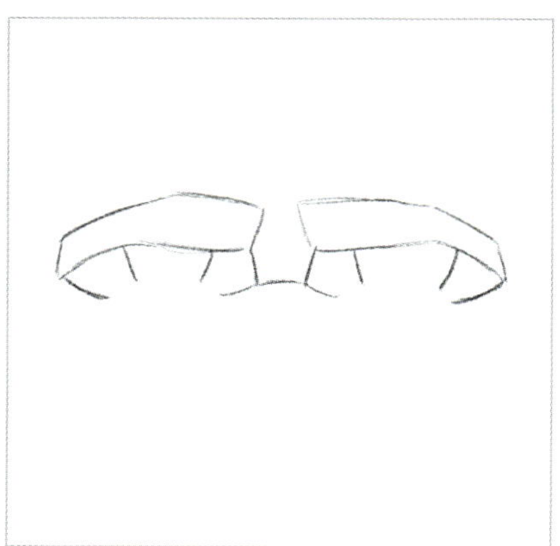

Pull down the frame lines that comprise the initial framework of the upper eyelid. This is the beginning of bringing out the three planes of the eye.

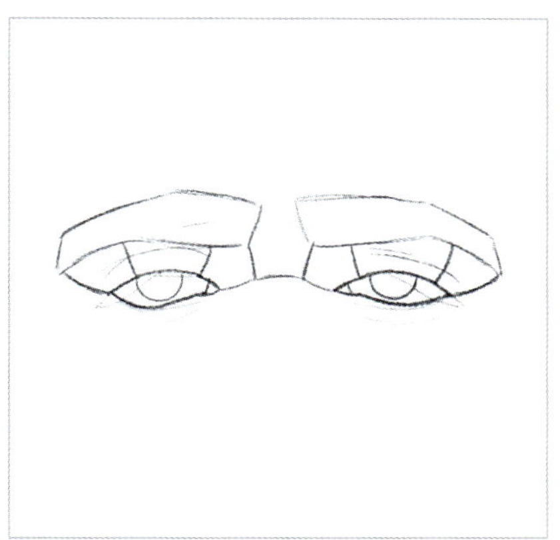

Draw the outline for the iris as well as the eyelashes, upper eyelid, and lower eye.

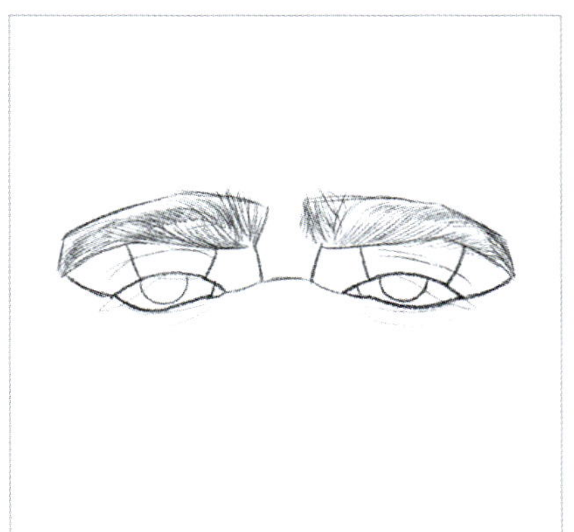

You can now start drawing in the linework of the eyebrows. Use medium charcoal for this step.

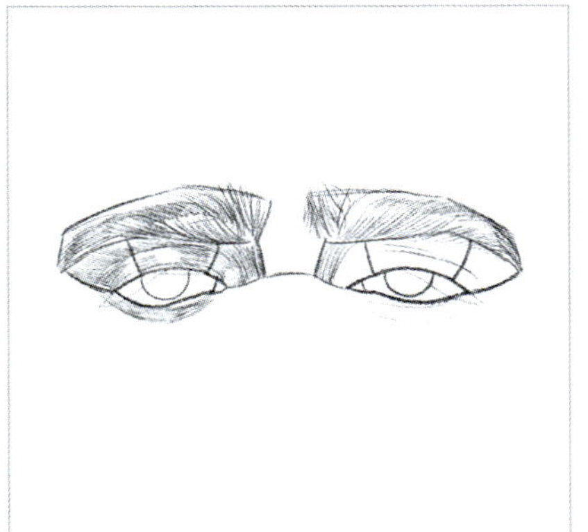

Start hatching or crosshatching. I am only hatching in the examples, but you can use either approach.

Best Practice: *If there are areas of the eyes that will require a much lower value, then you can crosshatch those areas in this step. That way when you smudge your hatching, your value in that specific area will already be lower.*

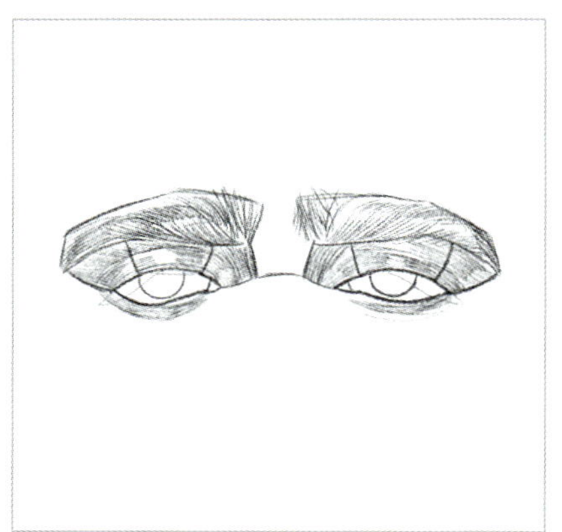

Hatch the Asaro planes individually to gain a thorough understanding of how the face is constructed. This, in turn, will also help you understand how light affects the portrait at different angles in varying light conditions.

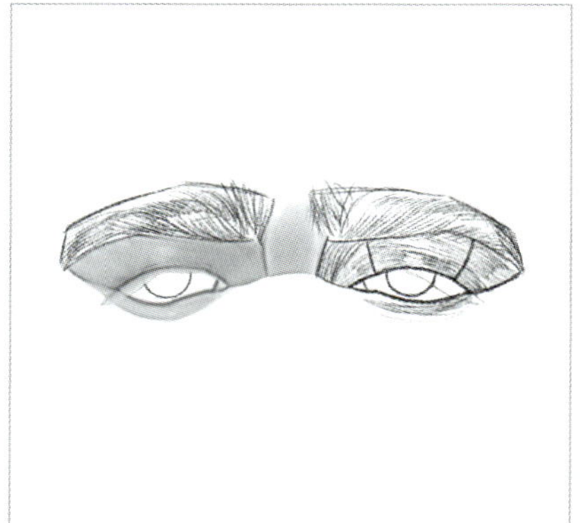

With your smudger and light pressure, start smudging the charcoal into the paper. The harder you press, the more the charcoal will be pressed into the pores of the paper and the lower the value will be.

Best Practice: *Always start with a light pressure.*

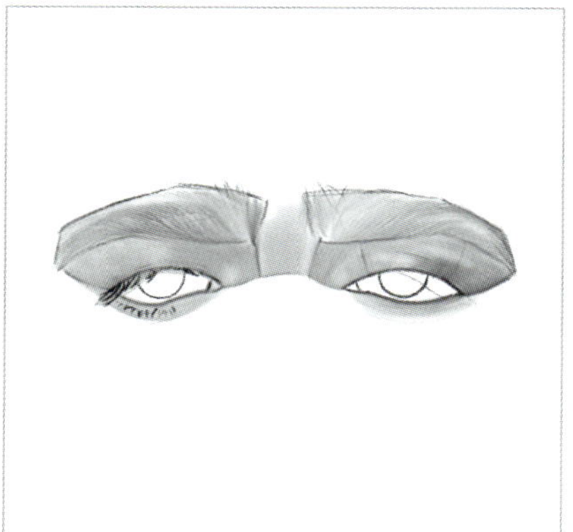

Once you have the entire drawing smudged, switch to a medium charcoal and start placing the eyelashes within their two-dimensional shape.

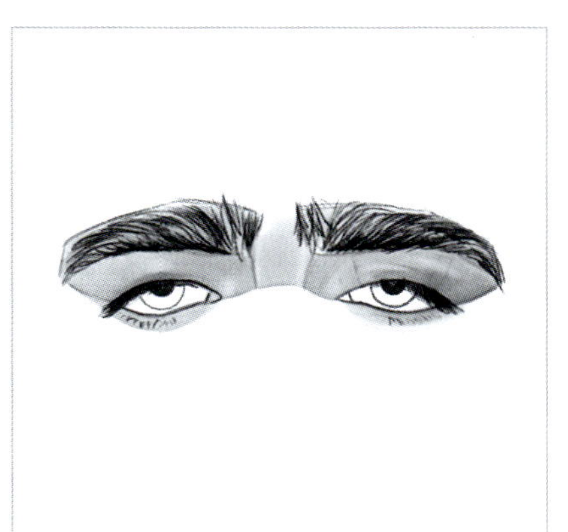

Continue to use your medium charcoal pencil for the other eyelashes and eyebrows. When you fill in the eye pupil, use a softer pressure. If you go in too hard. you risk scratching the paper.

> **Best Practice:** *The sharper you keep your pencil tip, the thinner the line quality you will be able to convey.*

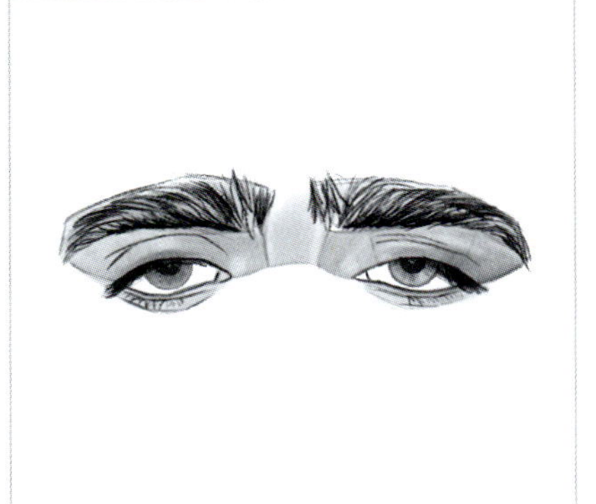

With a smaller smudger, pull the charcoal that you laid down for your eye pupil in a single motion to the edge of the iris. Then, switch to your medium charcoal pencil and reinforce the lower part of the eye with lower values.

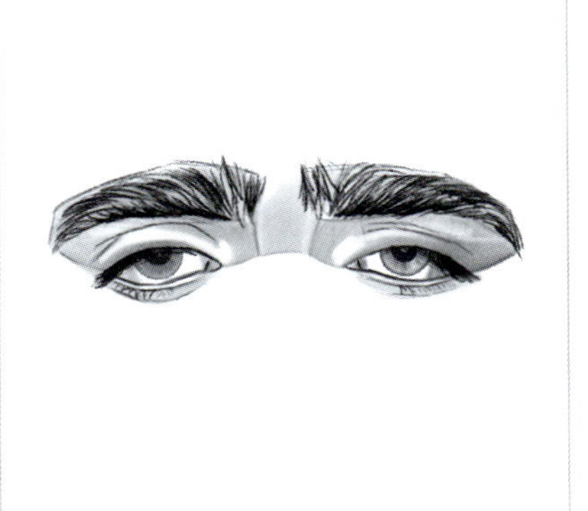

Use your MONO Zero Eraser to retrieve all your high and mid values. This will make your drawing more dynamic and start to showcase the value scale.

> **Best Practice:** *Vary your pressure control, so each eraser stroke will be a different tone. The harder you press, the higher the value retrieved. The softer your press, the lower the value retrieved.*

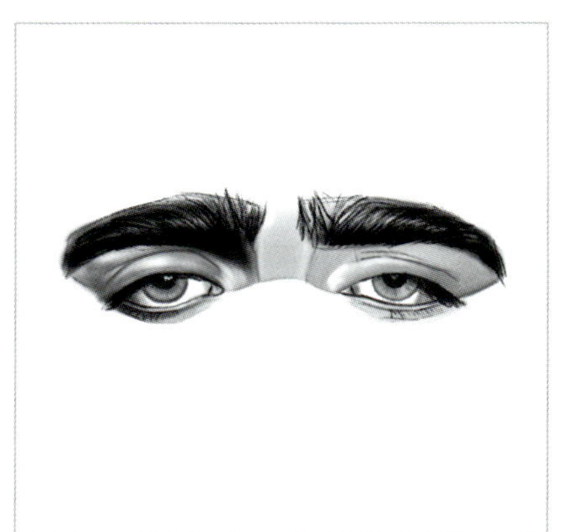

Bring out the low values in the eyebrows, eyelashes, and center of the pupil. Use your brush with your ground soft charcoal and do soft pulls. For the eyebrows, however, dab the paper with your brush to keep the integrity of your eyebrow hair lines while still lowering the value and producing a soft, airbrushed kind of aesthetic.

Best Practice: *If you can use complete black and all your tones leading to complete white, then you will have accentuated the value scale to its fullest potential and your drawing will pop.*

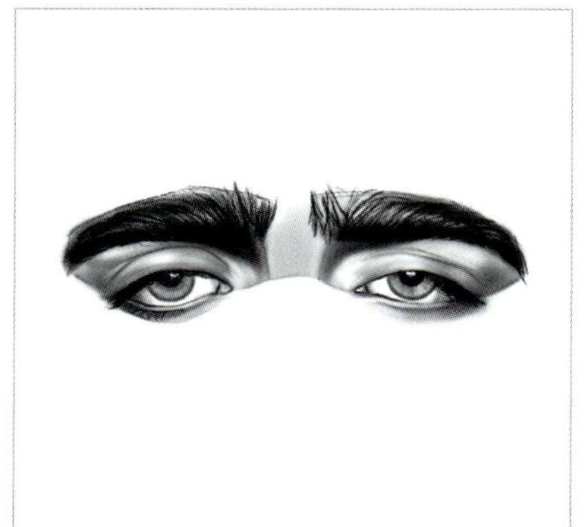

Continue to lower the values throughout the drawing with your ground soft charcoal and brush.

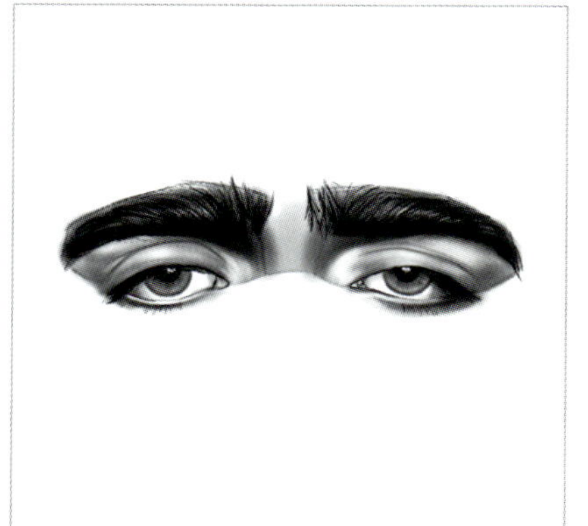

Finally, go through and cover your details. If you accidentally lowered the value too much somewhere, for example, you can hit that spot with a MONO Zero Eraser to retrieve the proper value.

Best Practice: *When you think that you are done with your drawing, take a 15-minute break, then come back to give it one last look over. Use your hard charcoal for any detail work, such as veins, skin blemishes, or fine hairs.*

The Three-Quarter-Turn Angle

The first step for constructing the eyes in a three-quarter-turn portrait is just like for a straight-on portrait.

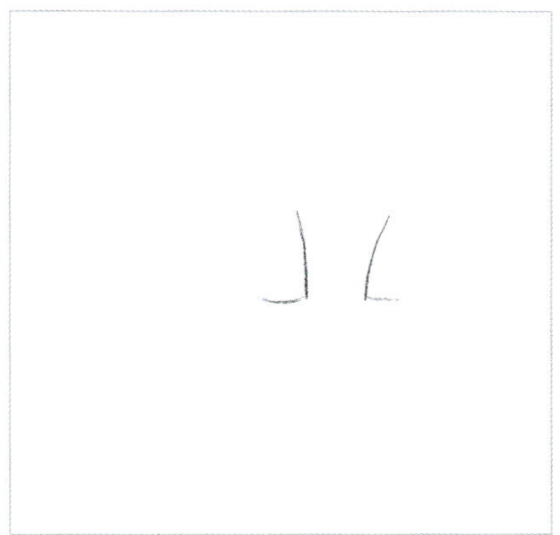

Draw two lines angled slightly towards one another, then draw a line to roughly where the tear duct resides. Notice how you don't necessarily need to connect the bottom of the nose bridge if you don't want to.

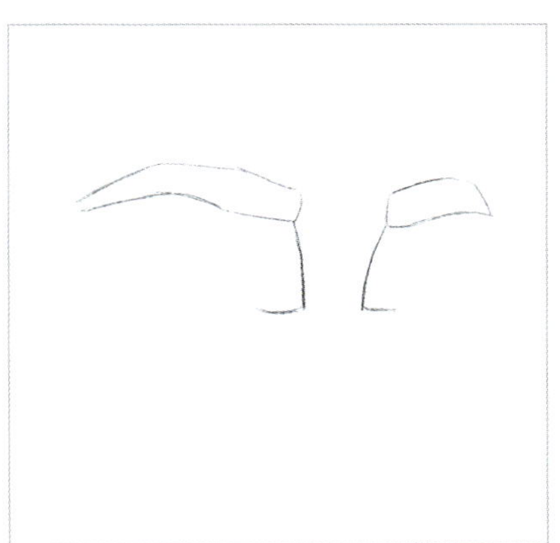

Draw in the two-dimensional shape of the eyebrows.

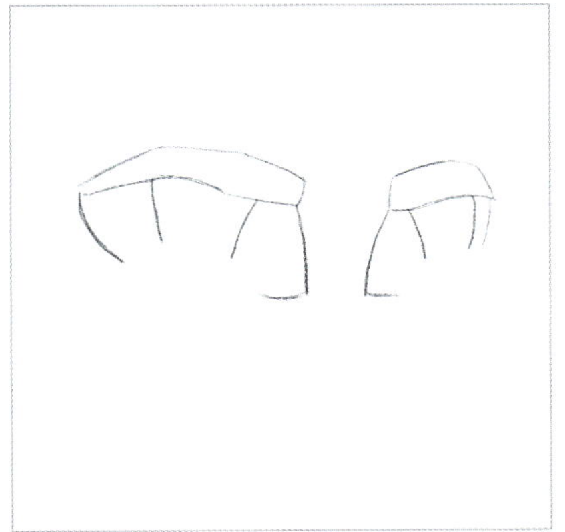

Now, pull down the frame lines that comprise the initial framework of the upper eyelid. Remember this is the beginning of bringing out the three planes of the eye.

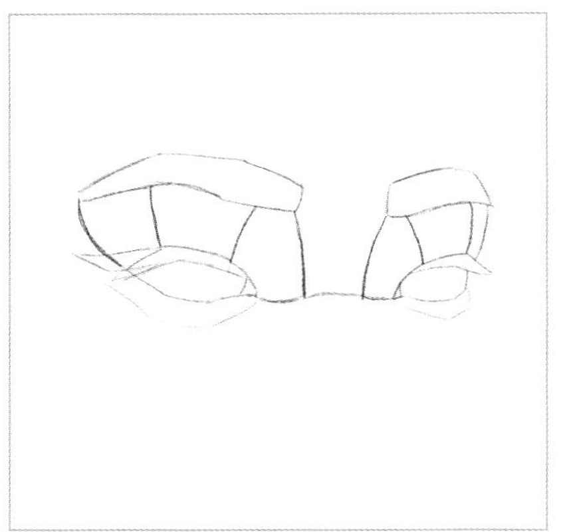

Draw the outline for the eyelashes, upper eyelid, and lower eye.

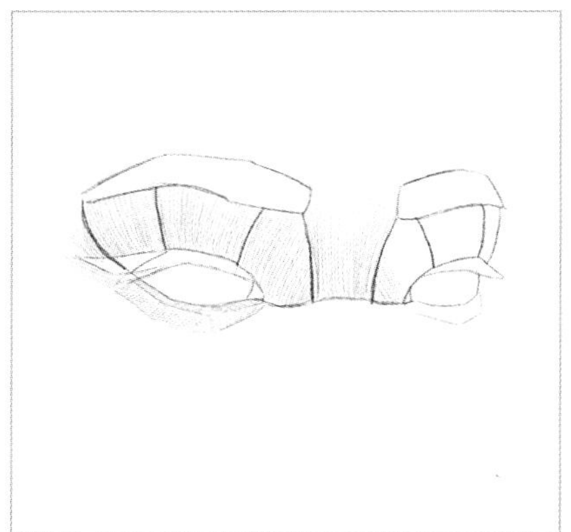

Using light pressure, start hatching the planes with your soft charcoal pencil. Remember to push or pull your pencil tip in the direction of your underlying form.

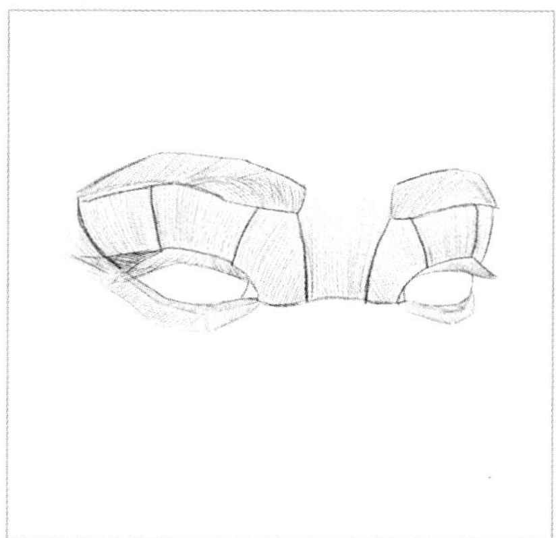

Continue hatching the eyelashes and eyebrows.

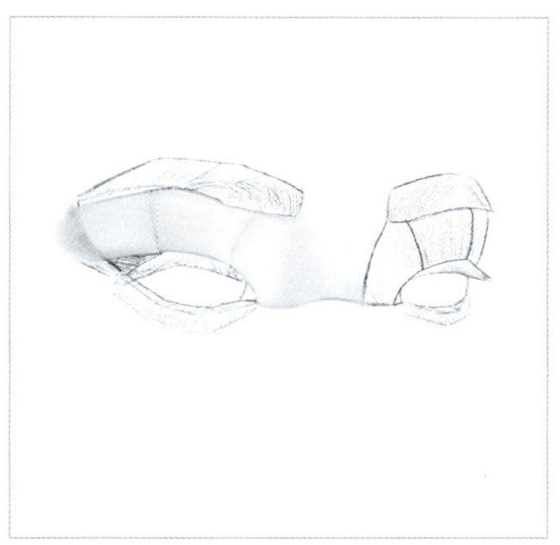

With your smudger and light pressure, start smudging the charcoal into the paper. The harder you press, the more the charcoal will be pressed into the pores of the paper, thus giving you a lower value.

> **Best Practice:** *For this step, carefully control your pressure. Always start off smudging with light pressure, because retrieving a high value is harder than saving a high value.*

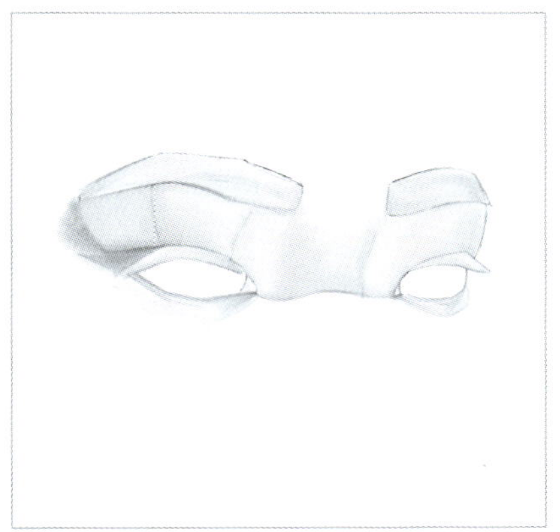

Continue smudging the drawing until it is completely smudged.

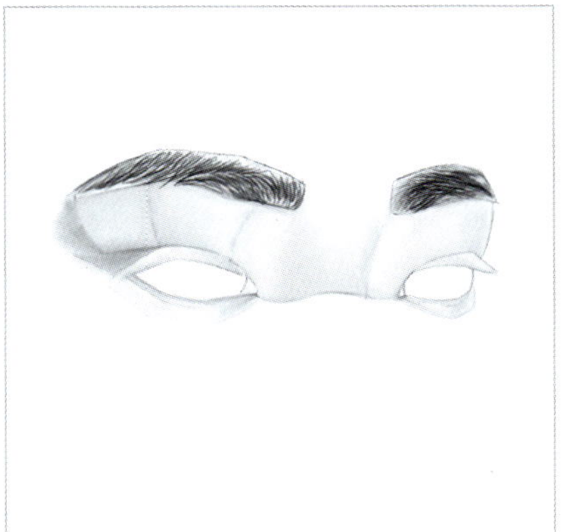

Switch to your medium charcoal pencil and start filling in the eyebrows.

> **Best Practice:** *When pulling or pushing the lines for your eyebrow hairs, lift as you conclude your line. This will give you a gradual thinning quality to the hair strand, making your hair look more realistic.*

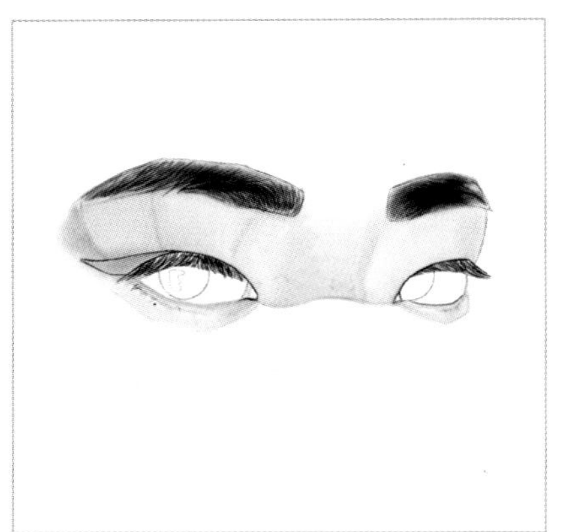

Continue to use your medium charcoal pencil for the eyelashes and tear ducts. After that, switch to your ground soft charcoal and brush the eyebrows. Remember to dab the eyebrows to help keep the line integrity of your eyebrow hairs and, in turn, make the eyebrows look more dynamic. Make sure to draw in the two-dimensional shape of the iris.

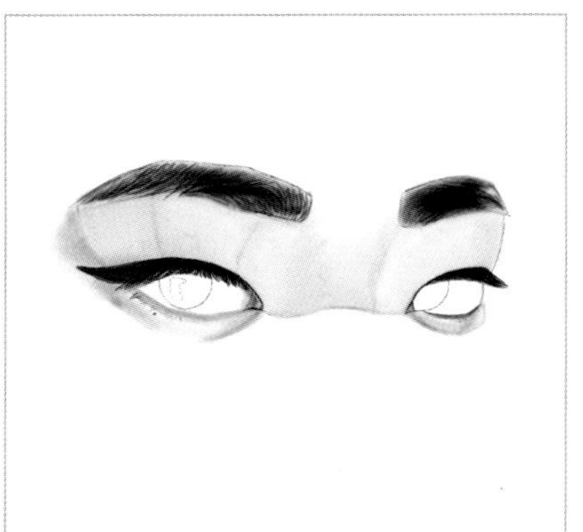

Switch to a smaller smudger and blend the eyelashes as well as the area in the reference that has eyeliner. Continue smudging to give the top of the eyelashes a lower value. Smudge the bottom of the eye to help the eye appear to sit in the head.

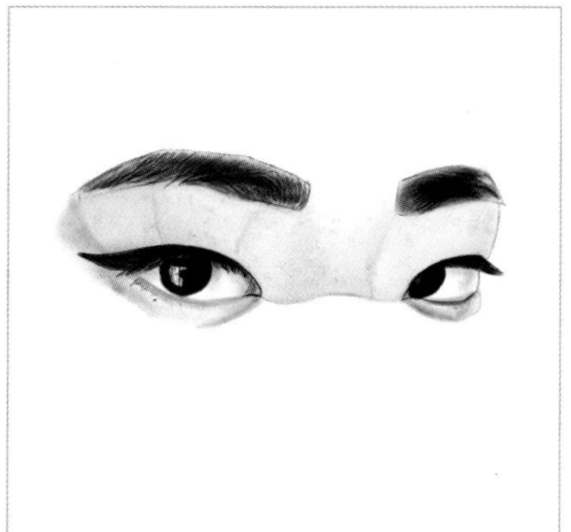

With a medium charcoal pencil, fill in the iris and pupil. Next, switch to your soft charcoal brush and lightly brush the inside and outside of both eyes. This helps the eyes look less flat outside of the iris.

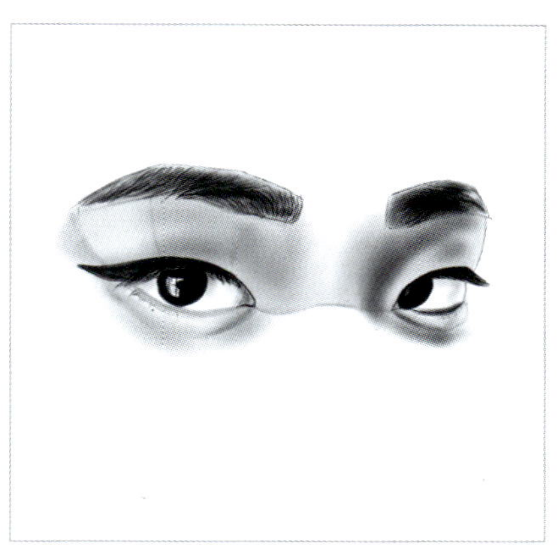

It's time to focus heavily on where your low values live in the reference. Push or pull your soft charcoal brush across the paper in those specific low value areas.

> **Best Practice:** *Much like when you first hatched your Asaro planes, pay attention to the flow of the face. Use the underlying form as your guide for the direction in which you think you should push or pull your brush.*

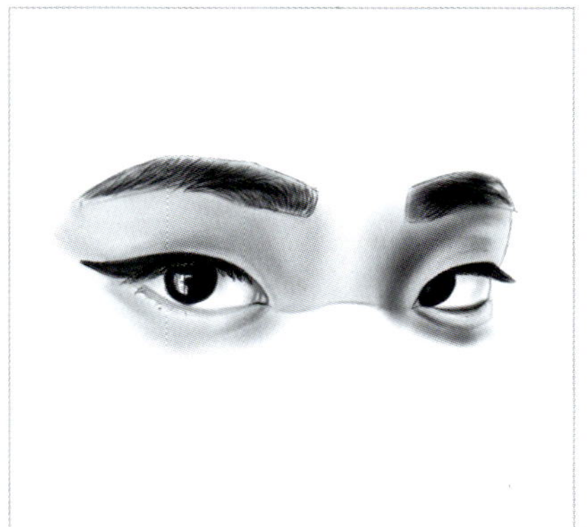

Using your MONO Zero Eraser, retrieve any high values that you need to. The direction that you pull remains an important element for the overall flow of the face.

> **Best Practice:** *You can use a kneaded eraser for bigger high-value retrieval areas if need be. The MONO Zero Eraser is great for detail work but not so much for bigger areas. Feel free to pivot between your tools as necessary.*

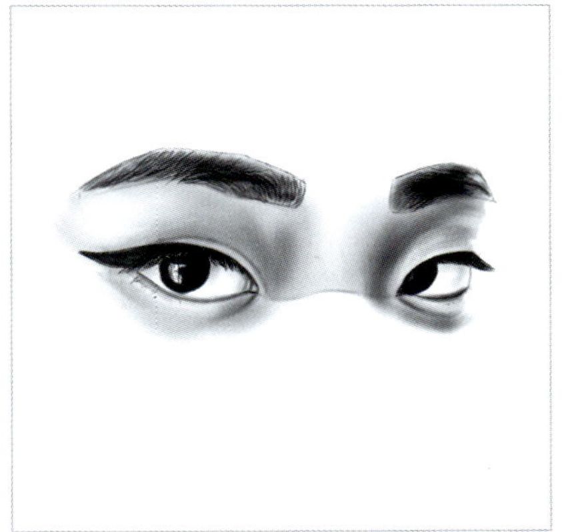

Finally, go over the details. For example, retrieve the highest values along the right side of the reference. You should also give your drawing a thorough examination of any mid tones and retrieve them as necessary with your MONO Zero Eraser. Remember, the longer you take on the detailing of your drawing the more realistic it will become.

Conclusion: Eye See What You Did There

In this chapter, we discussed the Asaro planes as they apply to the eyes. Just like the Loomis method gives you a basic shape from which to work, the Asaro method does the same for facial features. The more you draw this way, the greater your understanding will become, and you will know how to draw the eye planes from various angles without much thought.

CHAPTER 5

How to Draw *the* Nose

"I used to go and flatten my nose against that window and absorb all I could of his art. It changed my life. I saw art then as I wanted to see it."
—Mary Cassatt

While not as alluring or soulful as the eyes, the nose is very much the focal point of the entire face. There it is, right in the center, and you can use this to your advantage when drawing the rest of your portrait. The Asaro method can help. We covered drawing the bridge of the nose in the last chapter, and after you draw the bridge you can proceed in either of two ways: You can start drawing the basic two-dimensional shape of your eyebrows and drawing your eyes, as we did in Chapter 4, or you can start drawing your nose ridge plane and work your way down the nose. There is no right or wrong choice at this point in the process. If you prefer to draw one feature before the other, then that is what you should do. Every artist is different, and what works for you may not work for another. The Asaro method is adaptable enough to accommodate a subjective approach of varying comfort levels. For now, though, let's look more closely at the nose planes.

The Nose Planes

Just like with the eyes, focus on how to draw the nose before you worry about its placement. The Asaro method describes the nose using a few extremely adaptable planes, shown here in their most basic form in the profile, straight-on, and three-quarters angles.

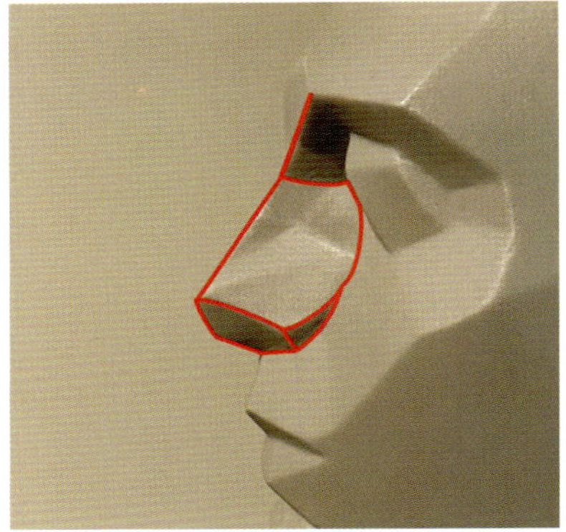
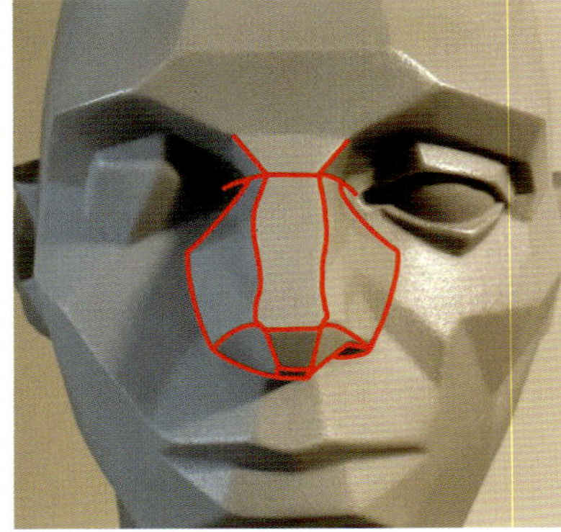
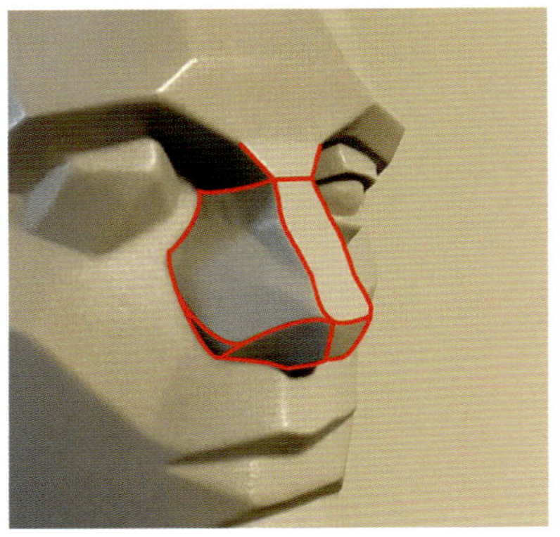

The planes you draw don't necessarily need to look exactly like the examples, so long as they help you accomplish a realistic drawing. The biggest thing to take from these references is the principal structure that the planes give you in these three angles.

The steps that follow will walk you through the process of drawing the basic planes. These simple lines will bring out the basic two-dimensional shape of the nose and cement the structure needed for hatching and blending later in the drawing process. Every person you draw will have a different nose shape, but the planes of the Asaro method will give you the best chance at drawing a realistic nose no matter the angle of the portrait.

Step 1: Draw the Nose Ridge Plane

The nose ridge plane extends from the bottom of the nose bridge and showcases the top of your subject's nose. From the bottom of the nose bridge plane, pull two parallel lines down the full length of the nose, converging slightly near the end. Draw one connecting line across the bottom of the lines and another slightly higher to indicate the nose tip.

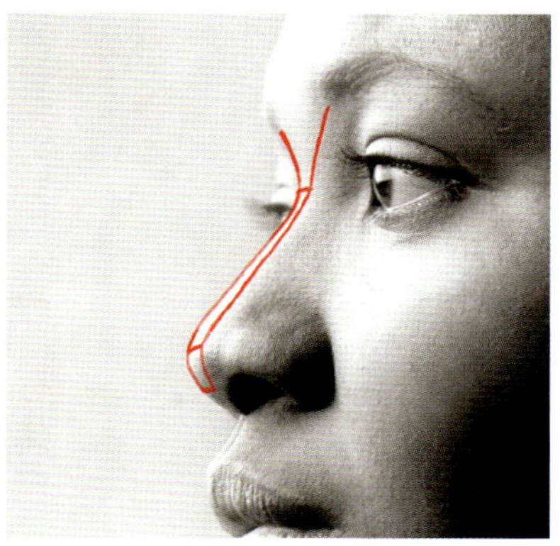
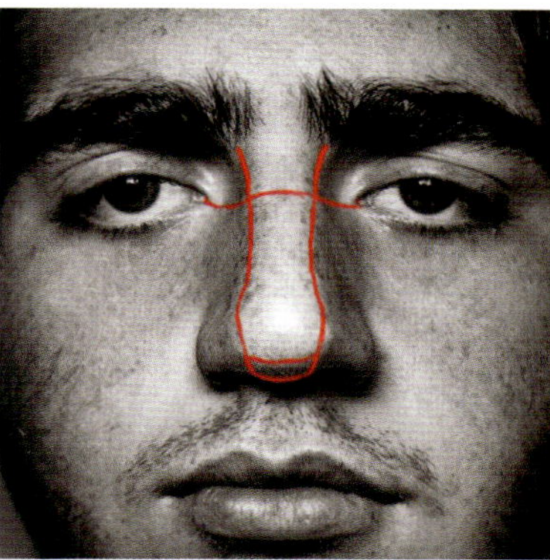
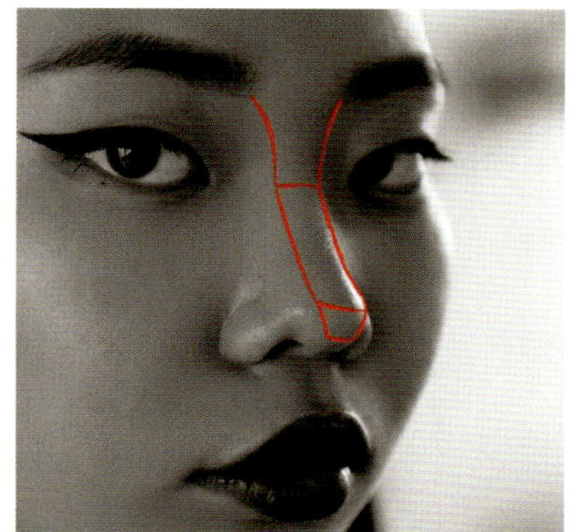

Step 2: Draw the Bottom Plane

In the examples, notice how the bottom plane starts where the nose ridge plane ends. On either side of this point in your drawing (at the nose tip), extend a line to where the side of the nostrils end. Next, draw a line across the bottom of your nose and up around the nostril to show the entirety of the bottom plane.

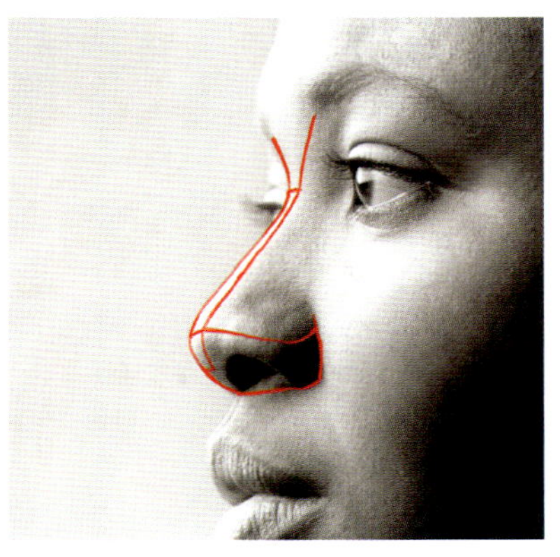
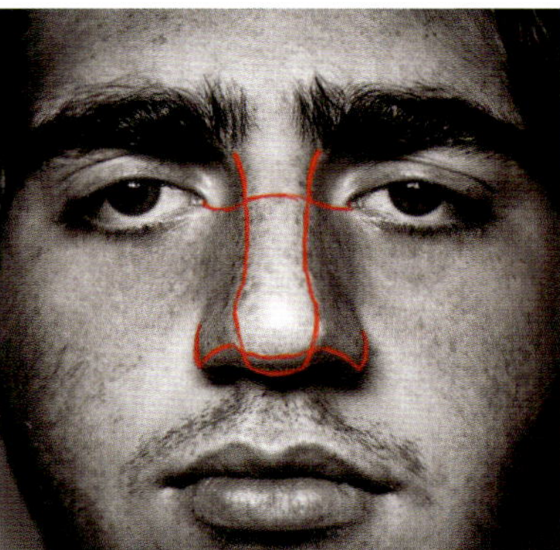
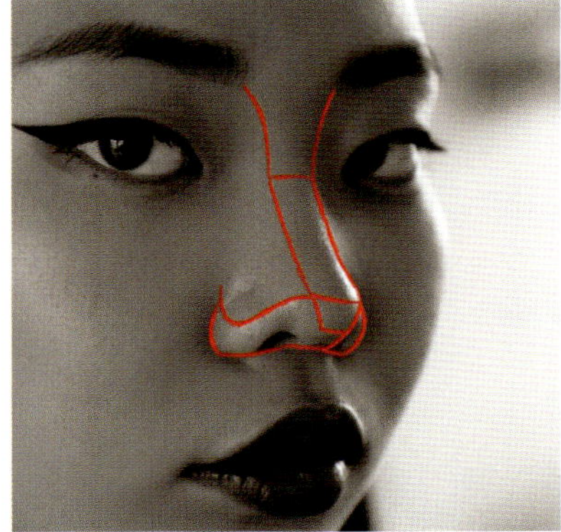

Step 3: Draw the Slope Planes

The slope planes are very much what they sound like: the planes that showcase the slope from the ridge of the nose down to the cheek plane. In the straight-on example, you can clearly see each plane due to the lighting in the reference. To draw these planes, first pull lines up from the edge of the nostril lines on each side and plug those lines into the bottom of the nose bridge plane. Use these references as your guide for the three angles.

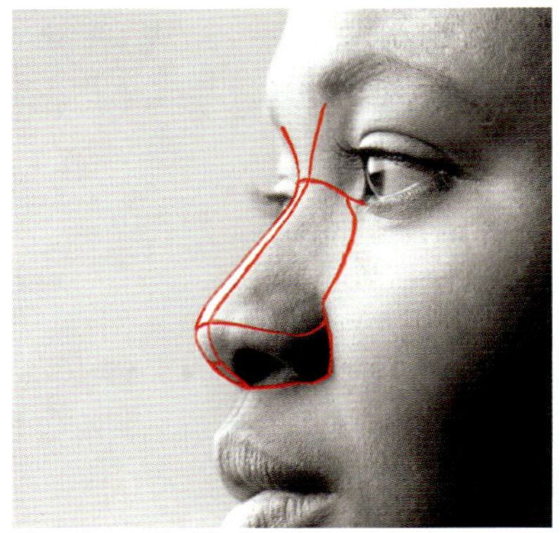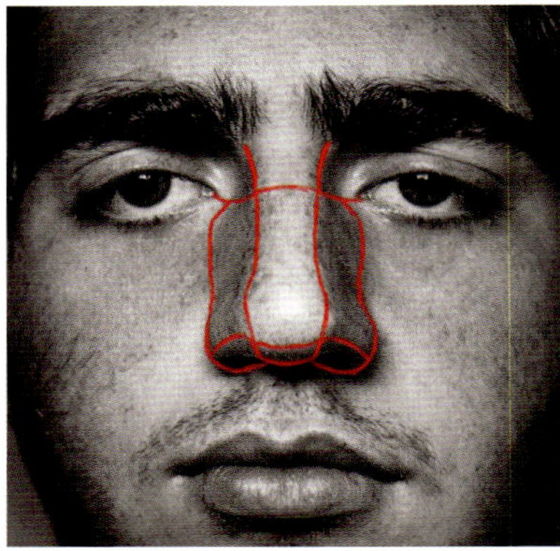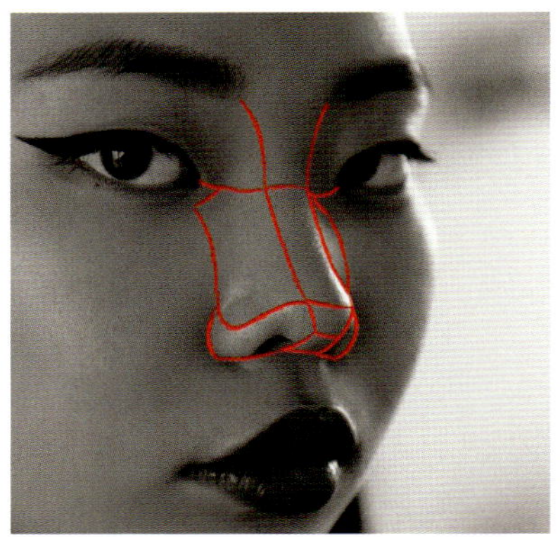

Drawing Noses with the Asaro Method

As you draw more and more noses with the Asaro method, you will discover that you need less and less structure. Eventually you may come to rely only on the ridge, bottom, and slope planes to help you draw any nose you choose. With that in mind, let's practice drawing. As for the eyes and other features coming up, we'll use the three references that Chapter 10's final project will be based on, so you can practice for the final project throughout the entirety of the book. Remember to take it slow and enjoy every stroke, smudge, blend, and adjustment.

The Profile Angle

The profile angle tends to be the easiest out of the three angles that we are covering in this book. The reason for this is because you have a lot less to draw when comparing it to the other two angles.

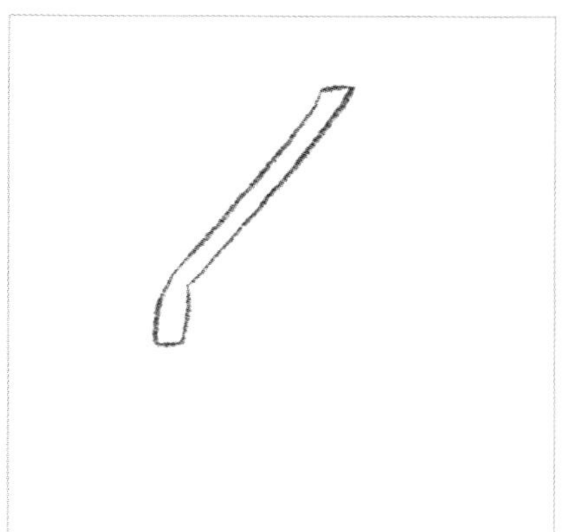

Using a soft charcoal pencil, draw your nose ridge plane down from the bottom of the nose bridge. Keep in mind the nature of the nose angle. Some noses may be closer to 45- or 65-degree angles, for instance. Do short pulls using light pressure, so you can more easily erase and adjust.

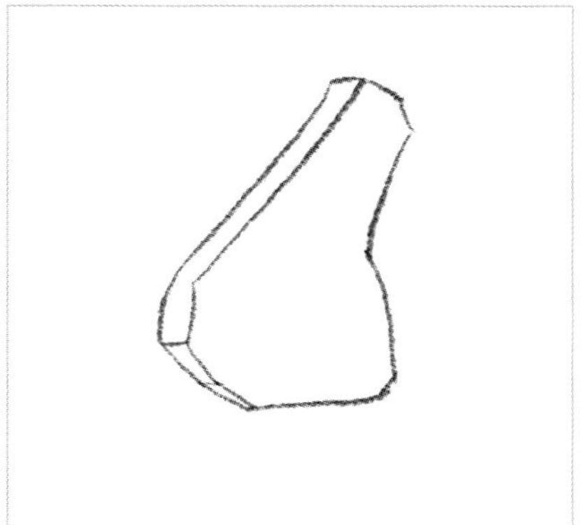

Draw the tip of your nose plane and connect it to your bottom plane. Then, extend the bottom plane line over to roughly where the sides of the nostrils are. Next, pull your line up and connect it to the bottom of the nose bridge line to showcase the slope plane of the nose.

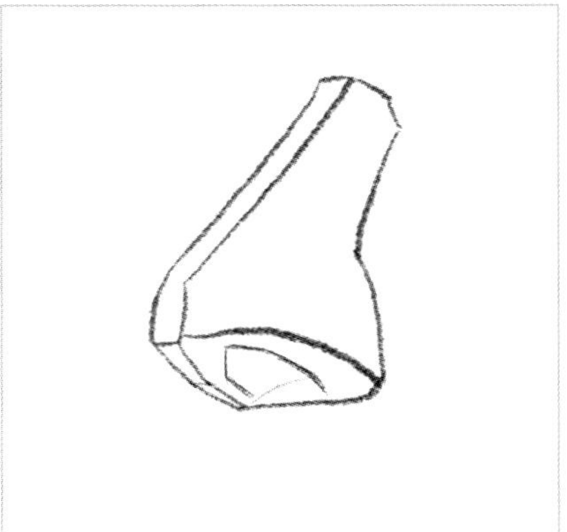

Draw in the bottom plane line, which extends from the bottom of the nose ridge line and over to the end of the side of the nostrils. In this step, you can also place the nostril.

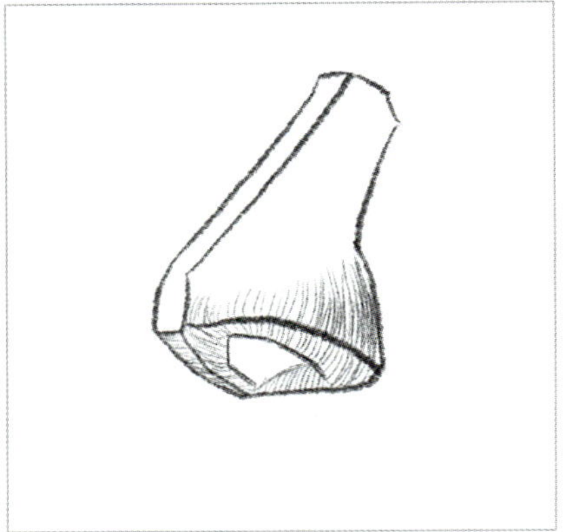

Still using your soft charcoal pencil, start hatching (or cross-hatching). Just like with the eyes, be aware of the direction that you push or pull your pencil when you stroke the paper. Follow the underlying form of your reference photo.

Best Practice: *Shorter strokes allow for more control; longer strokes give you less control.*

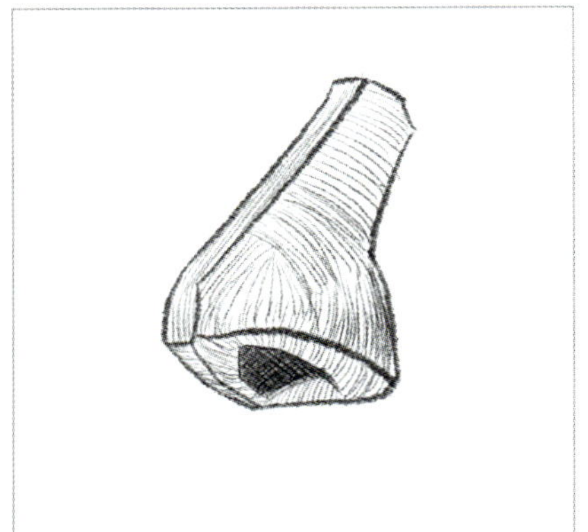

Continue hatching or crosshatching until the entire nose is covered.

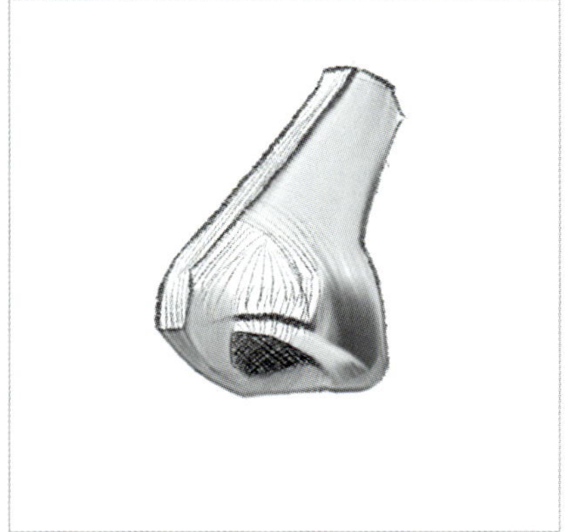

Switch to your smudger and start blending the charcoal that you laid down with your hatching. Remember to start with a soft pressure, because you can always push harder and lower the value later if need be.

Best Practice: *Start blending with a light pressure, finish blending with a heavy pressure.*

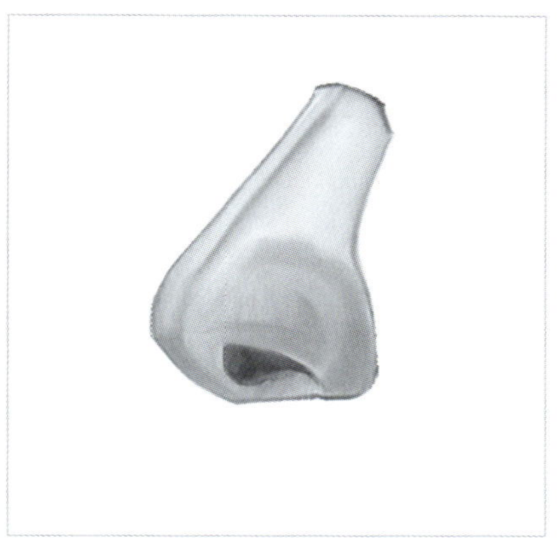

Continue blending your drawing until the hatch marks are no longer visible.

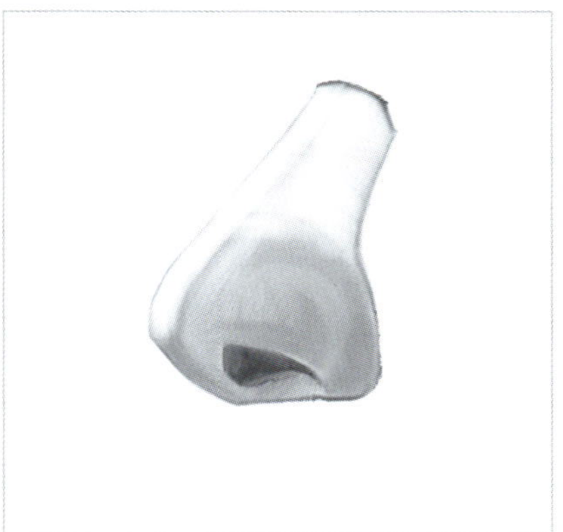

Identify the high values in your reference, then use either a kneaded eraser or a MONO Zero Eraser to retrieve the high values that you covered while blending the hatch marks.

> **Best Practice:** *When retrieving high values with your eraser work, be sure to start off with a light pressure control. Much like blending for lower values, you can always press harder to get your desired result. With eraser work you want to use a light pressure, so you can progressively retrieve a higher and higher value.*

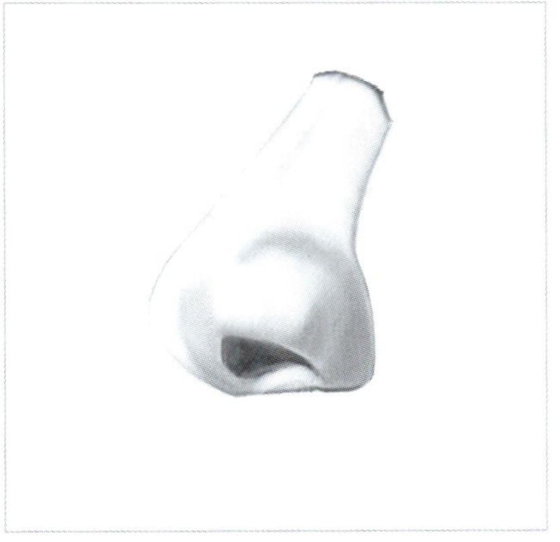

Continue to retrieve your high values until you are satisfied with the contrast.

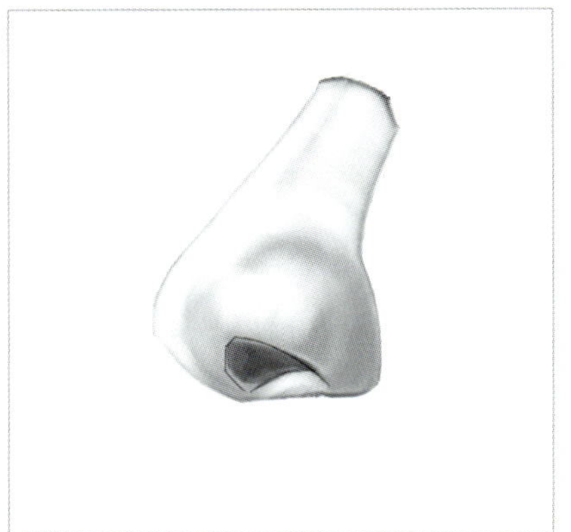

Now, outline the nostril with a medium charcoal pencil.

> **Best Practice:** *Always use a medium charcoal pencil for line work. Because it has more binder agent infused than soft charcoal, the pencil tips are less susceptible to breakage when you are pushing or pulling a line.*

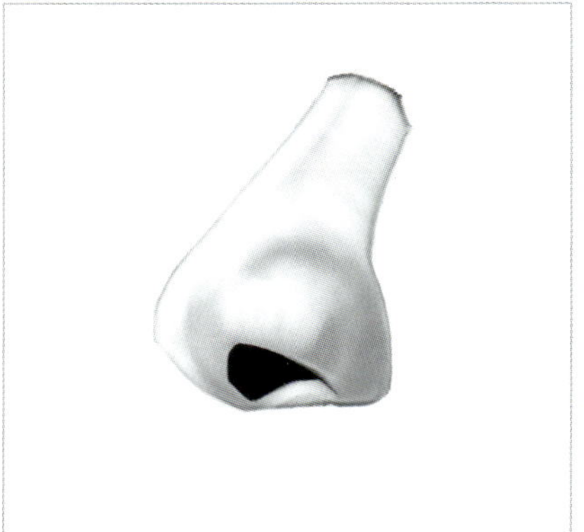

Fill in the nostril hole with your medium charcoal pencil, and then use a smaller smudger to blend the charcoal to a very low value. This is the lowest value in the nose, so make it completely black to accentuate the value scale.

> **Best Practice:** *To make your drawing as dynamic as possible, ideally you want it to contain complete black, complete white, and all the tonal variations.*

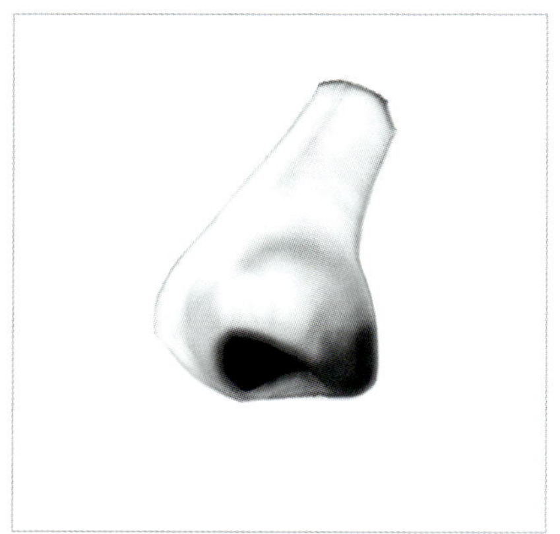

Dip your brush into your ground soft charcoal, test the tone on your scratch paper, and then start to strategically build up your lower values. (Remember, less is more.)

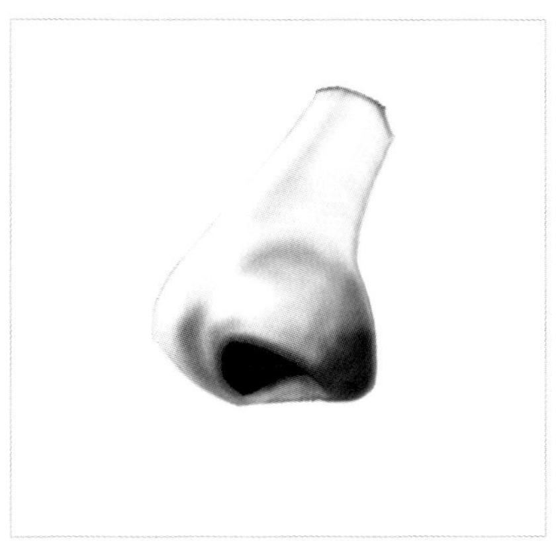

Continue using your brushwork to place your low values in the areas that need to be lowered.

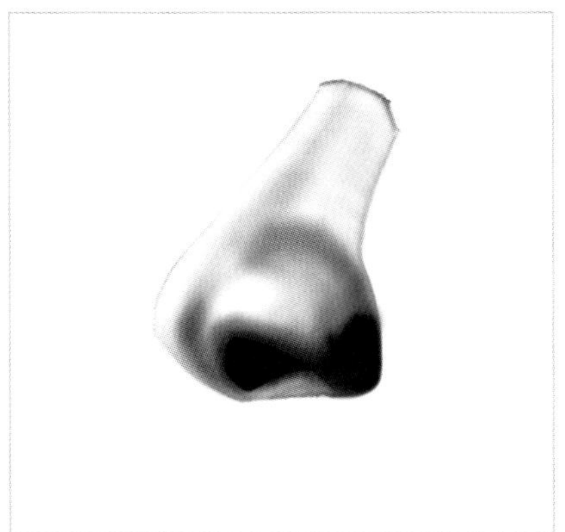

Now you can focus on building up the detail in the nose. Use your medium charcoal with light pressure for your base layer, then use a smaller smudger to place your blends exactly where you want them.

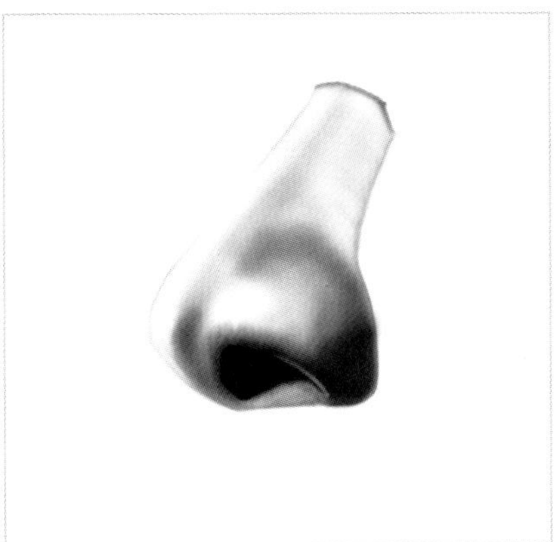

Finally, using a detail eraser, such as a MONO Zero, and very light pressure bring out the detail work. For a soft finish, make sure to go over your blends with an empty brush.

The Straight-on Angle

Keep in mind the nature of the nose angle. Straight-on portraits, such as this one, tend to give artists difficulty due to the angle's inherent symmetry, as compared to the profile and three-quarter-turn angles.

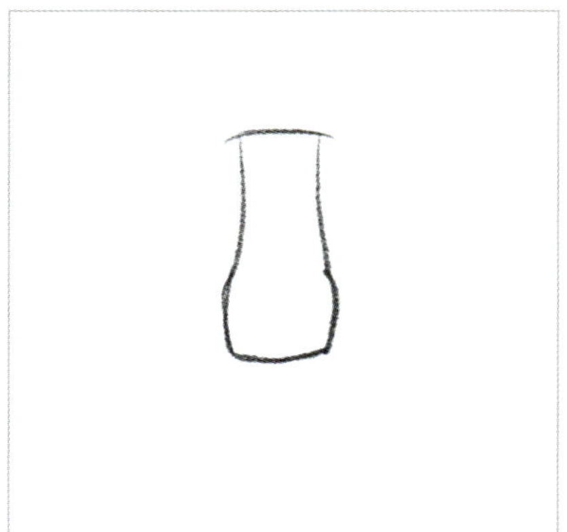

As for the profile nose, start by using a soft charcoal pencil to draw your nose ridge plane, which stems from the bottom of the nose bridge.

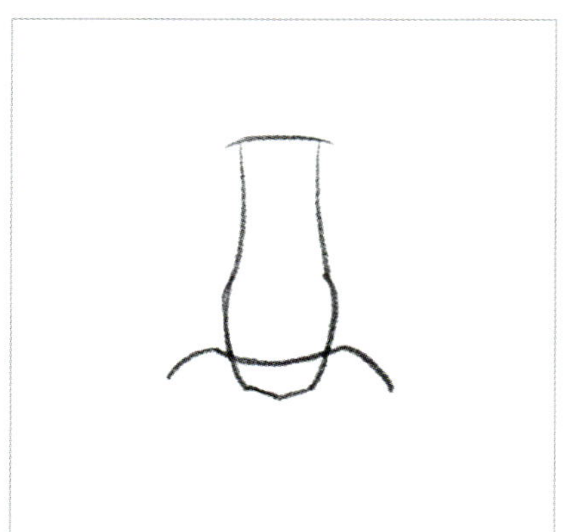

Draw the nose tip plane and extend the bottom of the nose ridge plane to the outside edges of the nostrils.

Best Practice: *Remember, if you need to erase to help you solidify your proportions, that is totally fine. I erase and adjust all the time. It's just part of the dance with drawing!*

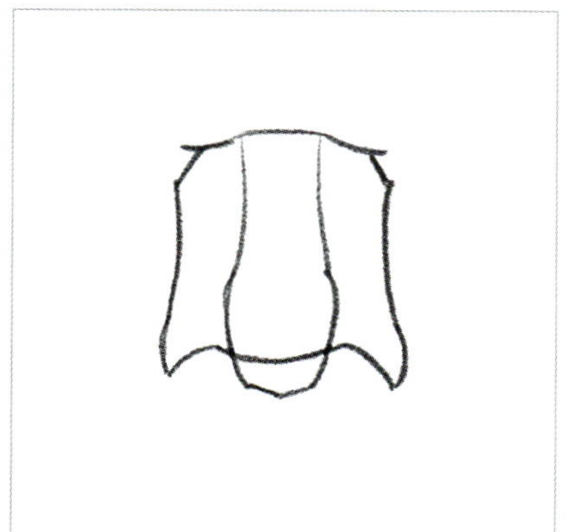

Extend the top of the nose ridge plane to roughly where the corner of the eyes lay. Pull your lines at a slight angle downward, then pull them all the way down to where they meet the top of the bottom plane, making sure to put a light curve at the end for the nostrils.

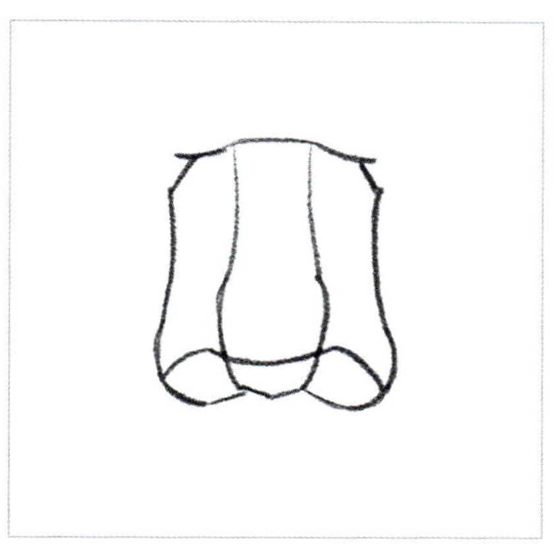

To finish up the framework for the basic two-dimensional shape, loop the slope plane lines you just drew up to the corners of the nose tip plane.

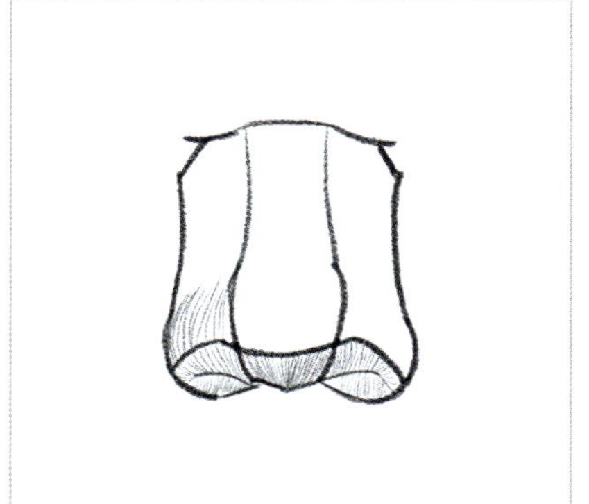

With your soft charcoal pencil, start hatching your nose. Remember to follow the underlying form with each stroke.

Best Practice: *If you are a beginner, try hatching each individual plane. This will help you build muscle memory to the basic flow of the face. With practice you won't need to hatch with this much structure.*

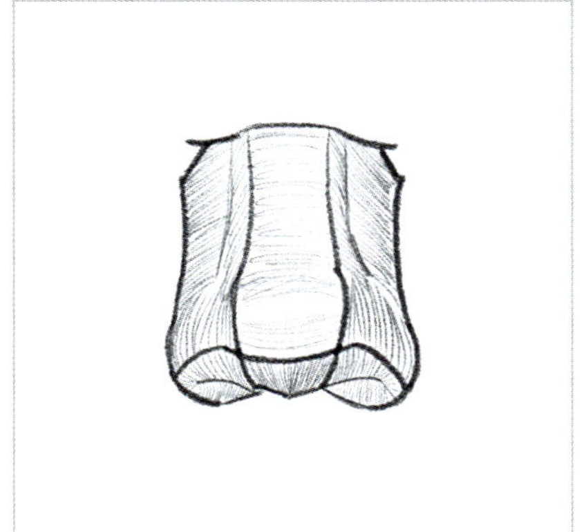

Now hatch or crosshatch the rest of the nose. Whichever option you choose, remember to keep a nice light pressure.

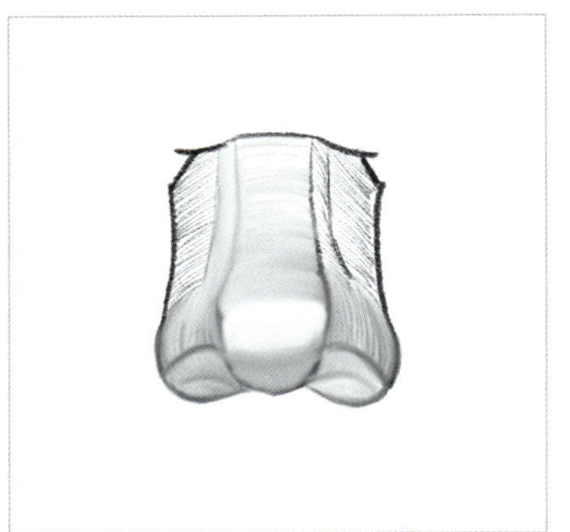

With a smudger, start smudging your hatch marks and blending them together.

> **Best Practice:** *If you push or pull your smudger with the grain of your hatches, the blend will be softer and you will retain more of the hatch marks. If you push or pull your smudger against the grain of your hatches, then the blend will be harder and the hatch marks less noticeable.*

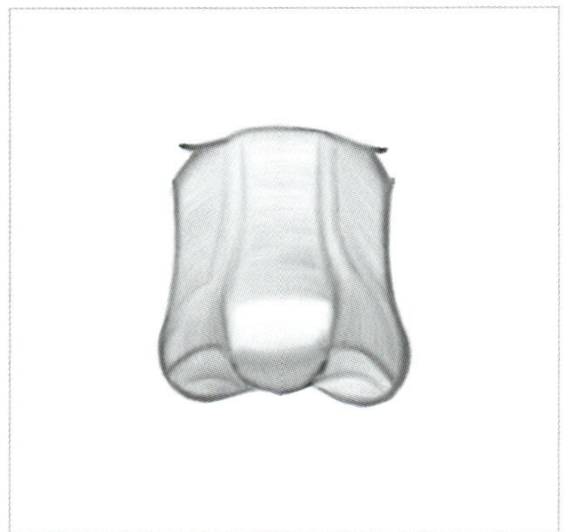

Continue blending your drawing until the nose is filled in.

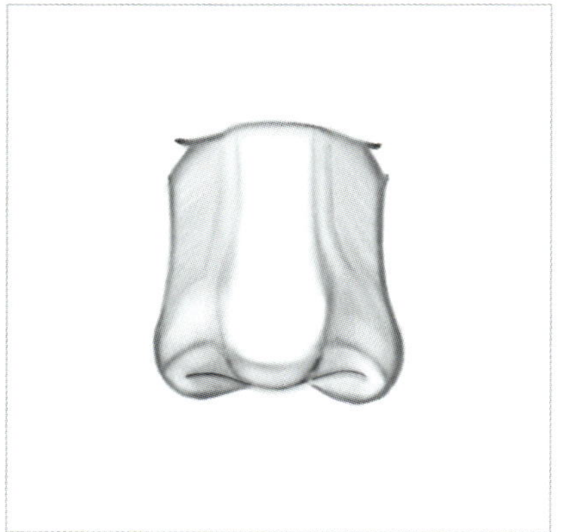

With a kneaded eraser or a MONO Zero Eraser, go through your drawing to retrieve your high values. Remember how pressure control affects the tones you retrieve: The more pressure, the higher the tone; the less pressure, the lower the tone.

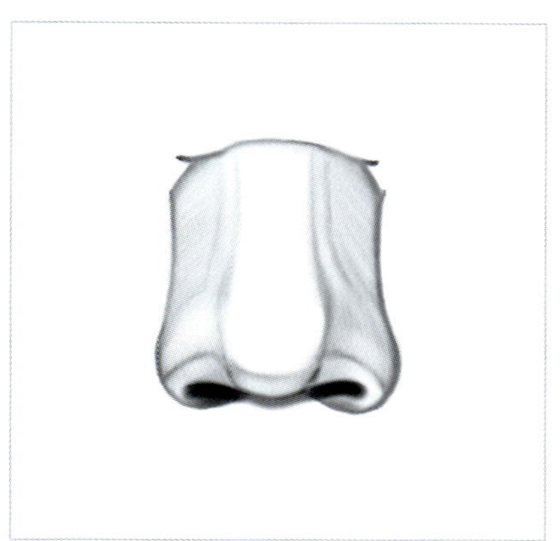

Switch to a medium charcoal pencil and fill in the nostrils. The blended soft charcoal provides a nice base for your medium charcoal so that you get a very low value, a richer black.

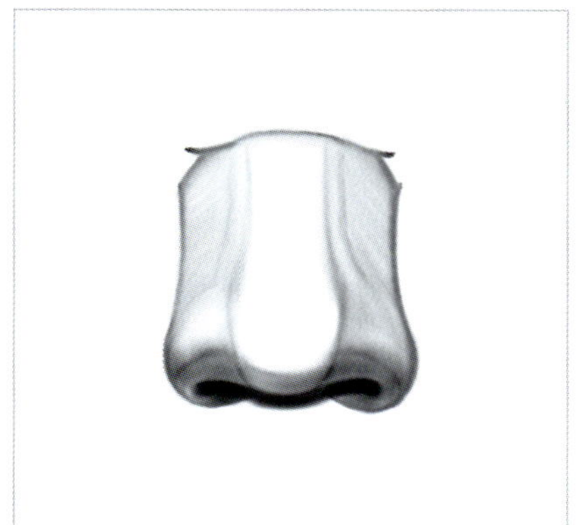

Dip your brush in ground soft charcoal, check the tone on your scratch paper, then lower the value at the bottom of the nose. In straight-on portraits, this area is the darkest because the least cast light reaches it.

Best Practice: *Sometimes it's better to dab the paper instead of swiping it. Try both techniques to see which look you prefer.*

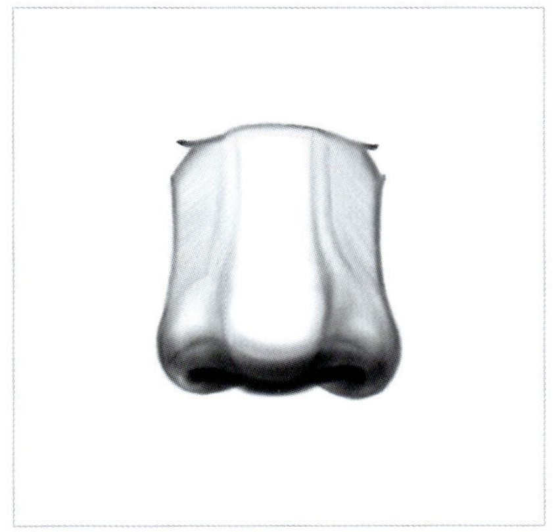

Keep lowering the value in and around the nostrils, and you will start to see the nose take shape.

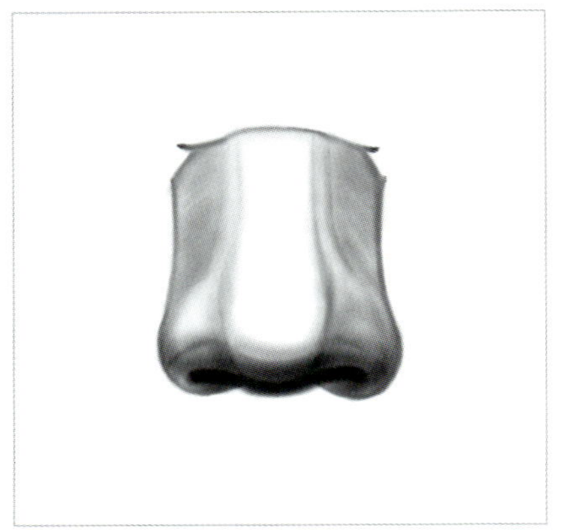

Continue to lower the value along the slope planes.

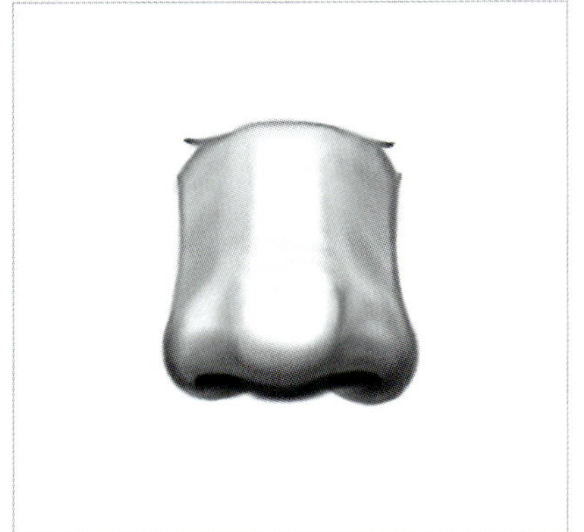

Trade your brush for a smudger and blend away any harsh or inaccurate values that you don't like. This will smooth the drawing and bring a nice gradation to your nose.

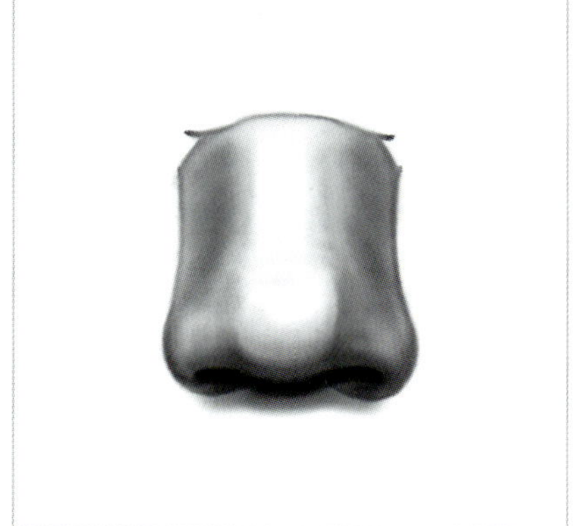

Finally, go through and cover your details with hard charcoal. Because it has the most amount of binder agent infused with it, hard charcoal holds together very nicely and rests on top of your layers of soft and medium charcoal.

The Three-Quarter-Turn Angle

The three-quarter turn angle is a very dynamic angle. It is not symmetrical like the straight-on angle, but it does have its own challenges, such as getting the far side of the nose in correct proportion to the rest of it.

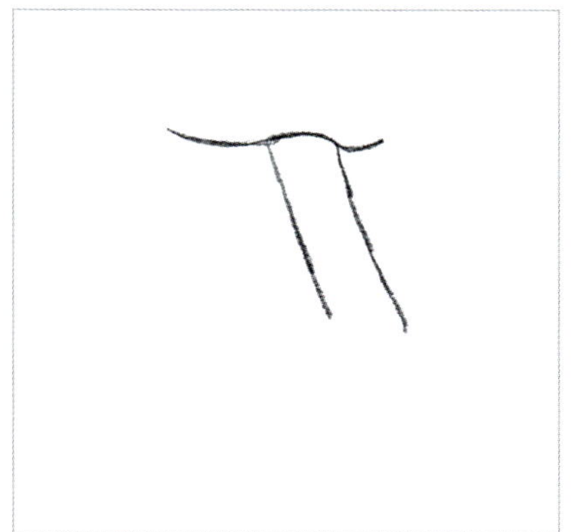

Start by drawing the top of the nose ridge plane and extending that line in both directions to roughly where the corner of your eyes lay. Then, pull two parallel lines down the length of the nose.

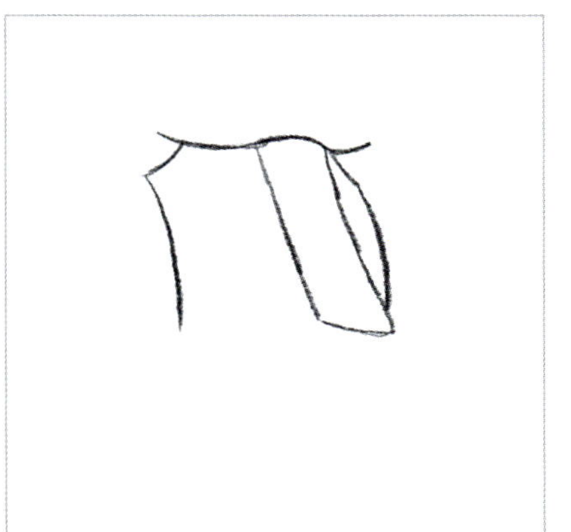

Connect these two parallel lines with a line to signify the bottom of the nose ridge. To bring out the slope planes, pull a line down on each side of the nose ridge. Keep the line on the right closer to the nose. On the left, angle the line out a short way and then down and inward at a slighter angle.

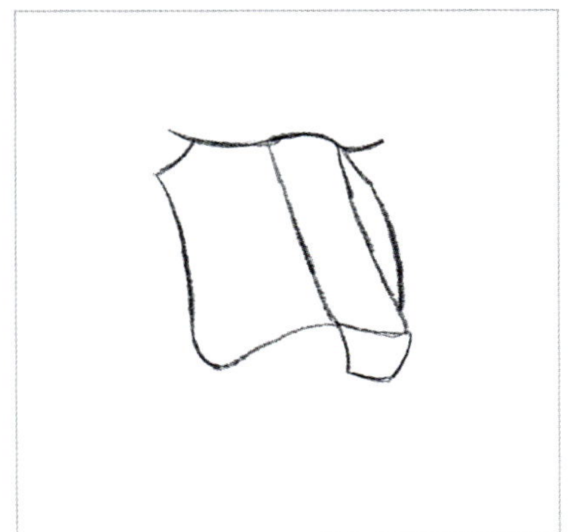

Draw your nose tip plane, and then connect the left slope plane line to the end of your nose ridge plane.

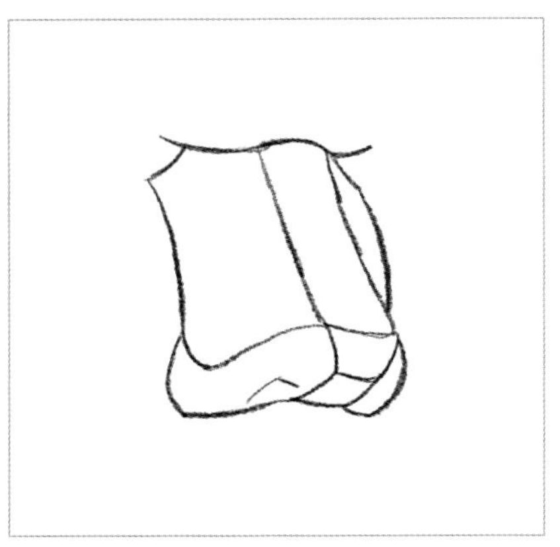

Draw in your bottom plane line, which should follow the outside edge of the nostril and connect to the bottom plane under the nose tip plane. Make sure to draw the bottom plane on both sides of the nose.

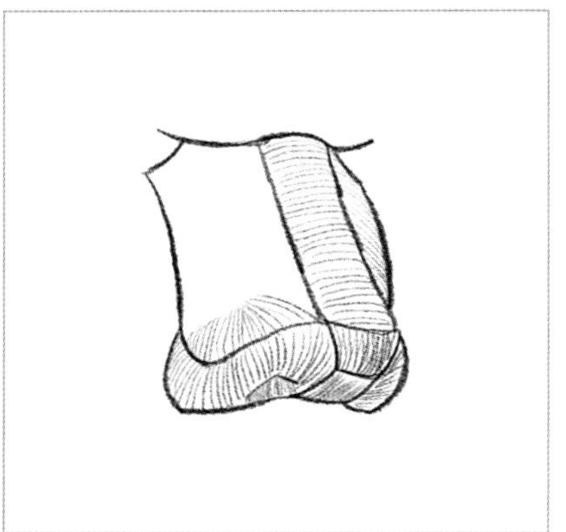

Now, start hatching the planes with your soft charcoal pencil. Remember to push or pull your pencil tip in the direction of your underlying form. Use light pressure for this step.

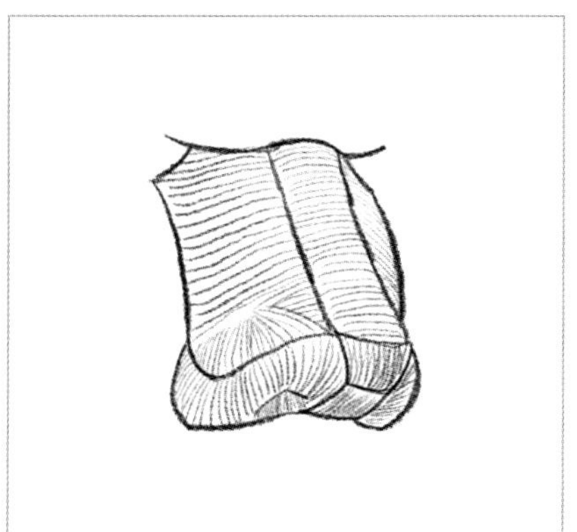

Continue hatching until you cover the entire nose.

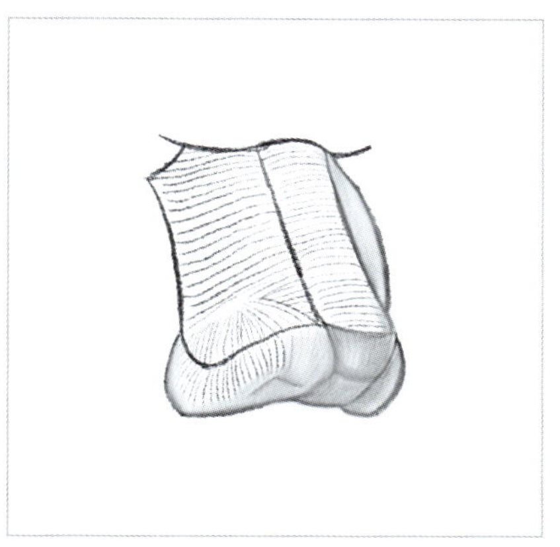

Swap your charcoal for a smudger and use light pressure to start smudging the charcoal into the paper. Remember the harder you press, the more the charcoal will be pressed into the pores of the paper, thus giving you a lower value.

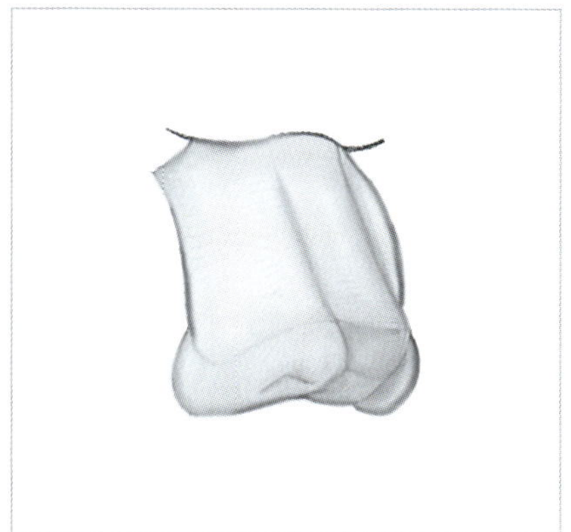

Continue smudging until the nose is completely blended.

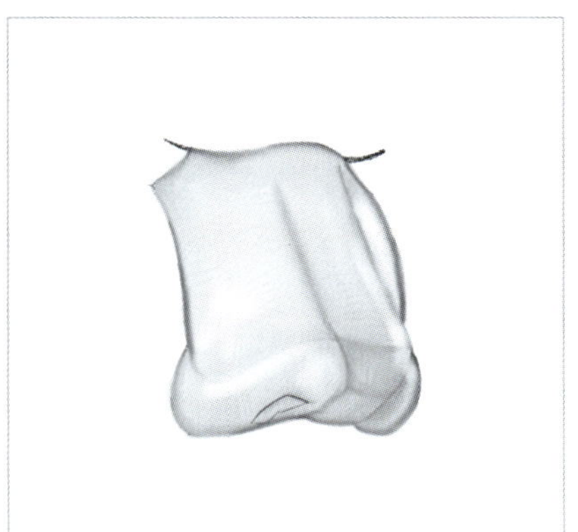

With your medium charcoal pencil, line out the nostril hole.

Best Practice: *Line out the nostrils before you start lowering the value inside of them. This way you can fill in and blend your low value right up to the line you laid down, giving you a clean break between your low value in the nostril and your mid tones for the rest of the nose.*

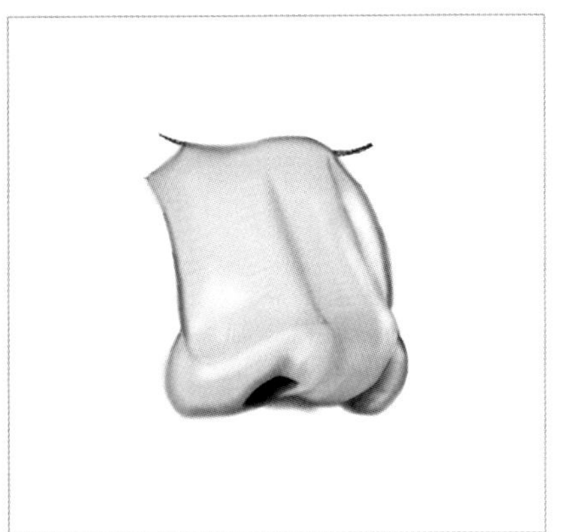

Fill in the nostril using the medium charcoal pencil, then switch to a smudger to start blending the tip of the nose. Notice that the plane lines start to dissipate as you blend more and more.

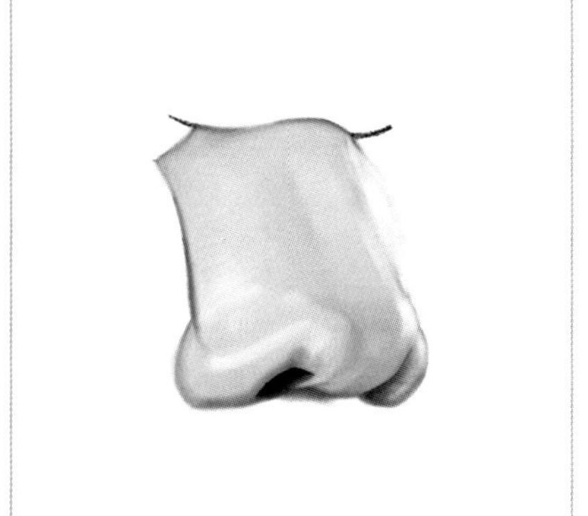

Continue smudging the rest of the nose so that you get a nice blend across its entirety.

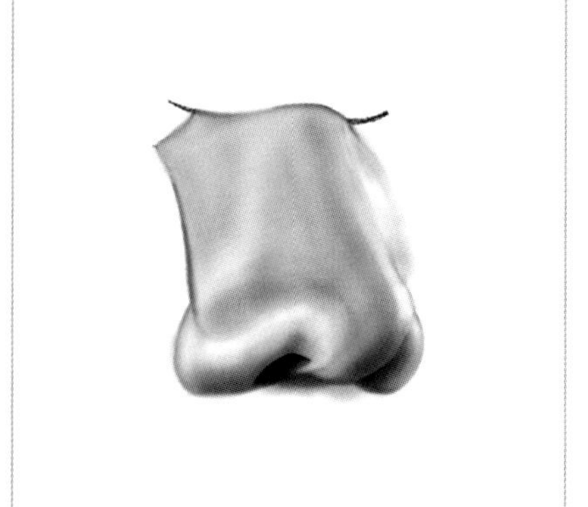

Now, switch to your brush and start building up the lower values. For the three-quarter-turn angle, you will see lower values around the nostrils, tip, and ridge of the nose.

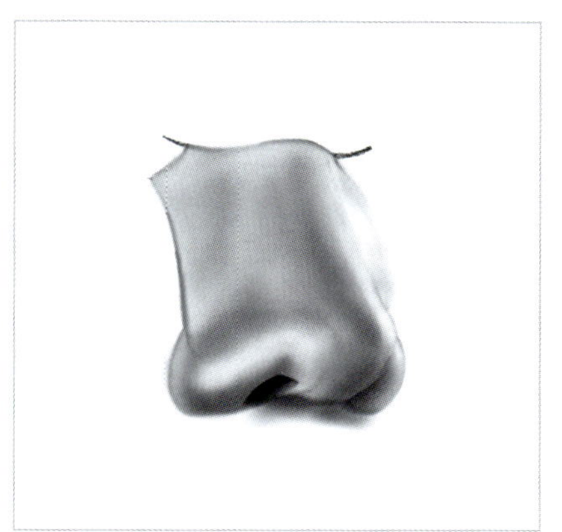

Time to focus heavily on where the low values live in the reference. Fill your brush with ground soft charcoal, test the tone on scrap paper, then push or pull your brush across the paper in the low value areas you identified.

> **Best Practice:** *Remember to pay attention to the flow of the face. Use the underlying form as your guide for which direction you think you should push or pull your brush.*

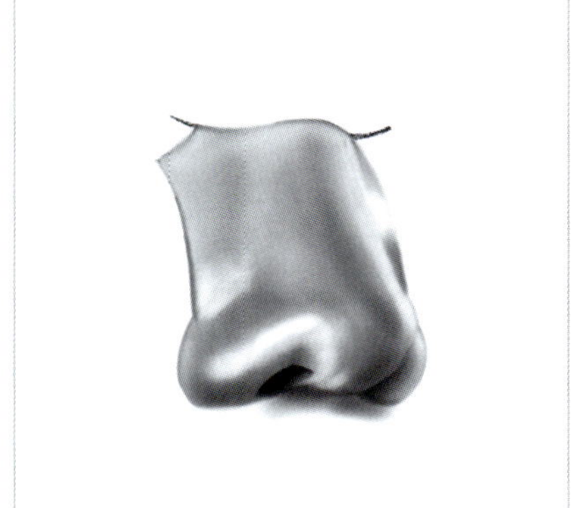

Using your MONO Zero Eraser, retrieve any high values that you need to. The direction that you pull remains an important element for the overall flow of the face.

> **Best Practice:** *A kneaded eraser is better for bigger high-value retrieval areas, but it offers less control. The MONO Zero Eraser offers more control so is great for detail work in smaller areas.*

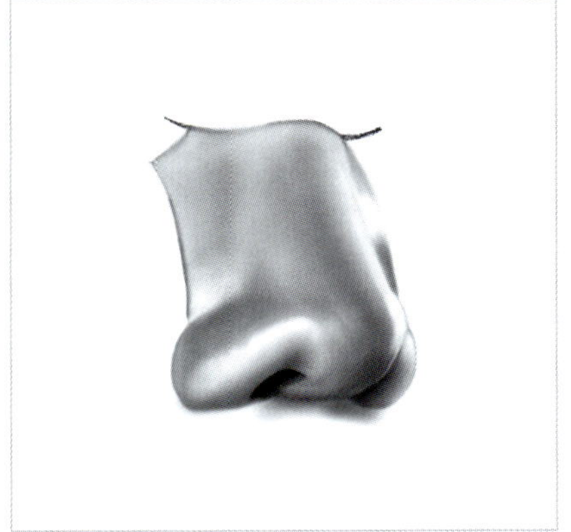

Remember, when you think that you are finished with your nose drawing, take a break. When you come back, check that everything looks like you want it to. Touch up values as needed.

Project 8: Draw Three Asaro Noses

For **Project 8**, draw three Asaro noses using the techniques and best practices you learned. If you need a more fluid explanation of the Asaro method or nose planes in particular, scan the QR code to view the video **How to Easily Draw Noses | Understanding the Asaro Method Part II**.

Conclusion: A Higher Plane of Understanding

According to Asaro, the nose and every other human facial feature has its own inherent planes that can help you understand your three-dimensional subject matter in two-dimensional space. The Asaro method is incredibly adaptable to any person you are drawing. Proportion is what separates the individual, but Asaro's planes bind us all to a common thread. Understanding this will help you become a better artist in your knowledge of portrait construction—and knowledge always transfers through to one's works.

CHAPTER 6

How to Draw *the* Lips

"My lips, two blushing pilgrims, ready stand
To smooth that rough touch with a tender kiss."
—William Shakespeare

Whether, like Romeo, you feel yours is the "unworthiest hand" that gives a rough touch to facial features, or you have a bit more confidence, the Asaro method will help you better frame the lips of your portraits. As with the eyes and nose, it is essential that you understand the basic planal structure of the lips so that you can give yourself the best chance at drawing them accurately. Once you identify the lip planes, you can get on with the artistic dance of hatching, blending, shading, and retrieving.

The Lip Planes

In the Asaro method, two planes comprise the upper lip and three comprise the lower. Use these as your guide to how you will construct your lips. Regardless of the angle that you are working with these foundational planes do not change, as the three examples illustrate. The only deviations are the proportions of the reference in question.

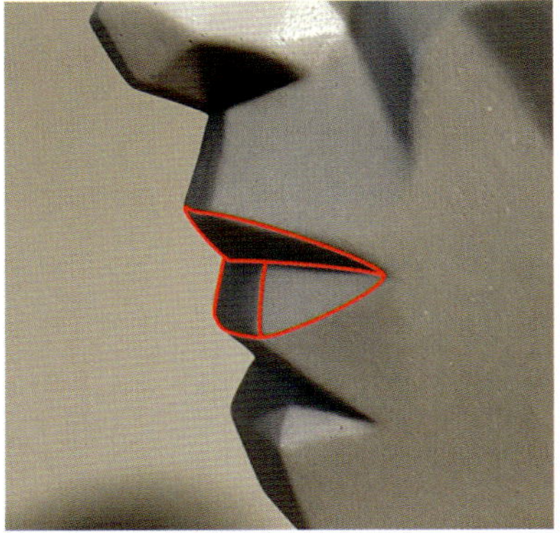 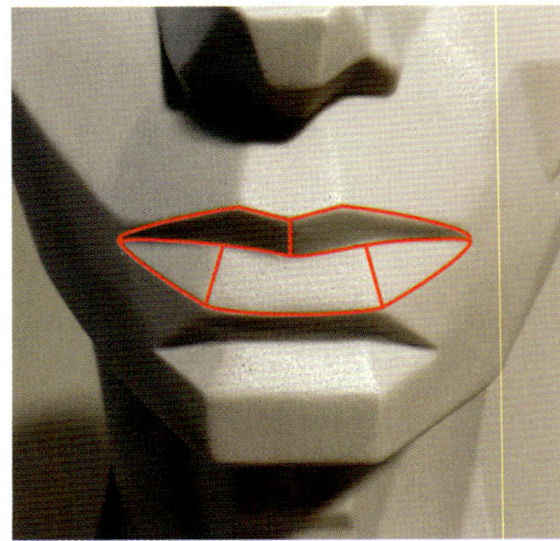 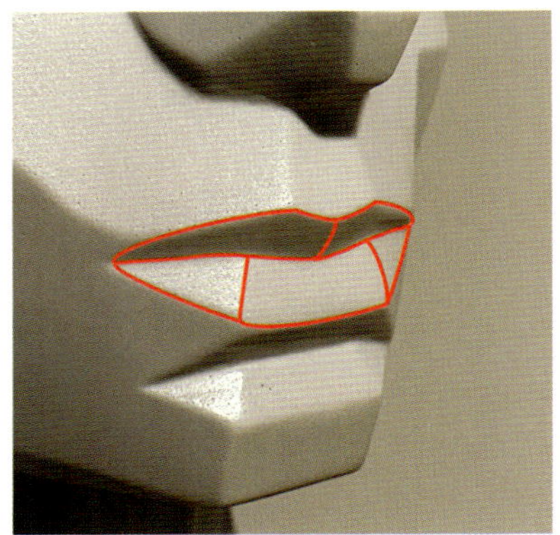

Let's take a closer look at the drawing flow for the lips based on the three references that your final projects are based on.

Step 1: Draw the Reference Points

To draw the most dynamic lips possible, start by roughly marking where you think the upper edge of the mouth lays. Next, draw the philtrum planes below the nose and use them as a guide to place two lines on the bottom lip that will frame the lower lip's three planes. After that, draw a single vertical line on the top lip that splits it into its two respective planes. Each portrait angle will dictate a slightly different approach to this drawing flow, but the basic principle remains the same.

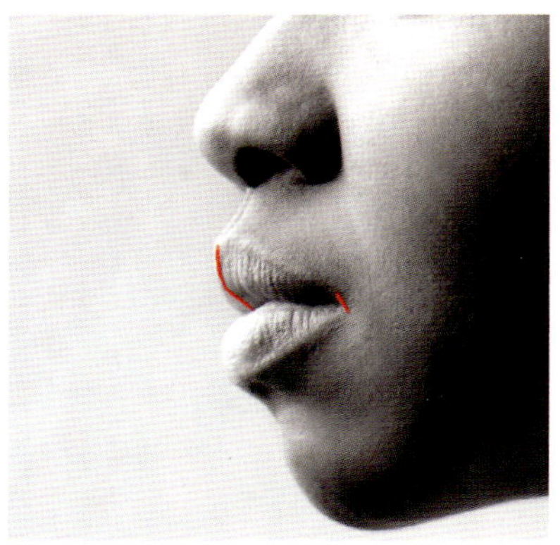 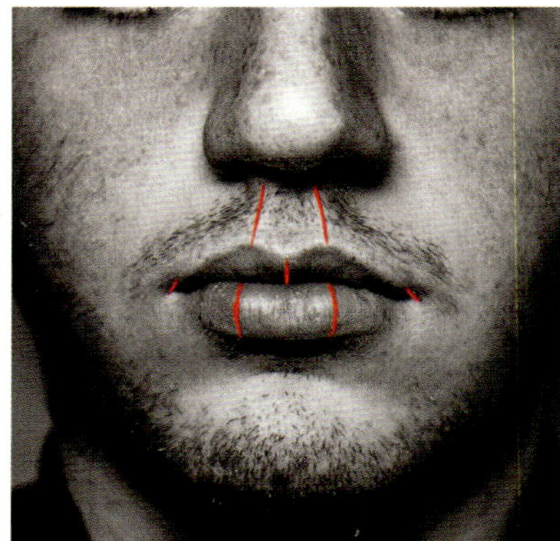 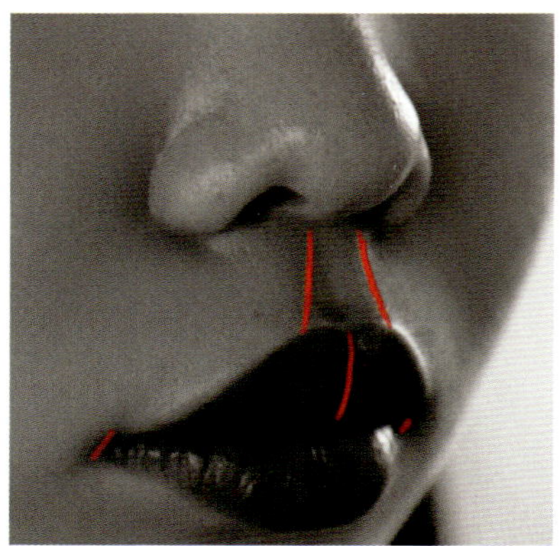

Step 2: Draw the Lips

Connect your reference points to form the upper and the lower lips. Remember, your drawing flow does not need to follow these examples exactly so long as the end framework ends up the same.

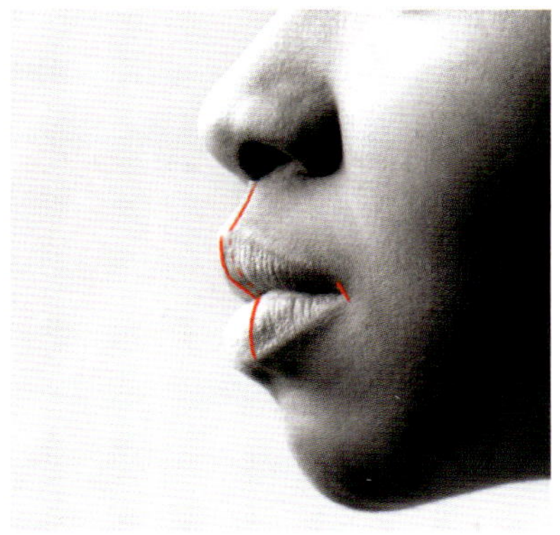
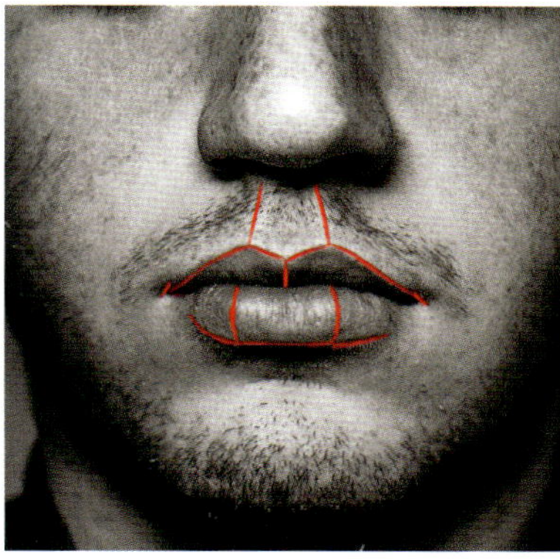
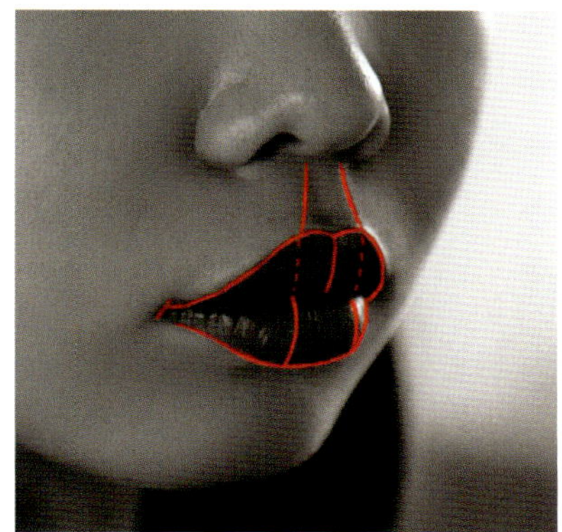

Step 3: Finish Up the Lips

Place a line that splits the upper and the lower lips and represents the opening of the mouth. At this point in the drawing process, you can erase your philtrum plane as you don't need it any longer. What remains is the complete two-dimensional shape you needed to draw lips.

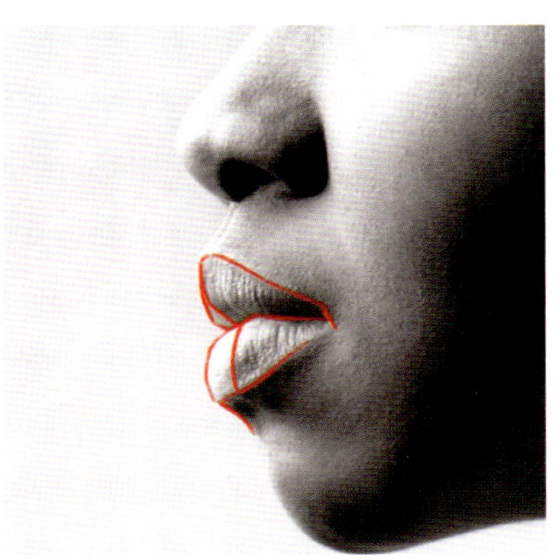
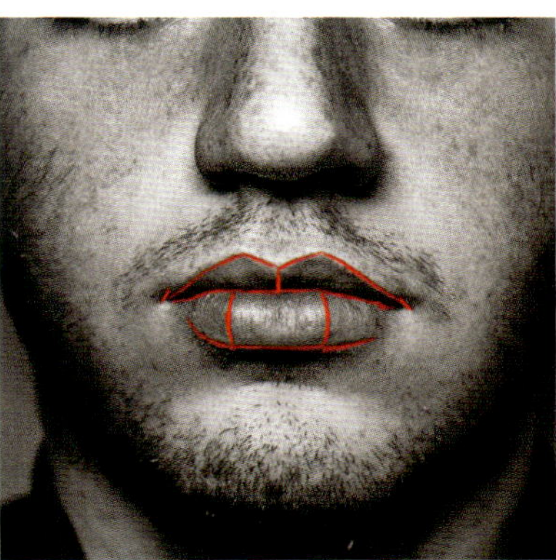
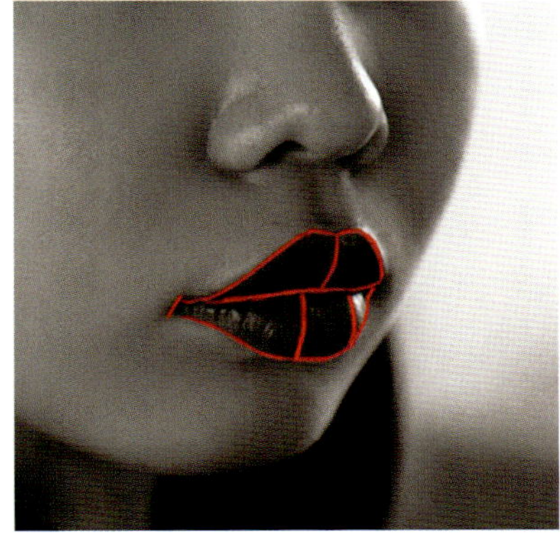

Step 4: Make Sure You Understand the Lighting

Light and shadow play a large part in conveying realistic lips. The pink shading in the three examples illustrates the darkest areas when light casts on the lips in most lighting situations for the three common reference angles.

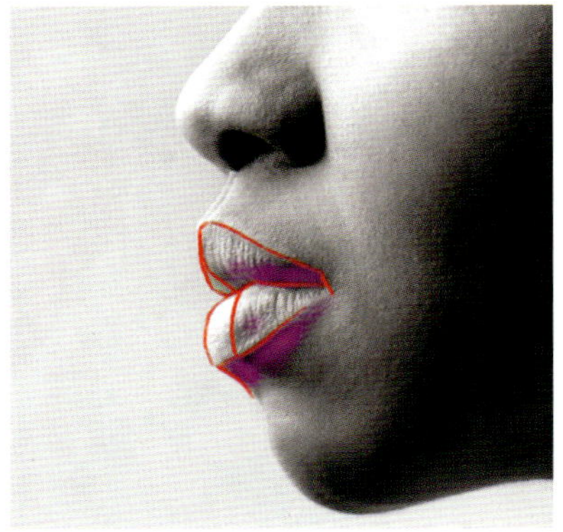

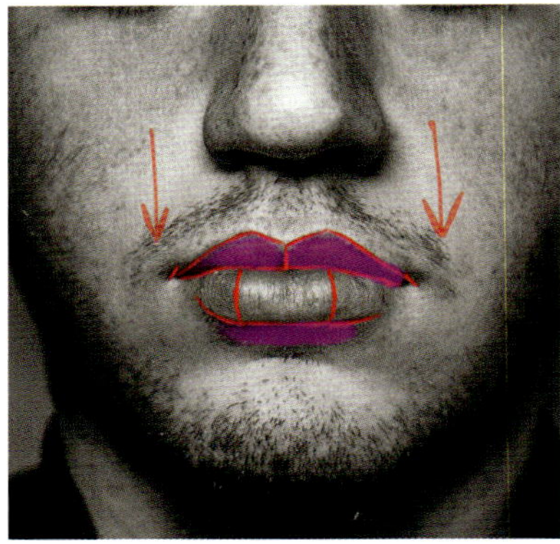

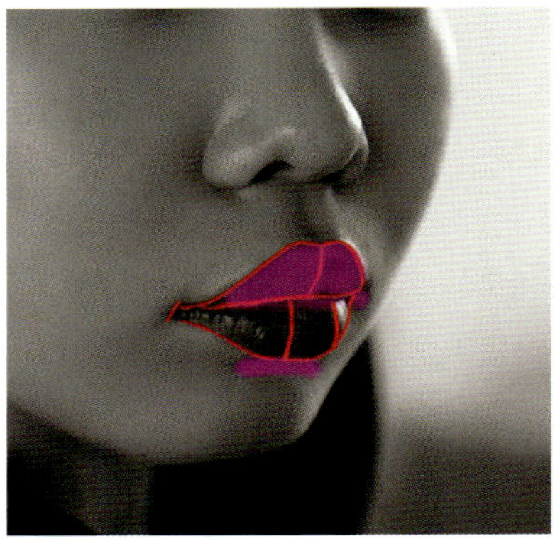

Notice where the lowest values exist for the profile angle. This is where your values should be the darkest in your drawing.

In this straight-on reference, most of the light is cast from directly above, so the lower values shift to the upper lip and beneath the lower lip.

In this three-quarter-turn angle, the lowest values are also the upper lip and beneath the lower lip.

Drawing Lips Using the Asaro Method

Remember you do not have to draw your lips verbatim like they are in the example drawing flows that follow. These are meant to be guides not absolutes. In addition, they offer practice creating profile, straight-on, and three-quarter-turn facial features for Chapter 10's final project. Remember to take it slow and enjoy every stroke, smudge, blend, and adjustment.

The Profile Angle

The profile angle is the only angle covered in this book where you cannot see the third plane of the lower lip. This is due to the nature of the angle. In the other two angles you will be able to see all the Asaro planes.

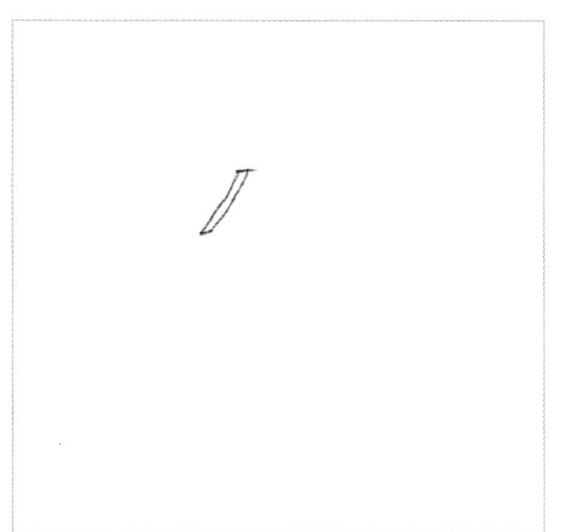

Draw two vertical lines parallel to each other at a slight angle. Connect the lines at the top and bottom.

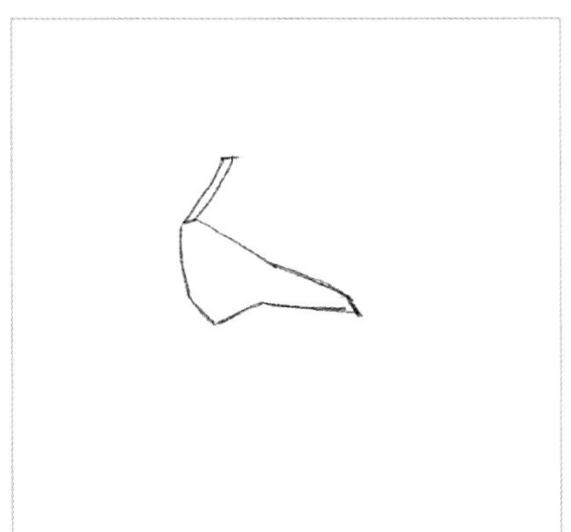

Draw the basic shape of your subject's upper lip.

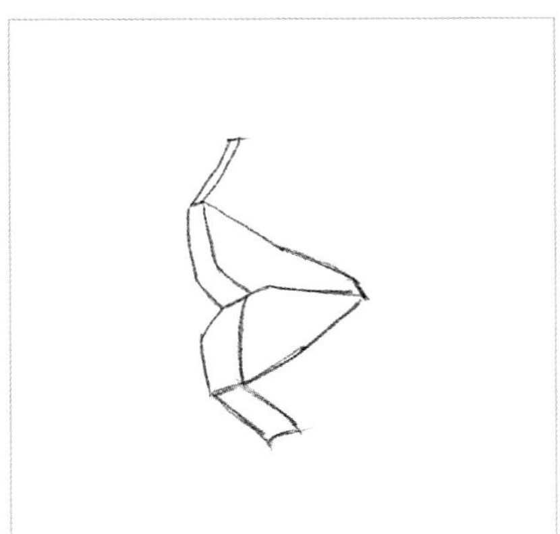

Draw the basic shape of your subject's lower lip. Next, draw a vertical line in the top lip shape to split it into two planes. Align the lower lip plane line with the philtrum plane line. This will give the lower lip its necessary shape.

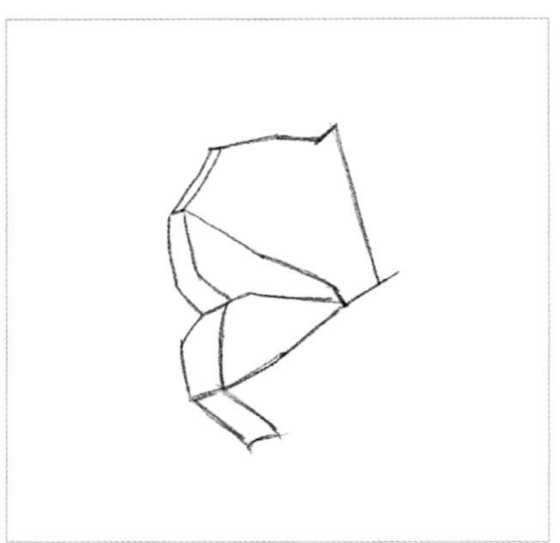

So that you have some room to work with, draw one of the Asaro planes for the face: Extend the corner of the mouth up at an angle, then pull the line up towards the edge of the nose.

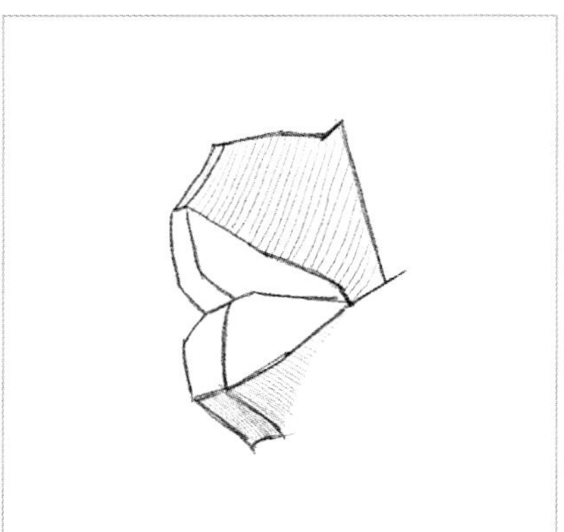

With the basic two-dimensional shape of the lips framed with Asaro planes, you can begin hatching. As always, push or pull your hatch lines in keeping with the reference. Remember your hatching should flow in the same direction as your underlying form.

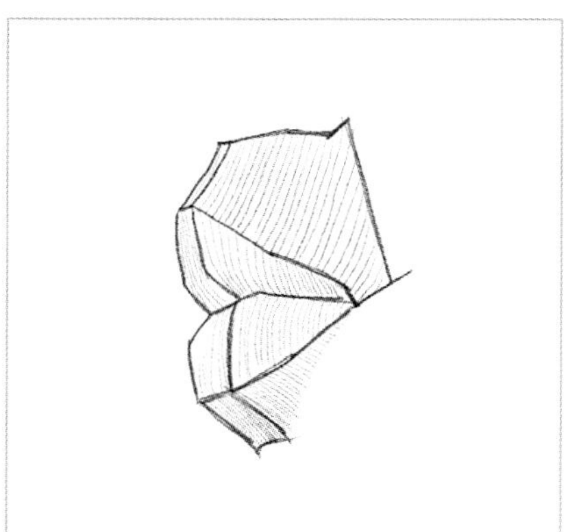

Hatch or crosshatch every plane in your drawing.

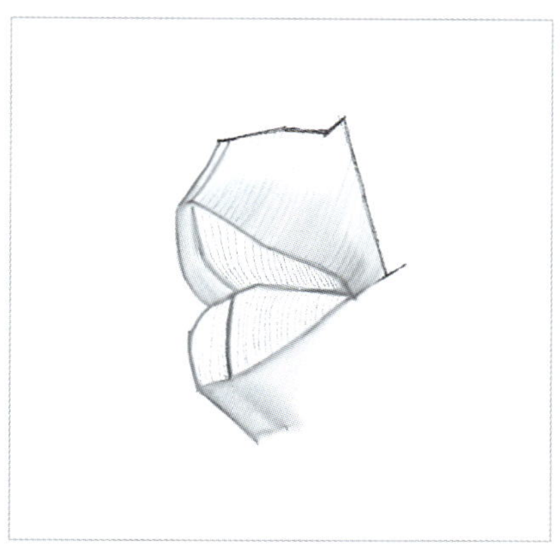

Use smudgers of varying sizes to blend the hatch marks. Remember, the shorter your smudger strokes, the softer the blend will be. Longer smudger strokes create a harsher blend with hatch marks still showing through.

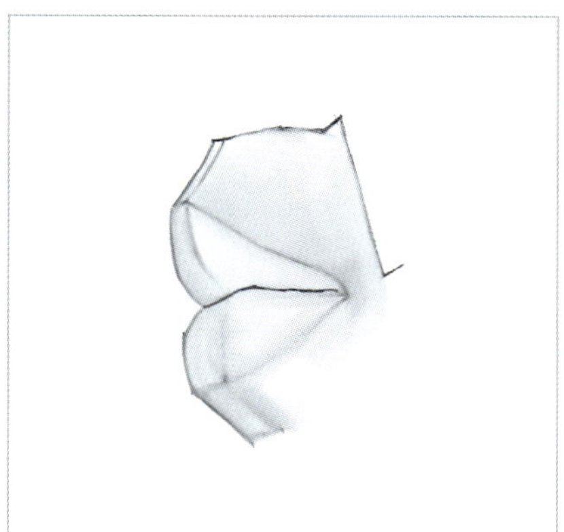

Blend the entire drawing, then draw a line with a medium charcoal pencil to separate the upper and the lower lip.

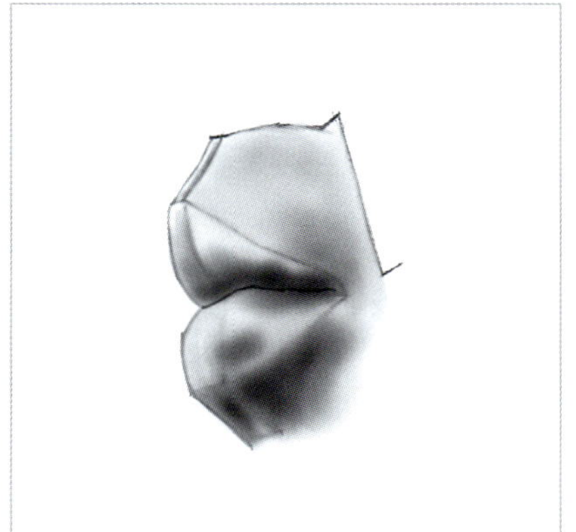

With your base layer blended, you can start to build up your lower values. Dip your smudger in your ground soft charcoal and use it to place your lower values. Focus on the bottom of the upper lip and bottom of the lower lip.

Best Practice: *Smudgers offer more control when building up low value areas than brushes do.*

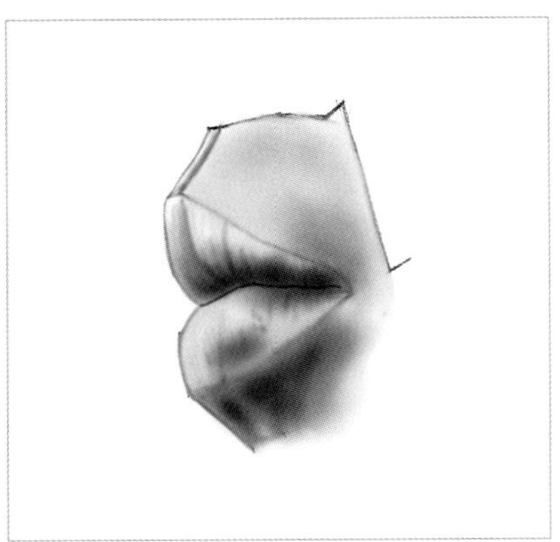

Push or pull up from the center line between the lips with your smudger, then do the same down from the center line to make the lips look more dynamic and creased.

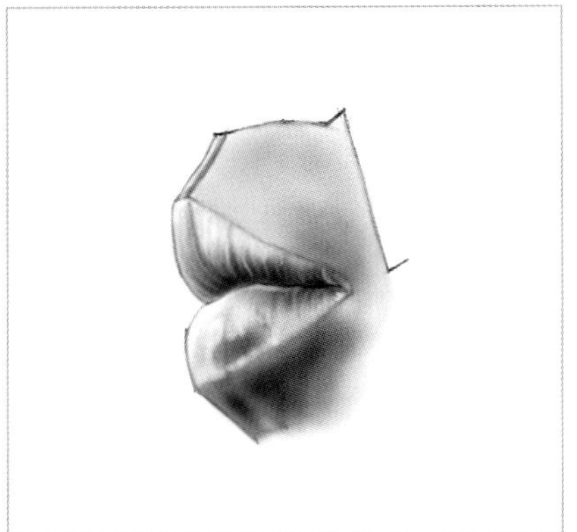

Trade the smudger for your MONO Zero Eraser, and work on retrieving the high values. Make sure you retrieve the highest values in the reference photo; this will help you accentuate the value scale when you start lowering the surrounding values.

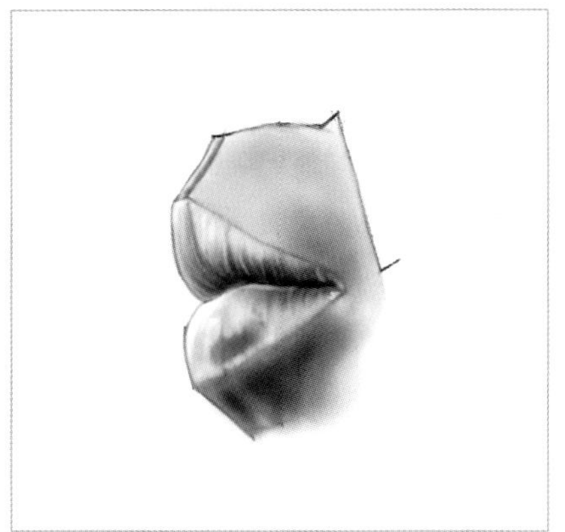

Time to swap tools again: Dip your brush in your ground soft charcoal, test the tone on some scratch paper, and then strategically build up the lower values, especially around the bottom of the upper lip and beneath the lower lip. (Remember, less is more.)

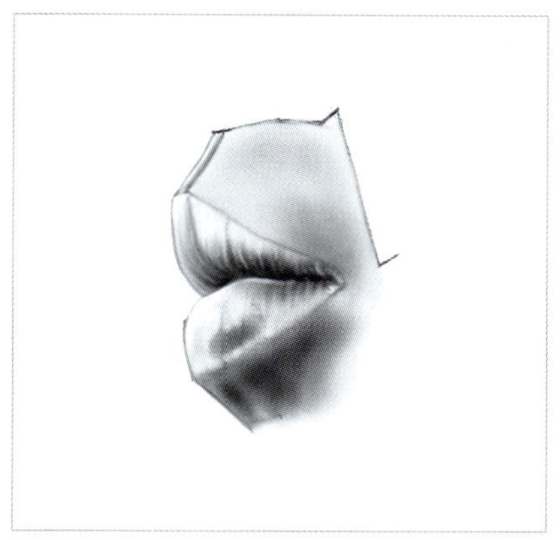

Finally, use a detail eraser, such as the MONO Zero, and very light pressure control to bring out detail. You could use a hard charcoal pencil for details, as well. To give the drawing a soft finish and to bring out gentle gradation, go over your blends with an empty brush.

> **Best practice:** *Always use a hard charcoal pencil for your detail work, because it lays on top of the soft and medium charcoals very nicely.*

The Straight-on Angle

The straight on angle is the only angle that you will draw that has inherent symmetry.

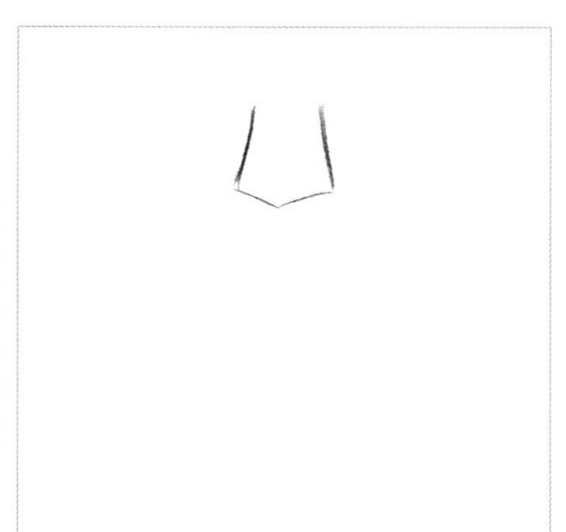

Start by drawing two lines angled slightly away from one another, then connect the bottoms to form a "cupid's bow."

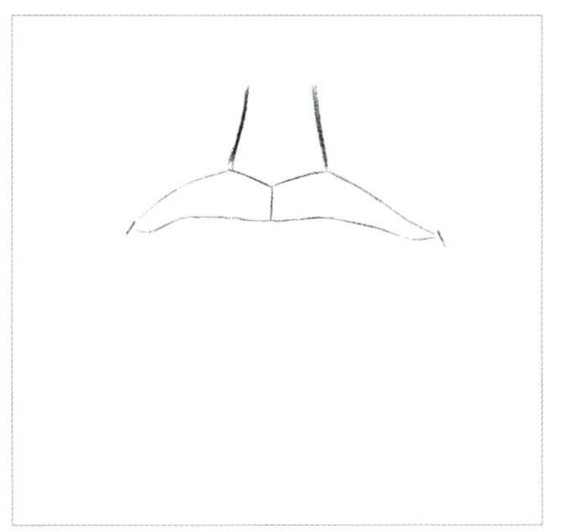

Draw the two-dimensional shape of the upper lip. I prefer the overhand grip for this, but use what feels the most natural to you.

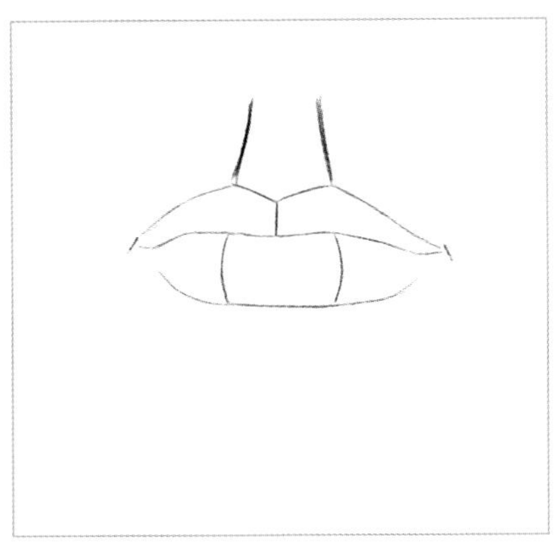

Using the philtrum plane lines as your guide, pull two lines down from the upper lip's lower edge to roughly where the bottom of the lower lip will be. Next, run a line from left to right to bring out the entirety of the lower lip.

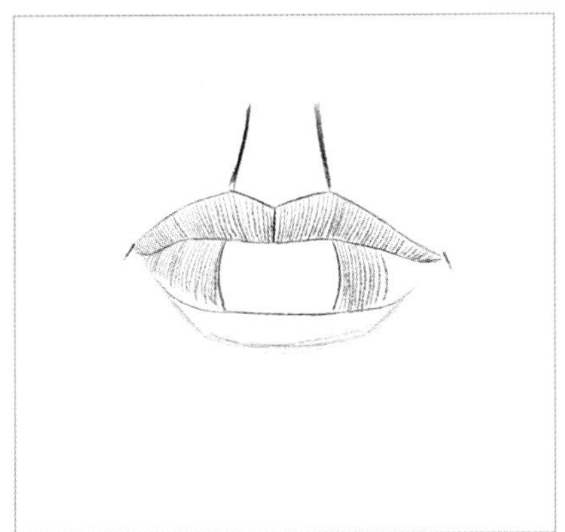

Using a soft charcoal pencil, lightly hatch (strokes in one direction) or crosshatch (crossing strokes in two directions) the lip planes. Be sure to follow the underlying form. Add the beginnings of a drop shadow for the lower lip, as well.

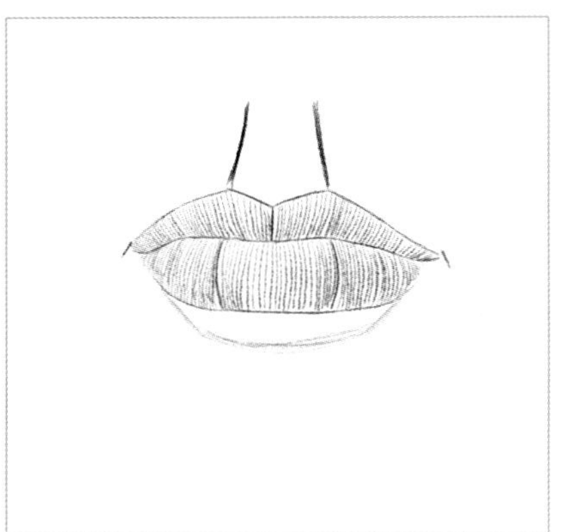

Continue to hatch or crosshatch until both lips are completely covered.

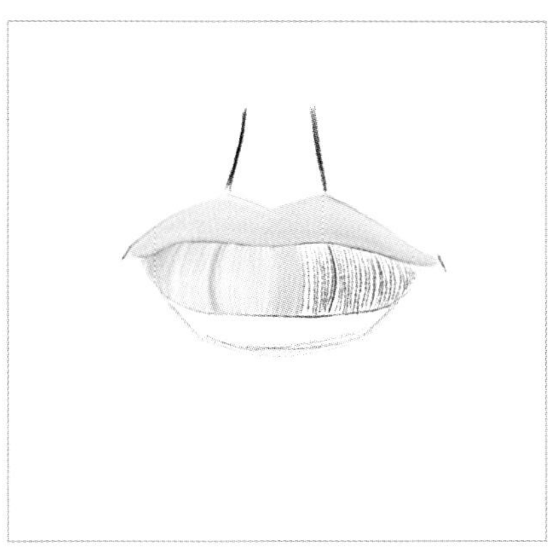

Switch your pencil for a smudger and begin blending your hatch marks.

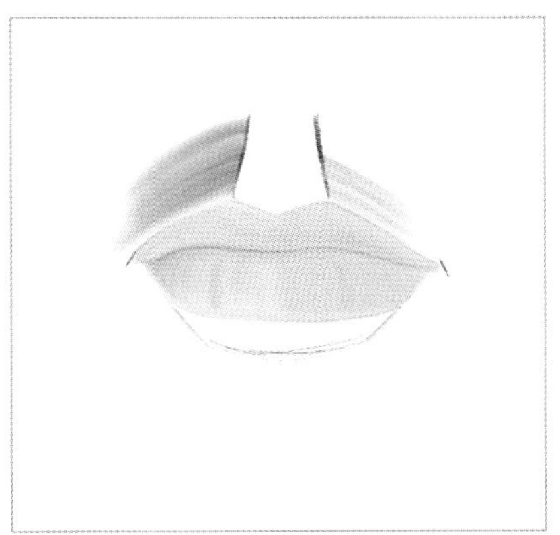

Pull the charcoal away from the philtrum lines and down at an angle. Follow the underlying form of your subject while pulling your smudger.

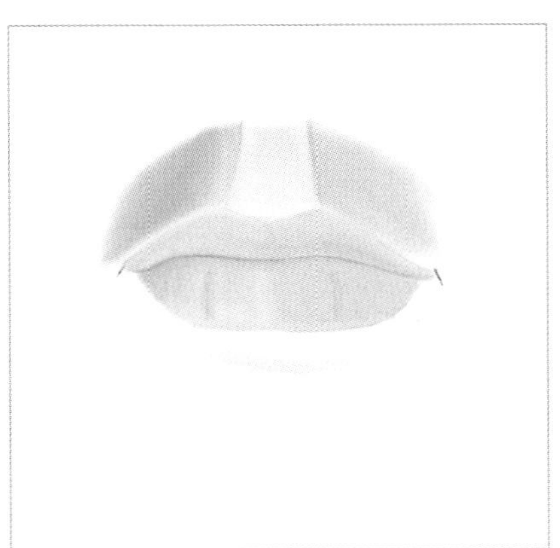

Continue to smudge the charcoal to bring out a smoother blend. Remember, always start with light pressure.

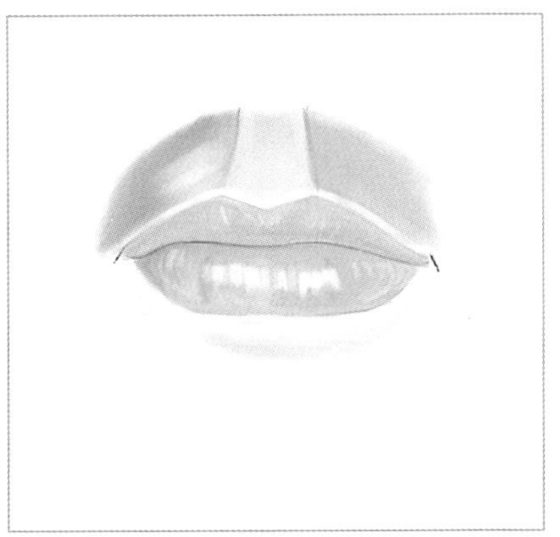

With your MONO Zero Eraser, start retrieving the high values. Remember that the harder you press, the higher the retrieved value, and the lighter the pressure, the lower the retrieved value.

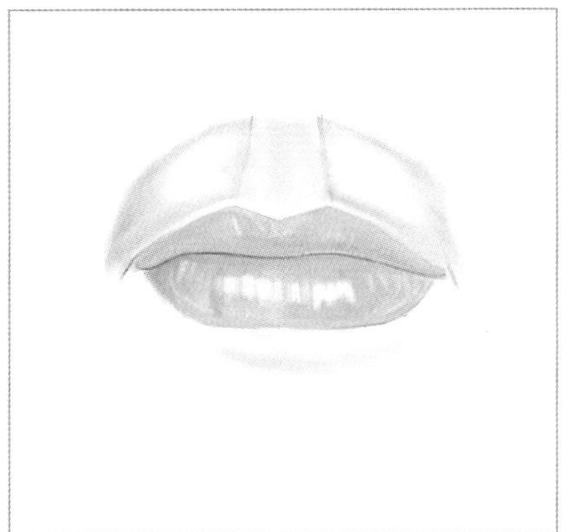

Continue retrieving higher values throughout the drawing as needed.

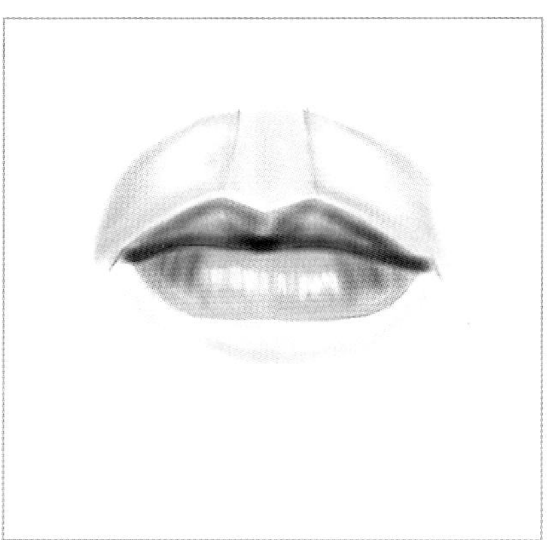

Dip a smudger in the ground soft charcoal, then start building up the low values on both lips.

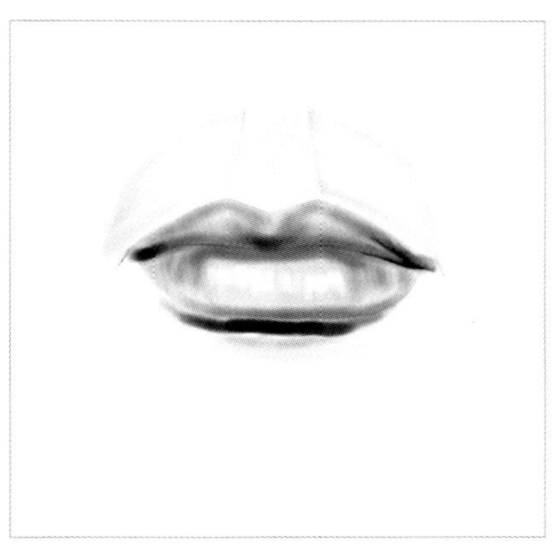

Continue building up your low values with your smudger, grabbing more soft charcoal powder with your smudger as needed.

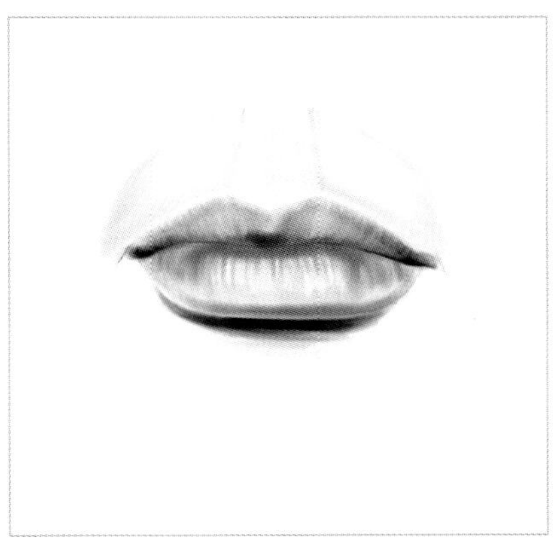

With your MONO Zero Eraser, continue to retrieve your mid tones and higher values. This is also a great time to erase any excessively low values in the drawing.

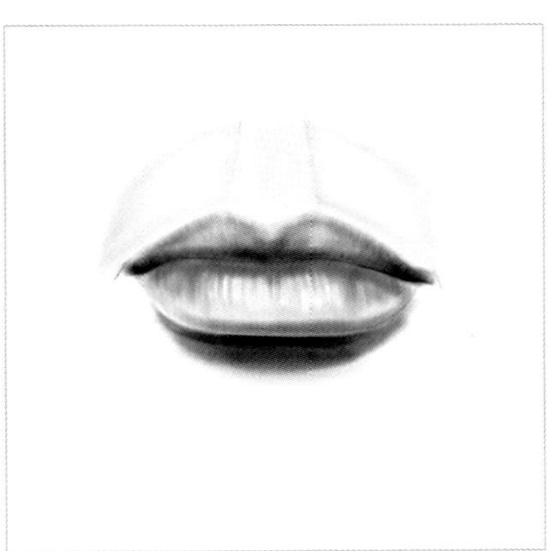

For a soft gradation across the entire drawing, switch to your brush, dip it in the soft charcoal powder, and blend the charcoal in the drawing. Make sure to focus on the lower values first. Focus on the center where the lips merge as well as beneath the lower lip.

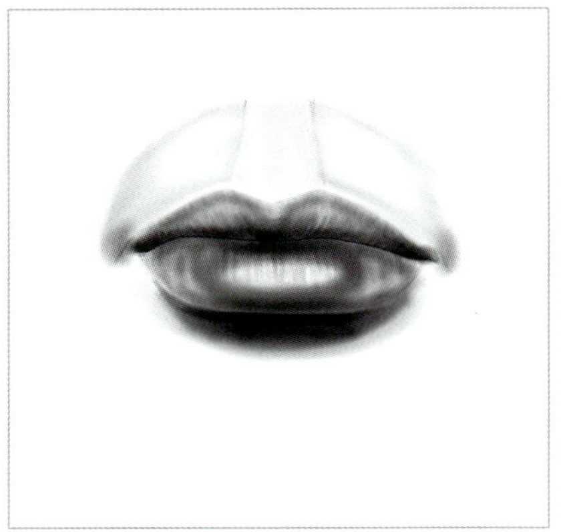

Focus on the lowest values now to bring out the three-dimensional form of the drawing. The more charcoal you throw down with your brush the lower the value will become.

Best Practice: *With a sharp medium charcoal pencil, extend a line from one corner of the mouth to the other. Make sure the line is intentional but with a thin line quality. This will make the lips look more dynamic.*

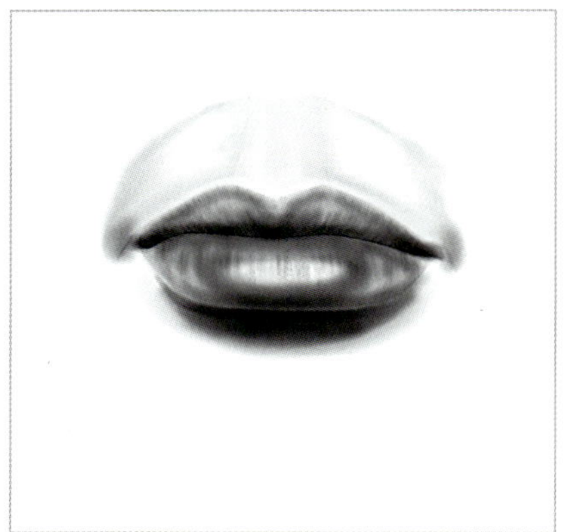

Finally, go through and cover your details. If you want to smooth out the entire drawing and bring out gradation even further, for example, you can hit it with an empty brush.

Best Practice: *When you think that you are done, take a 15-minute break, then give your drawing one last look over. If desired, use your hard charcoal to add detail work, such as veins, skin blemishes, or fine lines.*

The Three-Quarter-Turn Angle

The three-quarter turn angle is a lot of fun. The biggest thing to remember with this angle is to keep your far side proportional to the rest of the lips.

Draw two parallel lines for the philtrum plane, then connect them to form a cupid's bow.

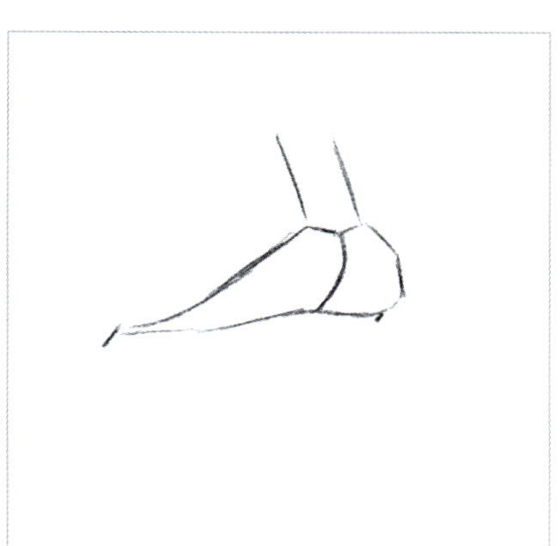

Draw the two-dimensional shape of the upper lip as well as the center line for the upper lip.

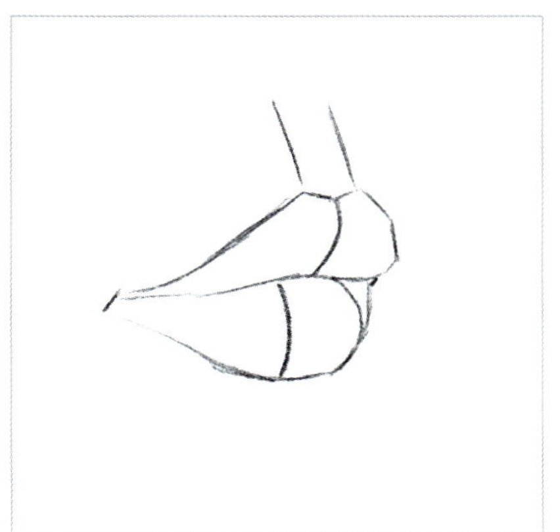

Using the philtrum plane lines as your guide for the bottom lip's plane lines, draw the basic shape of the lower lip, as well as the two lines that form that lip's three planes.

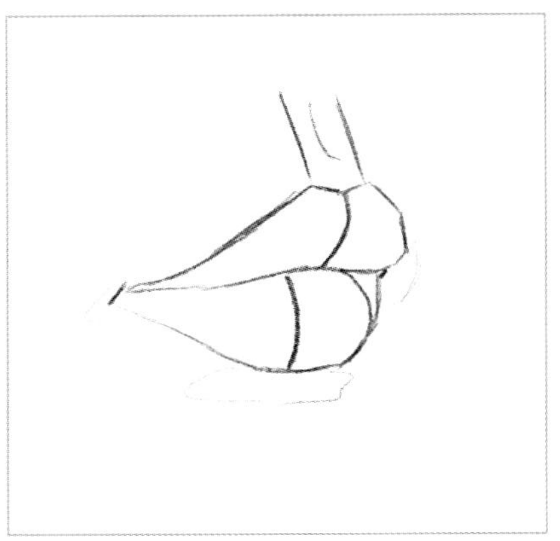

Draw some light outlines for the lower values around the corners of the mouth, underneath the lower lip, and the center of the philtrum.

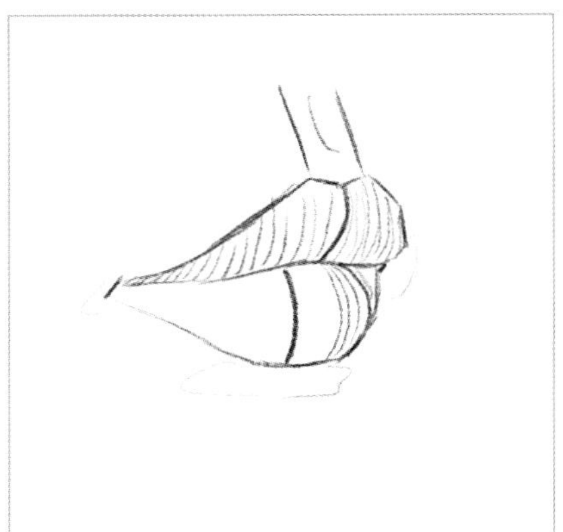

Start hatching the planes with your soft charcoal pencil. Remember to use light pressure and to push or pull your pencil tip in the direction of your underlying form.

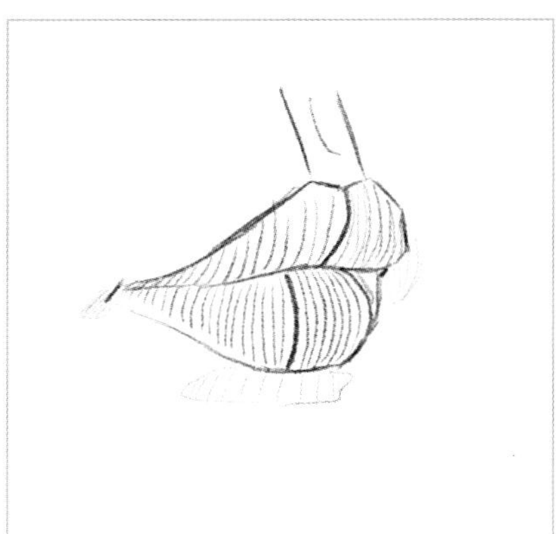

Continue hatching the lips until they are completely covered. This is also a great time to hatch the shadows around the lips.

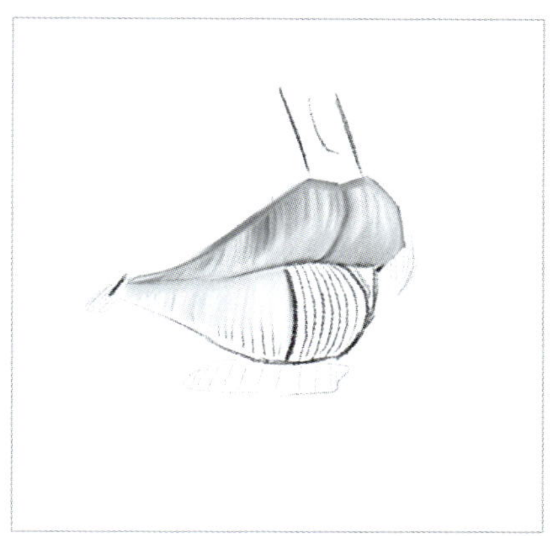

Using a smudger with light pressure, start smudging the charcoal into the paper. The harder you press, the more the charcoal will be pressed into the pores of the paper, thus giving you a lower value.

> **Best Practice:** *For this step, always start off smudging with a light pressure control, make sure to pull the charcoal in the direction of the underlying form.*

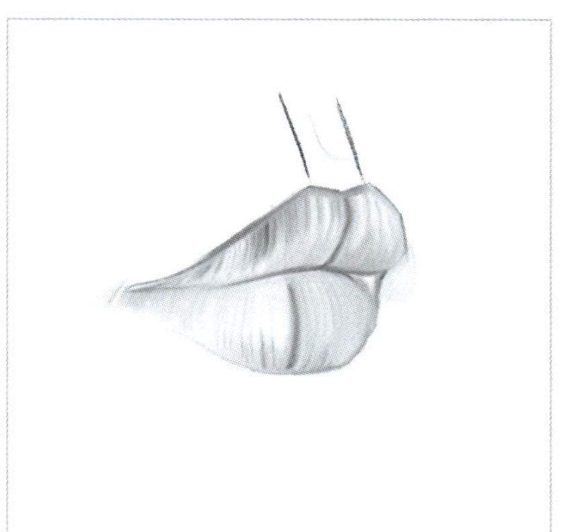

Continue smudging the drawing until it is completely smudged, including the shadows around the lips.

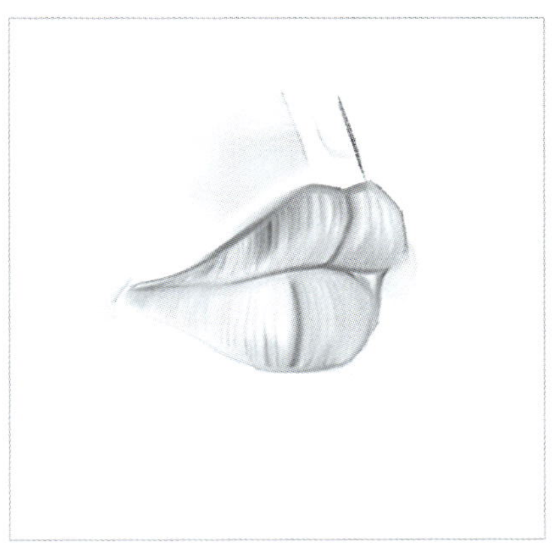

To give the lips more dimension, pull the charcoal away from your philtrum lines with your smudger.

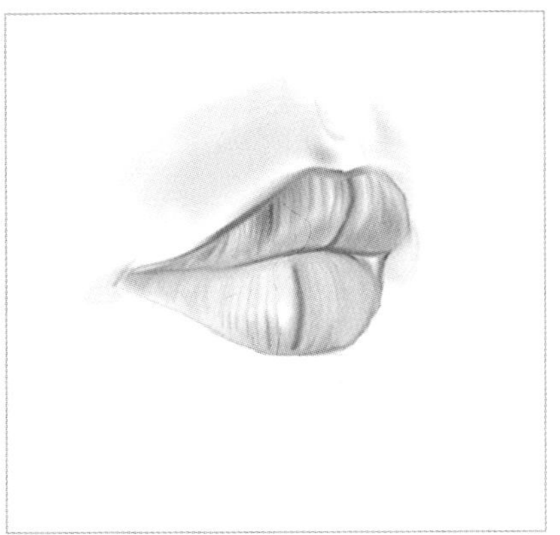

Continue lightly blending the charcoal on the other side of the philtrum.

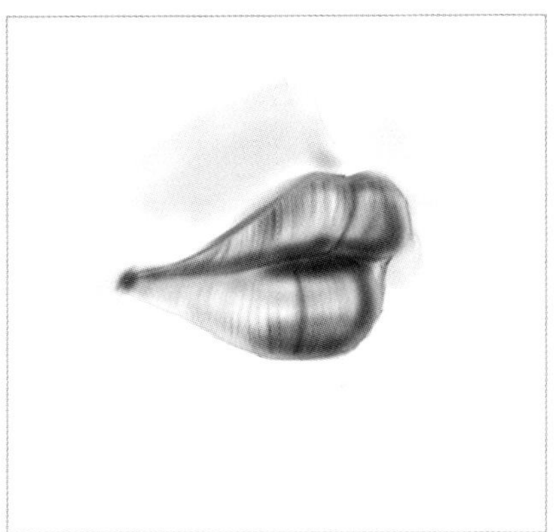

Load your brush with soft charcoal powder and target the lowest value on the upper and lower lips. Give the center of the lips the most attention, as this section is the lowest value in a three-quarter-turn drawing.

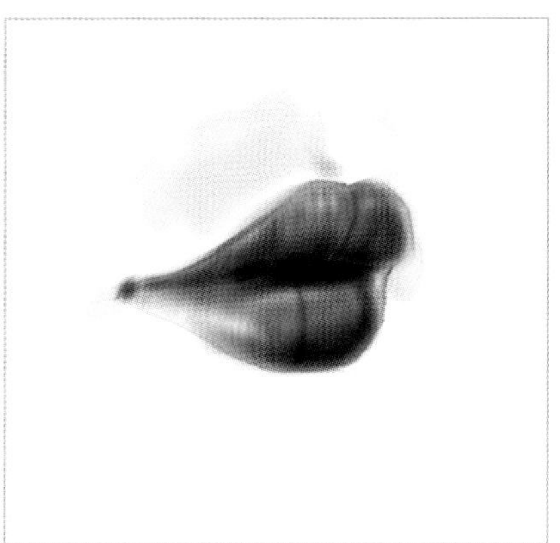

Continue blending the lips with your brush; dab the paper in the areas that require a lower value.

Focus heavily on where the low values live in the reference. Push or pull your brush with soft charcoal across the paper in those low-value areas.

> **Best practice:** *Much like when you first hatched your Asaro planes, pay attention to the flow of the face. Use the underlying form as your guide for which direction you think you should push or pull your brush.*

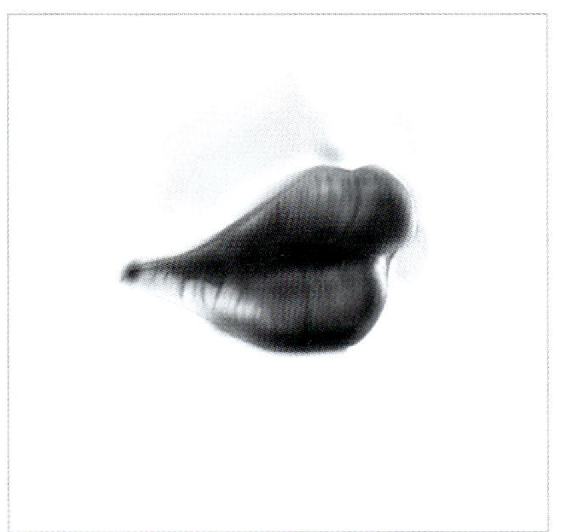

With your MONO Zero Eraser, retrieve any high values that you need to, such as the slight cracks in the lower lip's side. The direction that you pull remains an important element for the overall flow of the lips.

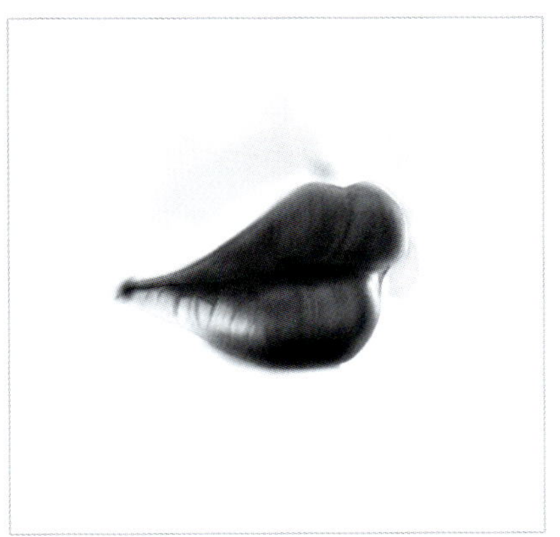

Switch to your hard charcoal to bring out such details as cracks in the lips, skin blemishes, and so on. When you think you're done, take a 15-minute break. When you return to your drawing with refreshed eyes, you will more easily see any adjustments that should be made before you call your drawing finished.

Project 9: Draw Three Sets of Lips

For **Project 9**, draw three sets of Asaro lips using the techniques and best practices you learned. If you need a more fluid explanation of the Asaro method or lip planes in particular, simply scan the QR code to watch the video **How to Easily Draw Lips | Understanding the Asaro Method Part III**.

Practice Your Planes

The biggest thing to take from this chapter is the Asaro method's planal structure of the lips: two planes for the upper and three for the lower lip. Once you have the planes of the lips drawn the rest is simple hatching, blending, and value building via the Three-Layered method. if you need to take a deeper dive into the lips, the Asaro method, or the three-layered method of drawing with charcoal, please jump on YouTube through the chapter's QR code and check out my videos with detailed audible narration. The more you practice, the greater your understanding will become, and you will soon be drawing the lip planes from various angles without much thought.

How *to* Draw Ears

"A powerful person has big ears."
—Japanese proverb

Ears, like other facial features, have their own Asaro planes that will help you frame and understand them in three-dimensional space. Unlike the eyes or nose, however, your subjects' ears may not be a focal point—or even visible. It all depends on the angle and reference you are working with. Whether the ears are on full display, partially obscured, or completely covered, though, the principal structure of the Asaro planes remains the same. In this chapter, I'll walk you step by step through plane construction as well as how to draw ears from the three most common portrait angles: profile, straight on, and a three-quarter turn.

The Ear Planes

When studying the ear planes, you'll notice something reminiscent of the rest of the planes of the head of the Asaro model. The right side offers a slightly different variation of the ear planes from the left. For example, compare the right ears in the figures below with the left ears. You can clearly see a difference in planal structures. The ear lobes of the left and the right ears, for example, have different planes drawn in. This is the adaptability of the Asaro method in action. Again, which planes you choose to identify when drawing will depend on the proportional differences found in the reference that you are using, as well as the angle at which you're drawing your subject.

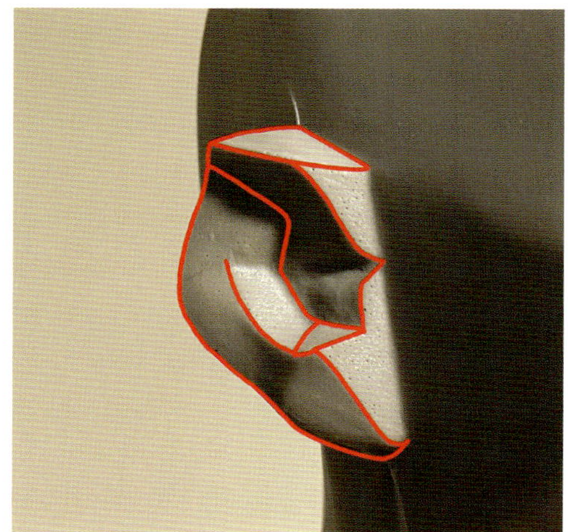
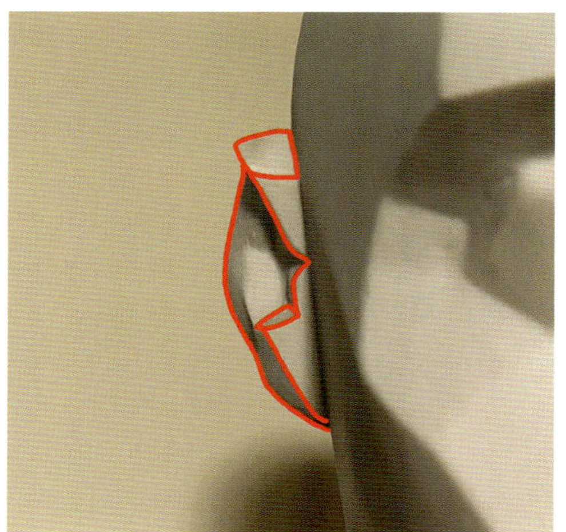
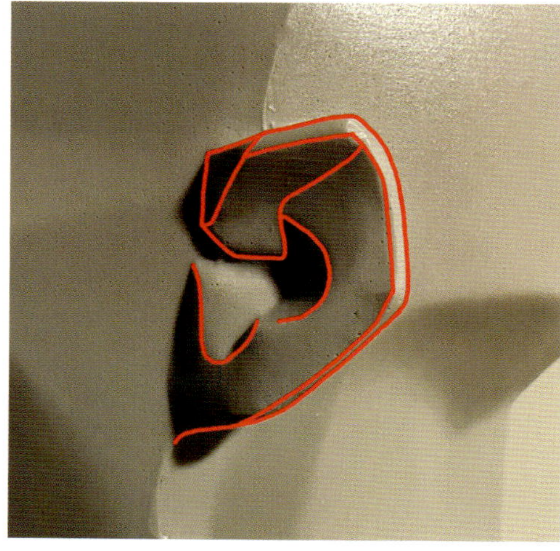
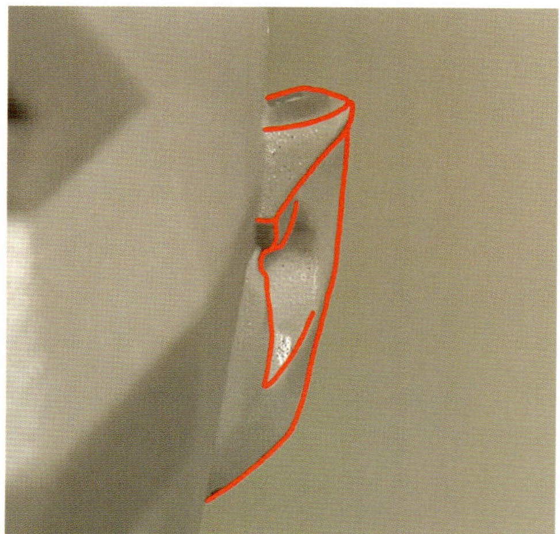

Step 1: Identify the Planes

Each set of ears covered in this drawing flow will have a slightly different approach, because each ear is not only proportionally different to the next but also is viewed from a different angle. The Asaro method itself is adaptable enough to handle this, but you also must be adaptable with its application to be successful.

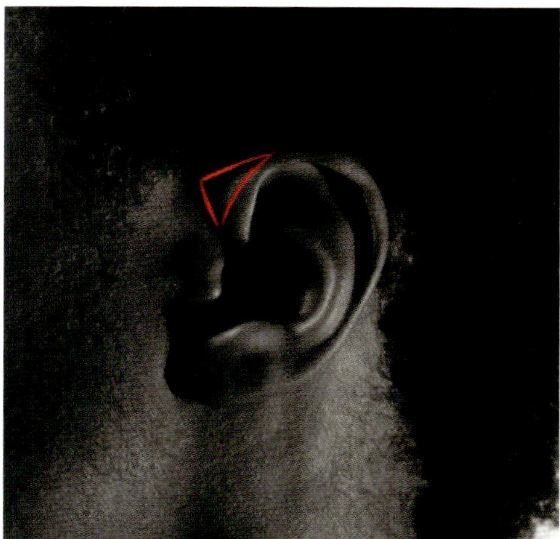

For the profile angle, start by drawing the ear one plane at a time, slowly building out the ear. This way you will not get overwhelmed and have a much more accurate shape as you draw further.

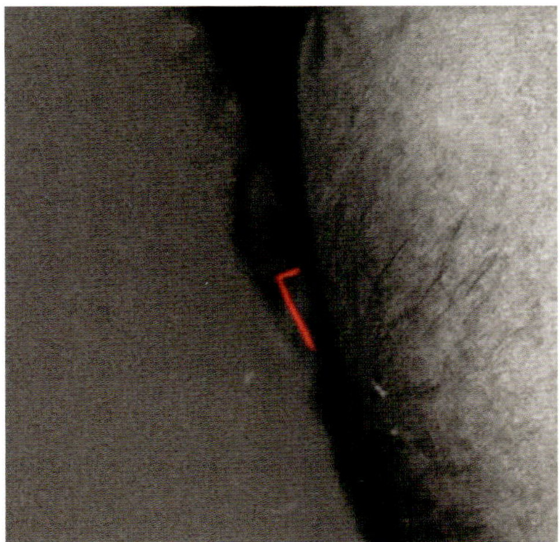 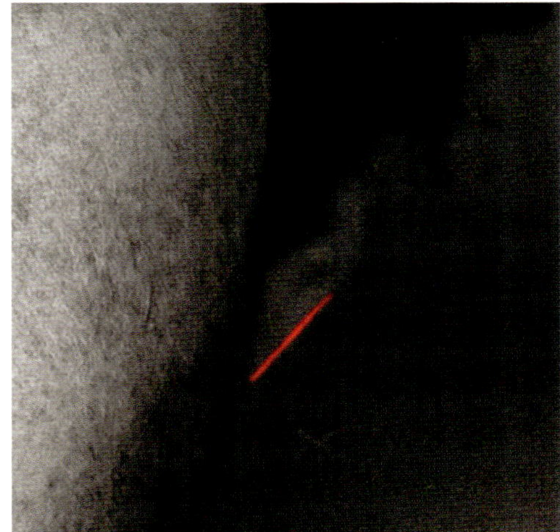

For the straight-on angle, start with what your viewer will see the most: the plane of
the ear lobes.

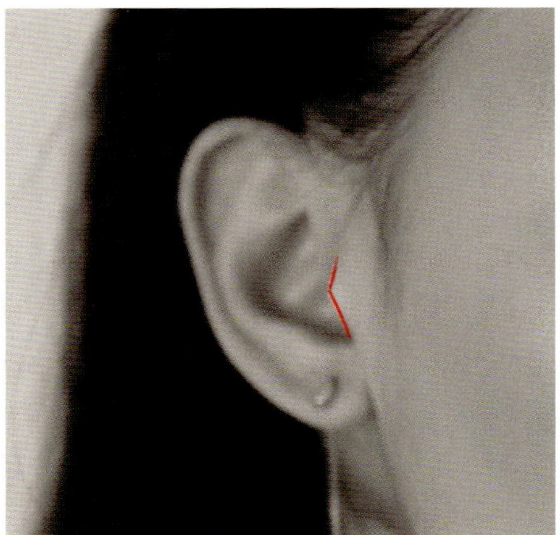

For the three-quarter-turn angle, first identify where the ear plugs into the side of
the head. This way you can start to build out your ear by using the head as your
anchor point.

Step 2: Follow the Flow of the Ears

Now that you have your first plane drawn, you can extend it into the overall flow of the ear. Each plane that you draw will be an extension of the plane that came before. By drawing your ear one plane at a time, you can better see and understand the way the ear is structured.

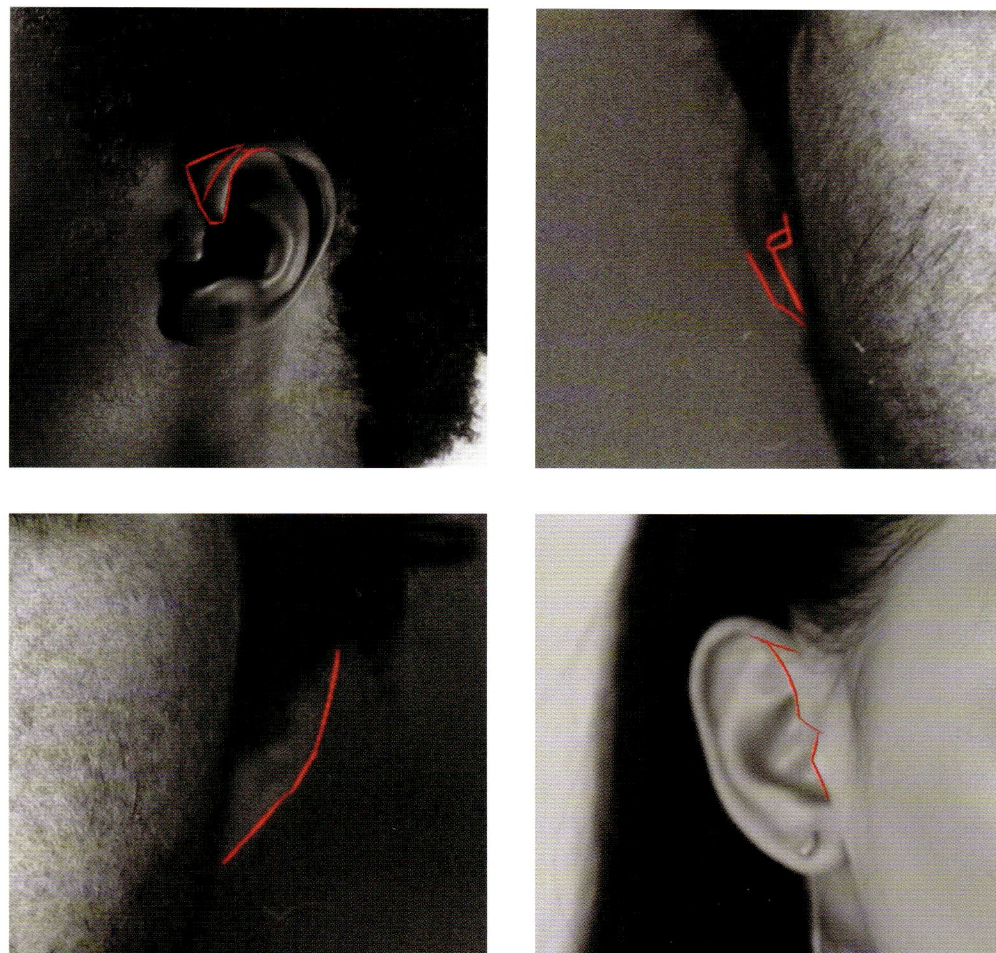

Step 3: Draw the Outline of the Ears

As you continue to extend your line work, focus on drawing the basic two-dimensional shape of the outer ear first. Once you have the shape secure, then you can start focusing on the inside planes of the ear. This will vary slightly depending on the angle you are drawing.

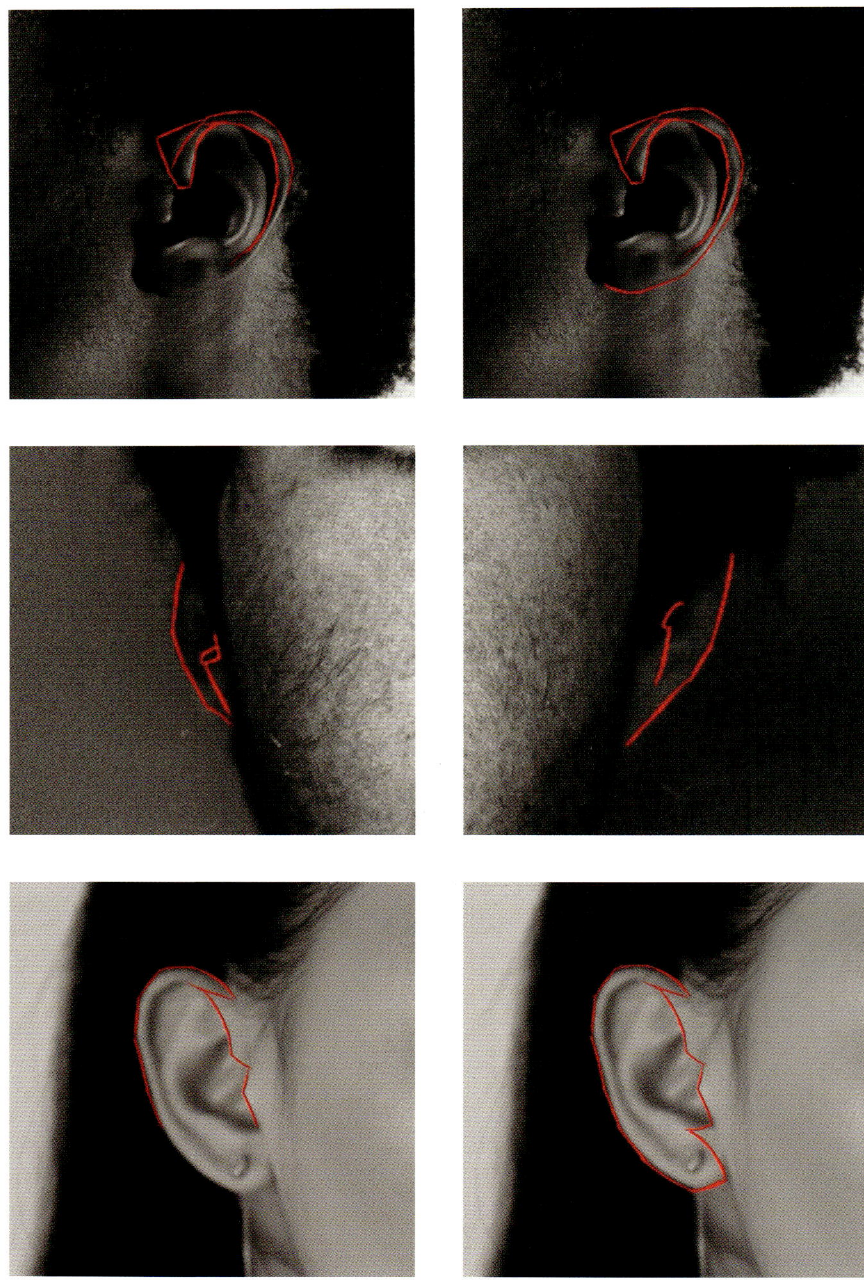

Step 4: Draw the Planes of the Inside Ear

After you draw the whole of the ear's outside, identify the planes that comprise the inside of the ear. This will solidify your ear's shape and allow you to move onto the next phase in the drawing process.

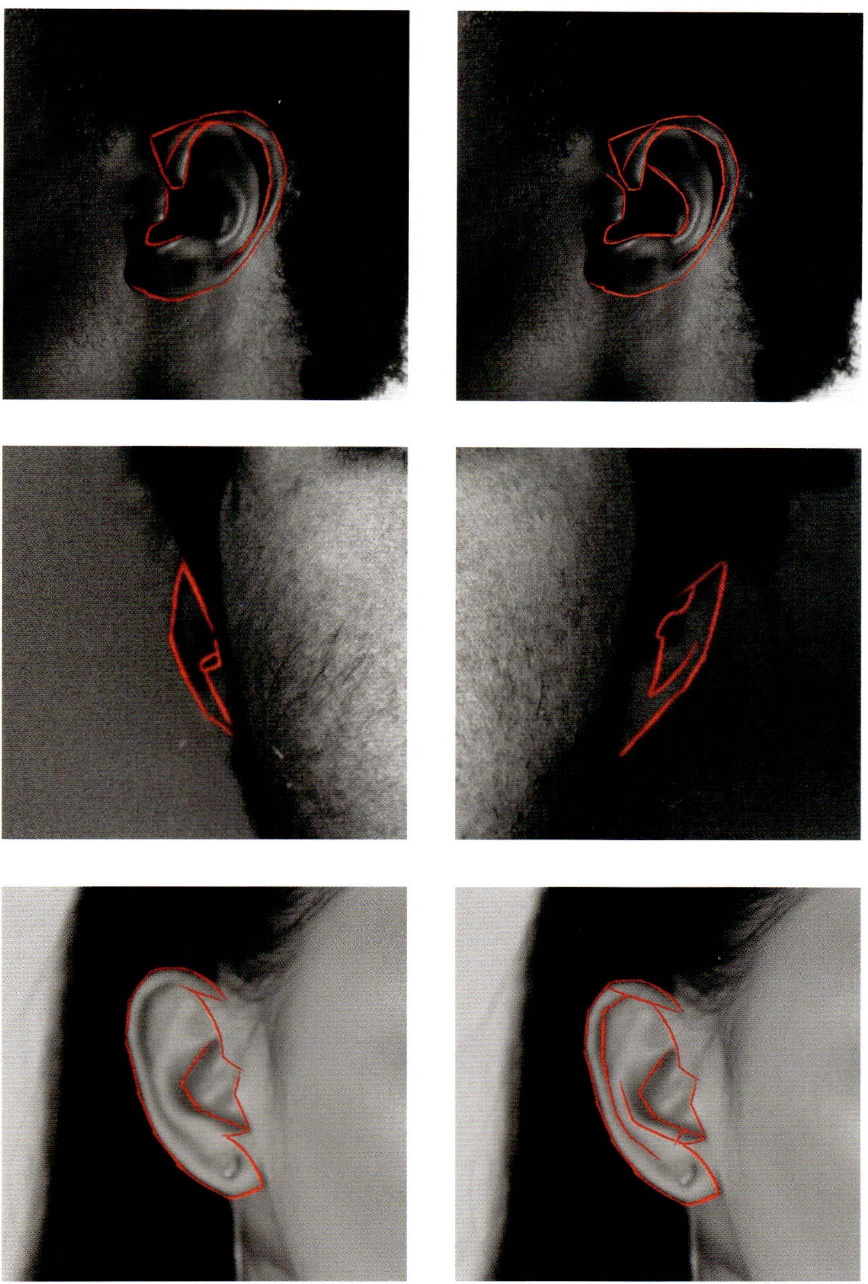

Drawing Ears Using the Asaro Method

Now that you have a grasp of working with the ear planes, I'll walk you through the flows for drawing ears from the profile, straight-on, and three-quarter-turn angles with the Asaro method. Just like with the other facial features, you have flexibility and some autonomy for how you would like to approach the drawing of your ears—just think of your reference from the perspective of the planes that comprise it. Use single, short strokes, and extend your first plane into your second plane and so on. Remember to take it slow and enjoy every stroke, smudge, blend, and adjustment.

The Profile Angle

Remember that by drawing your ear one plane at a time, you can better see and understand the way the ear is structured.

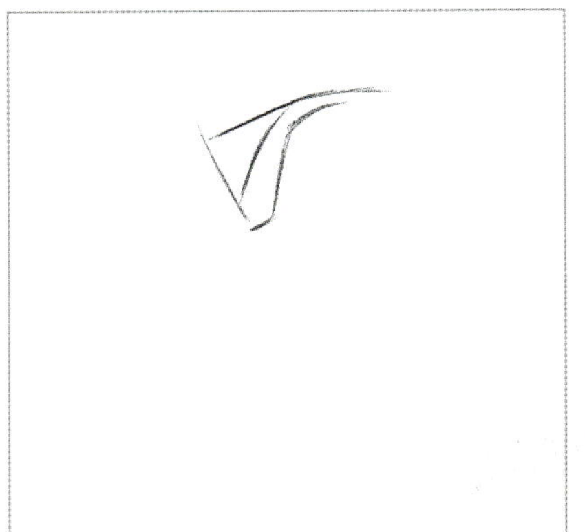

With a soft charcoal pencil, draw the top plane where the ear extends out from the side of the head, then draw the second plane that brings out the fold of the ear.

> **Best Practice:** *Use very light pressure, so you can easily make adjustments with your eraser.*

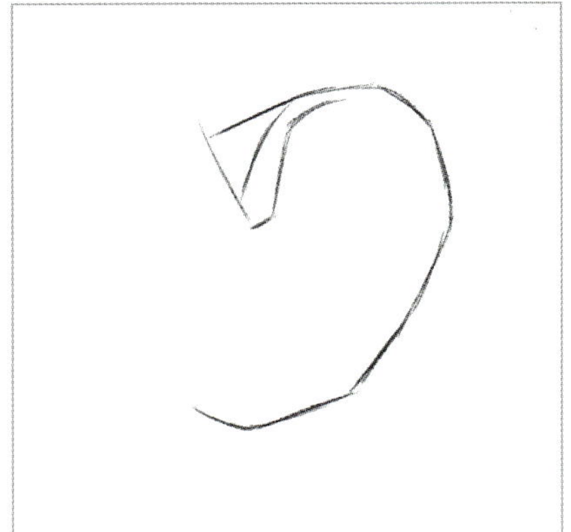

Extend your line down and around the full length of your subject's ear to create the ear's outside edge. Remember, you want to work from the outside in with the profile angle.

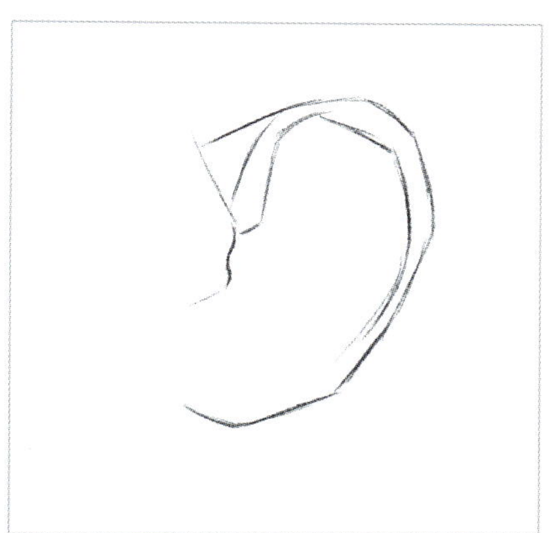

Draw a line inside and parallel to the curve you just drew, stopping when you get just past halfway down the outer ear slope. Also draw in an S-shaped line from the lower tip of the first plane you drew.

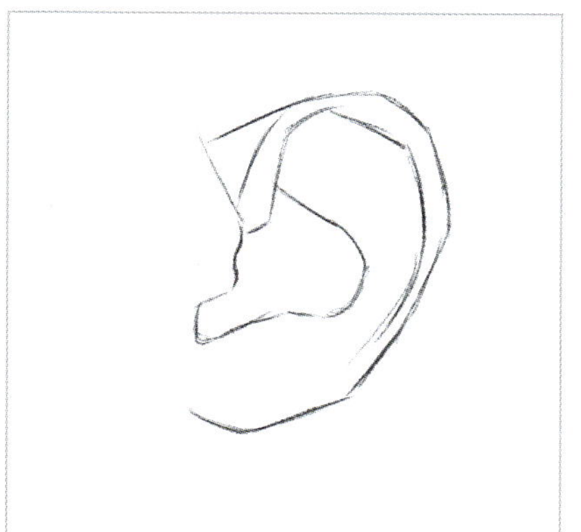

Bring that S-shaped line down, over, and up to outline the inner plane of the ear. This is the entirety of your basic two-dimensional shape.

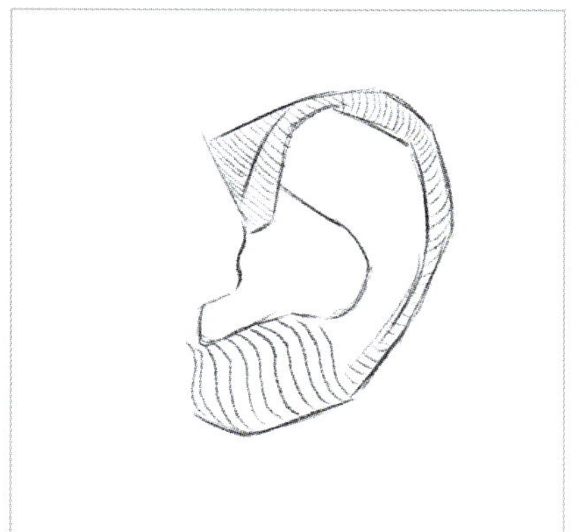

With your soft charcoal pencil, start hatching or crosshatching the individual planes of the ear.

Best Practice: *The underlying form of the ear is everything, so make sure you follow it with your hatching. This will help you later when you blend your hatch marks with a smudger.*

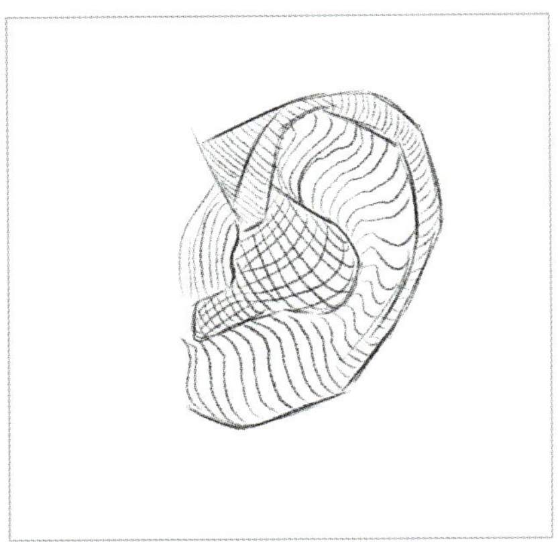

Be sure to crosshatch the inner ear due to its inherently lower value.

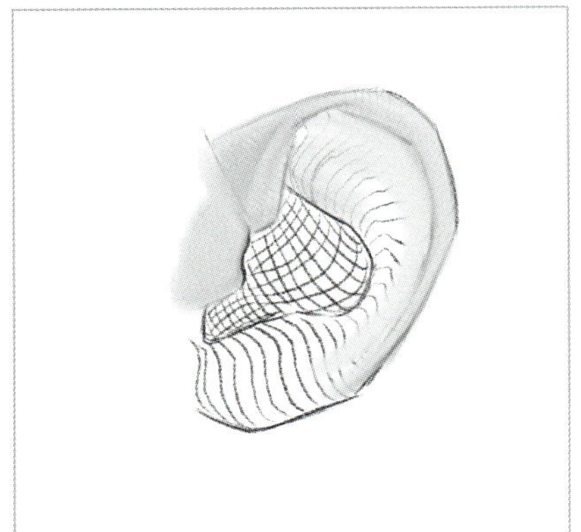

Switch to your smudger and start blending your hatch marks. Remember to push or pull your smudger in the direction of the underlying form.

> **Best Practice:** *When you smudge, start with light pressure, and then slowly start increasing the pressure. This will teach you how to control the values that you convey through smudging.*

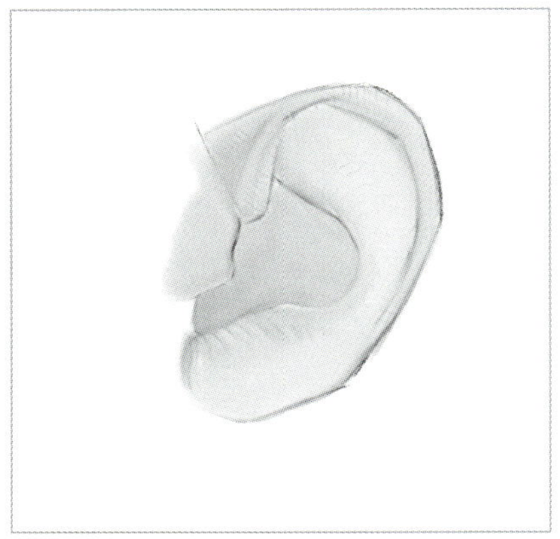

Continue to blend the entire drawing until none of your hatch marks are visible. Notice how the inner ear already has a lower value? Crosshatching usually produces a lower value when blended.

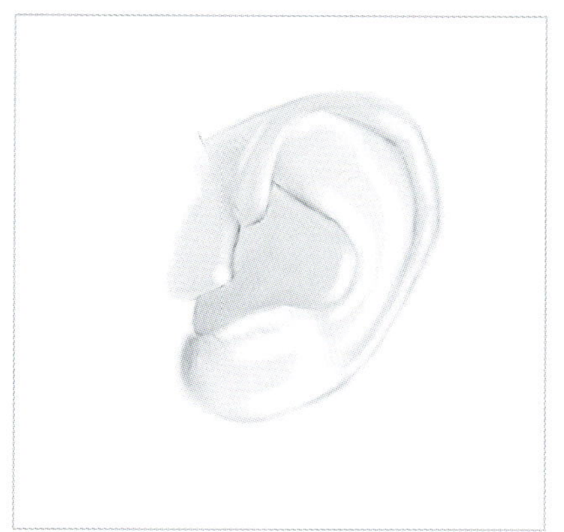

Trade your smudger for your MONO Zero Eraser and start retrieving your high values. Remember, heavy pressure will retrieve higher values and vice versa.

> **Best Practice:** *Smaller erasers, such as the MONO Zero Eraser, offer more control but retrieve a smaller area. Larger erasers, like a kneaded eraser, offer less control but retrieve larger areas.*

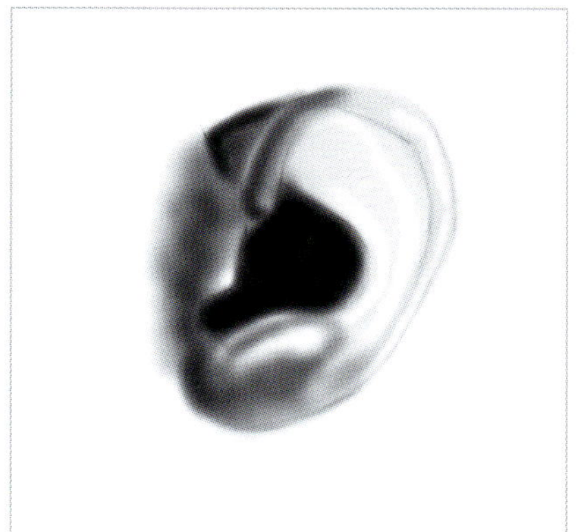

Switch back to your smudger and dip the tip into your soft charcoal powder. Check your tone on scratch paper, and then start building up your lower values. Make sure you follow the underlying form.

> **Best Practice:** *Keep your pressure light. You can always go back over areas with more charcoal and more pressure to continue lowering your values.*

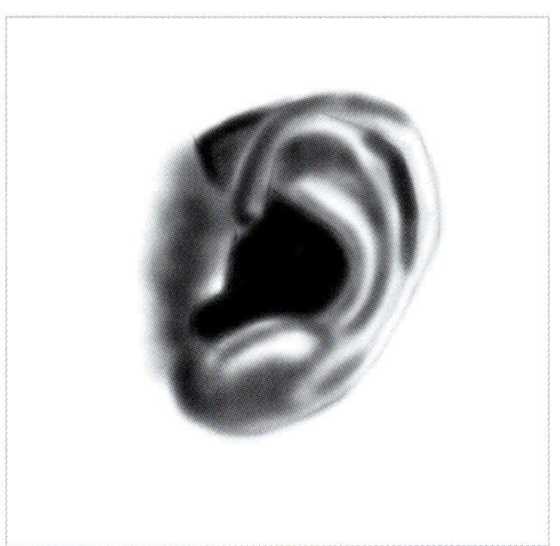

Continue to build up your lower values throughout the ear, keeping in mind your pressure control.

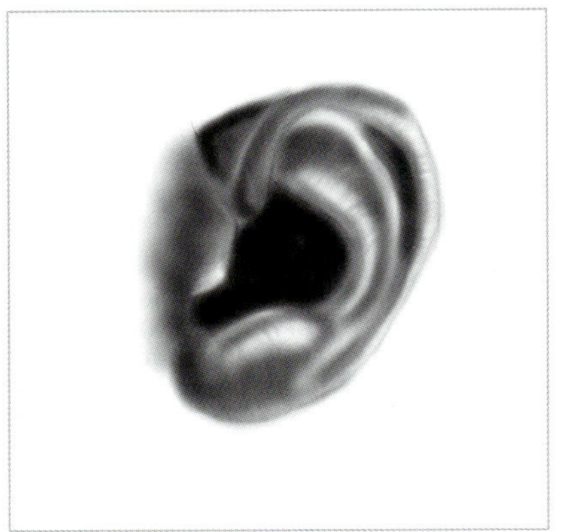

Very lightly go through your drawing with your MONO Zero Eraser to retrieve just a hint of the underlying form. Make your pushes and pulls the same as your original hatch marks. This helps your viewer's eye pick up on that three-dimensional shape a bit more.

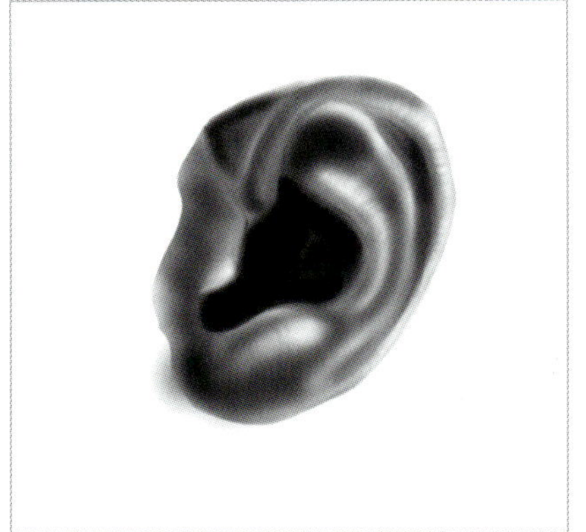

Brush the whole ear lightly with an unloaded brush to soften the look and produce a nice gradation across your different values.

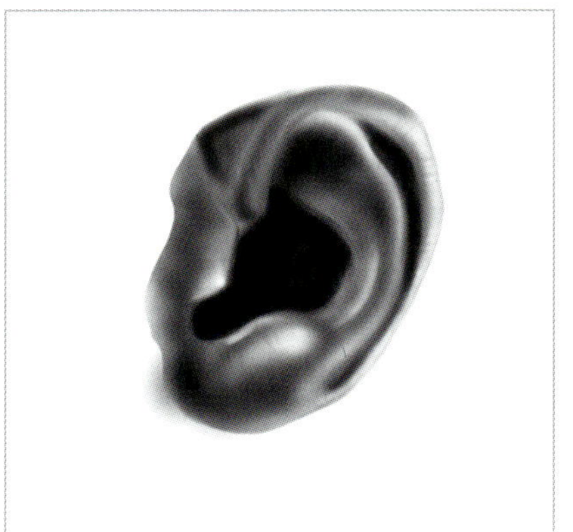

Continue to build up your lower values throughout the ear. Remember you want areas of complete black and complete white so that all your mid tones pop and the ear looks as dynamic as possible.

> **Best Practice:** *For smaller areas of intense low value, use a sharp, medium charcoal pencil. Not only will it give you more control, you also will be able to get into much smaller areas than with a brush or smudger.*

The Straight-On Angle

With this specific angle you won't be able to see much of the ears. However, you still need to abide by the principles of planal structure for what is visible.

Draw an arch that extends from the bottom of the left ear to the bottom of the right ear. The arch will give you a basic structure to work from and help you keep a sense of proportion for the head between the ears.

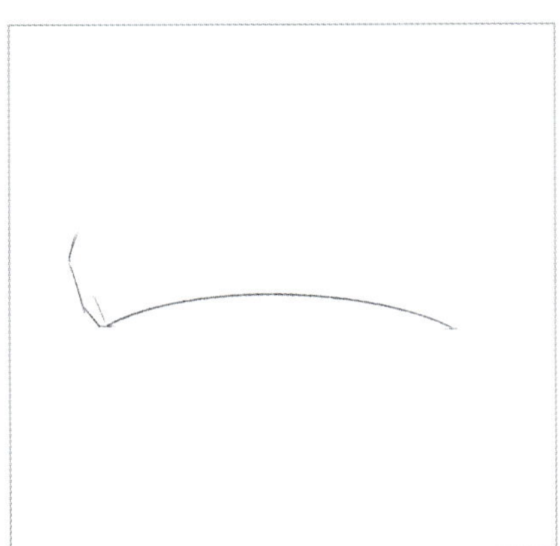

On one side of the arch, start drawing the basic shape of the bottom of the ear lobe. Remember that you want to draw the outside edge of the ear as well.

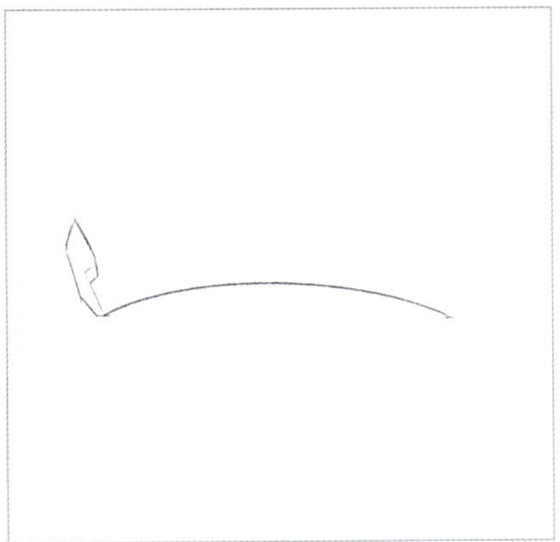

Continue to draw the outside edge of the ear, and then place the inner ear plane.

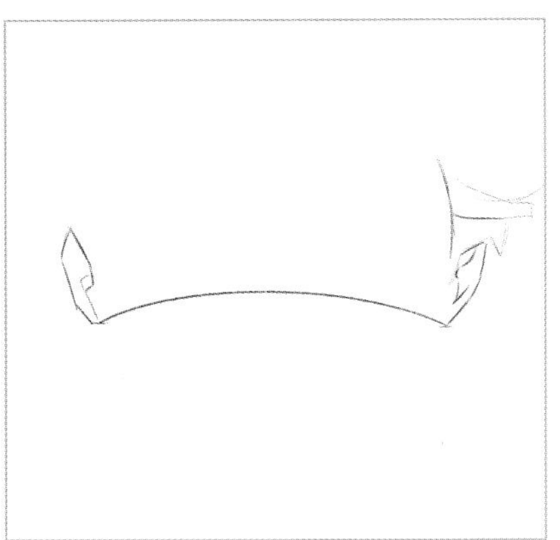

Now, draw the same on the other side of your arch. I encourage you to draw the beginnings of your subject's hair, as well, so you can see how the two features affect each other.

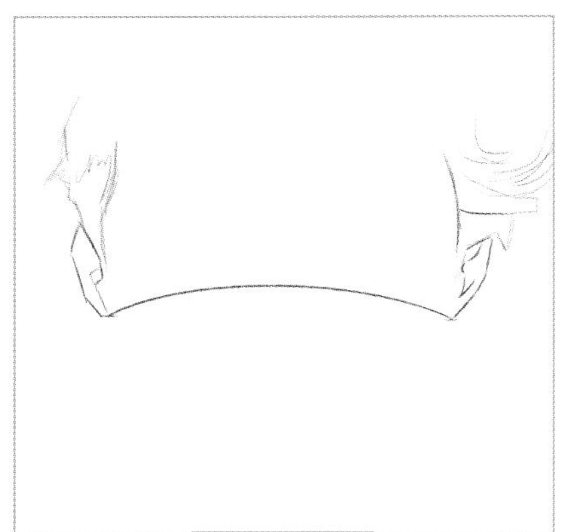

Draw the basic shape of the hair on both sides of your subject's head.

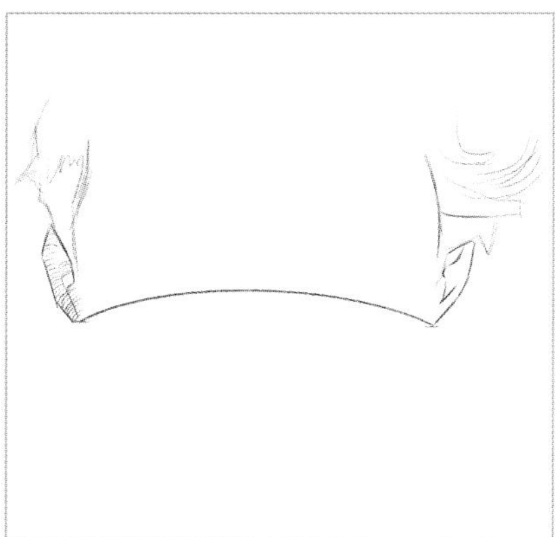

With a soft charcoal pencil, start hatching or crosshatching the ear planes.

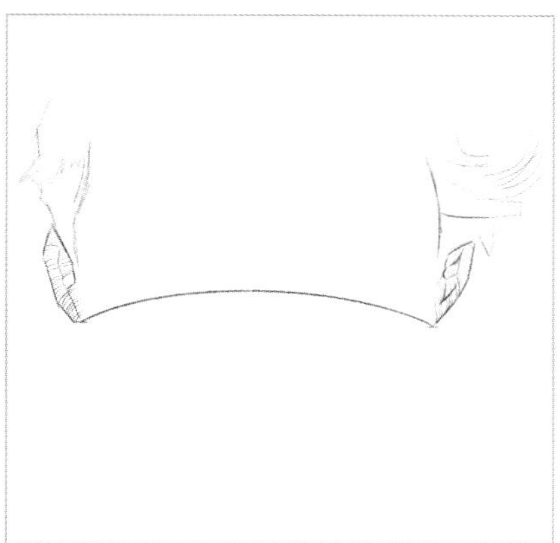

Hatch the other ear until both ears are completely covered.

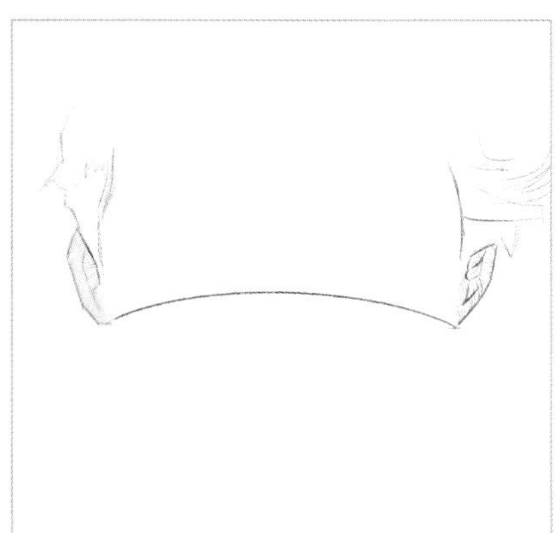

Switch to your smudger and begin to blend your hatch marks. Remember to follow the underlying form of your ears using your planes and reference as your guides.

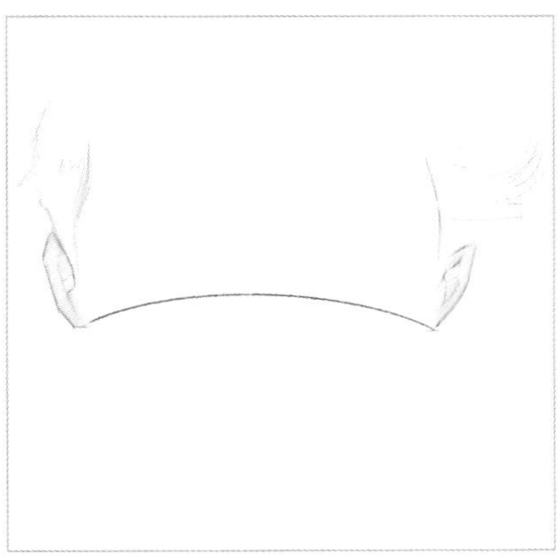

Continue smudging your hatch marks until they are completely blended and there are no more or very few hatch marks visible.

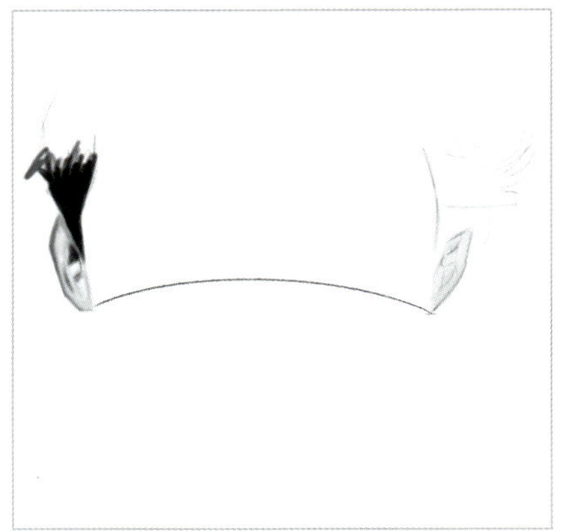

Dip a smudger into the soft charcoal powder, and check your tone to make sure it is a very low value. Starting on the left, begin lowering the value of the inside of the ear as well as the hair. To get the lowest value possible in the hair, you may want to switch to your medium charcoal pencil.

Best Practice: *With light pressure, continue to go over the areas in the hair that need a very low value, then blend those areas with your smudger and brush for a soft gradation.*

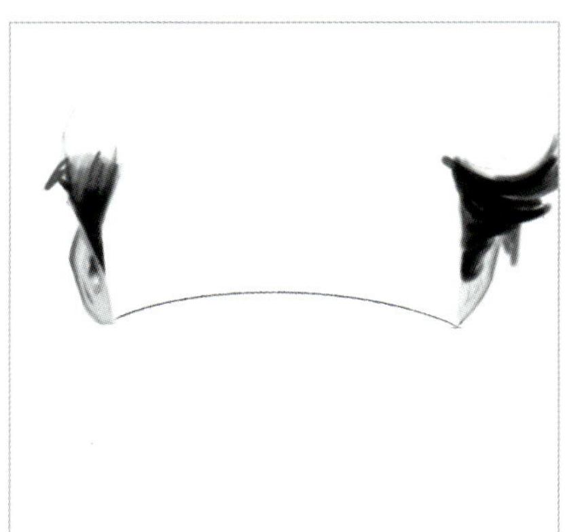

Continue the process on the other side of the head. Once you are happy with the hair's low values, retrieve some higher values with a kneaded eraser to bring out the sharpness of the hair flow.

Best Practice: *The MONO Zero Eraser gives you more control when retrieving your high values in clumps of hair and hair texture.*

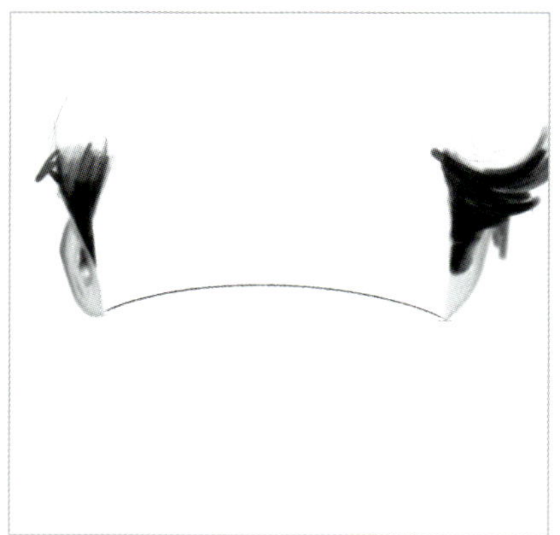

Continue retrieving the high values throughout the hair to give it some dimension and character.

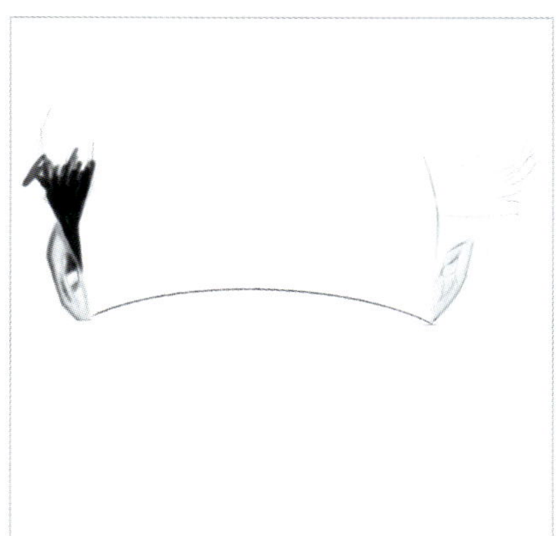

Continue to retrieve your mid tones and higher values with a MONO Zero Eraser. This is also a great point to erase any excessively low values in the drawing, too.

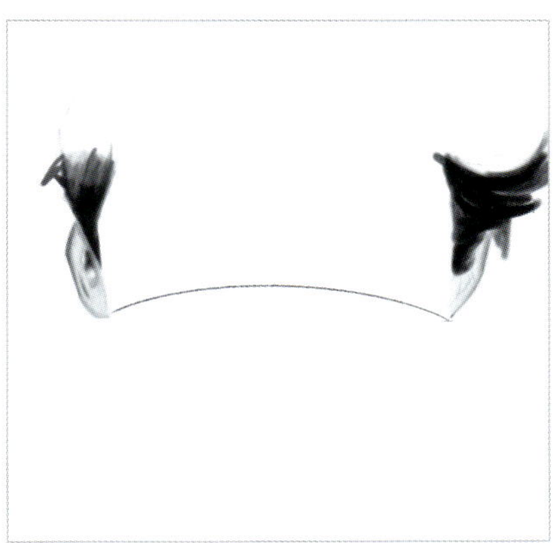

Finally, blend the ears and the hair with an unloaded brush, following the underlying flow of each feature. The ears in this angle take a back seat to the hair in the straight-on portrait, so it's important to understand how the two interact in their construction.

> **Best Practice:** Use a hard charcoal pencil to draw in small details in the inner and outer ears, as well as flyaway hairs on your subject's head.

The Three-Quarter-Turn Angle

The three-quarter-turn angle will be very similar to how the profile angle ear was constructed.

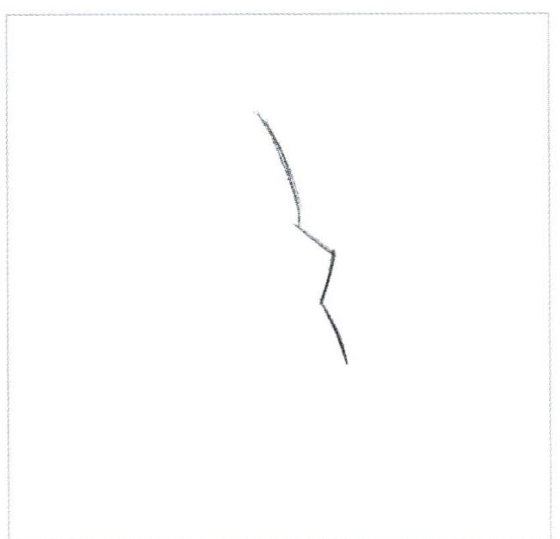

With a soft charcoal pencil, draw a zigzag line to represent where the ear attaches to the side of the head.

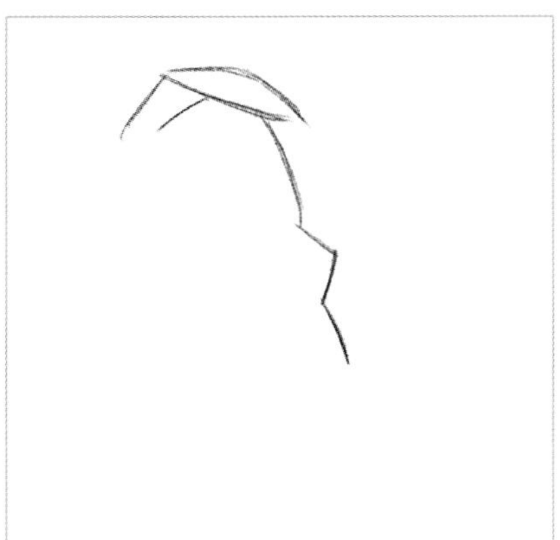

Draw your first plane to showcase the ear's top, then extend this plane so it leads to the top of the backside of the ear.

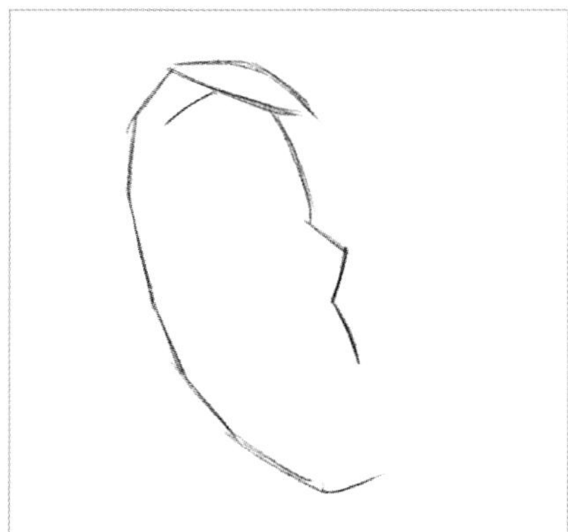

Continue to draw the line down to create the outer ear's basic shape. Remember to use short light pulls.

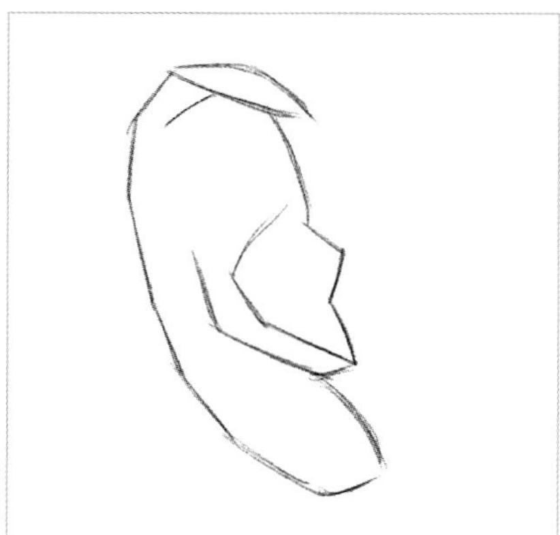

Bring the outer line up and around to bring out the ear lobe's outline, then draw the inner ear plane.

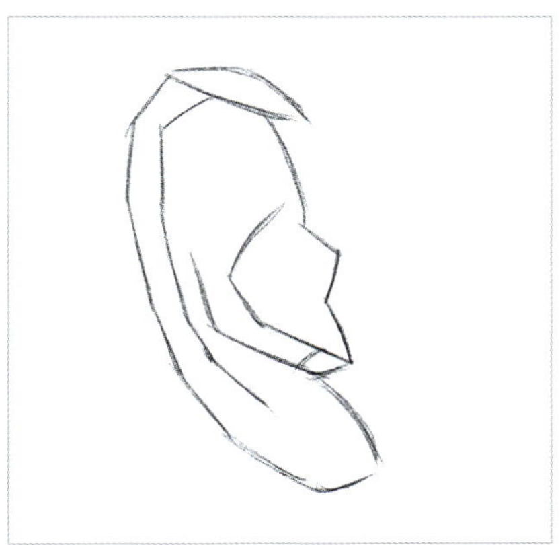

To help you better see the underlying form of the inner ear plane, draw a small line across it.

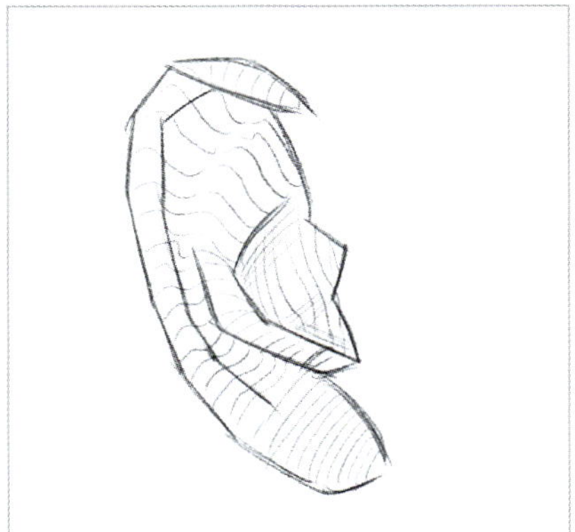

Start hatching or crosshatching the planes of your ear with a medium charcoal pencil.

> **Best Practice:** *For lighter values, spread out your hatch marks. For darker values, place your hatch marks close together. For the inner ear and other areas with extremely low values, crosshatch.*

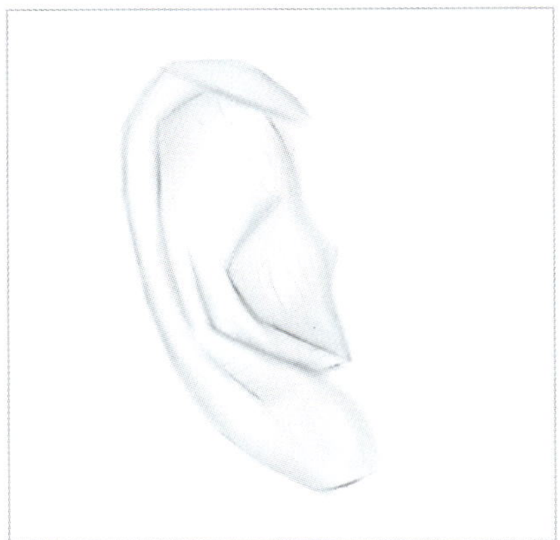

Using a smudger and light pressure, smudge the charcoal into the paper. Take your time and blend away all your hatch marks.

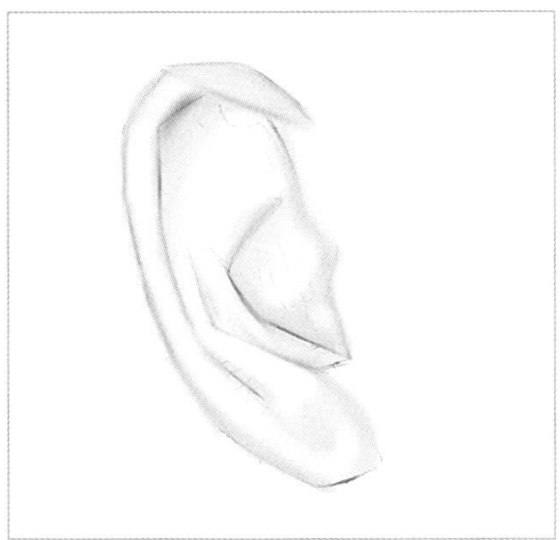

Switch to your MONO Zero Eraser and start retrieving your high values. Remember, you can use a kneaded eraser for bigger areas.

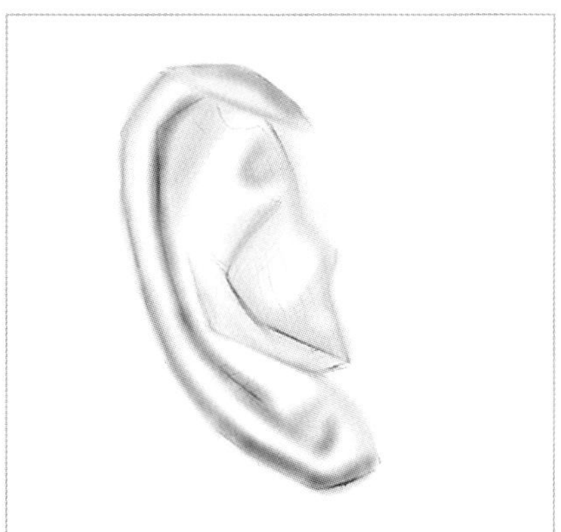

Give your ear some more dimension: Dip a smudger into your soft charcoal powder, check the tone on scratch paper, then start building up the lower values along the backside of the ear and the bottom of the ear lobe.

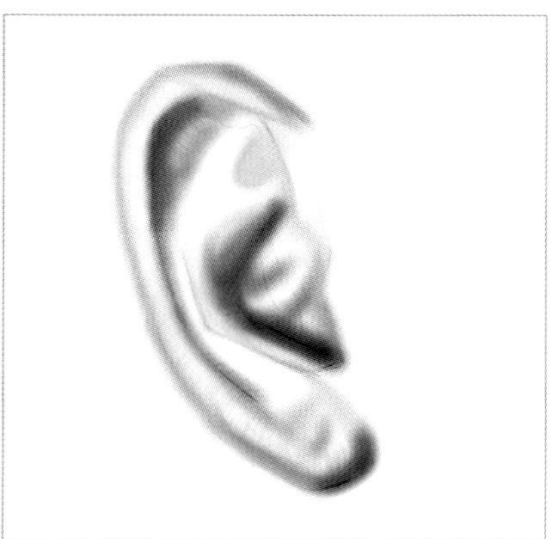

Continue lightly building up the low and mid values throughout the drawing. Notice how your ear is slowly become more and more dynamic? Keep going!

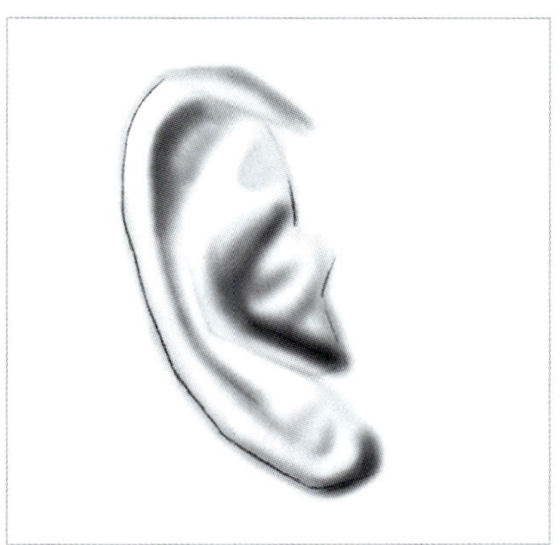

Now, switch to your medium charcoal pencil, and line the back of the ear and the inside of the ear where it connects to the head. Remember, less is more for this step.

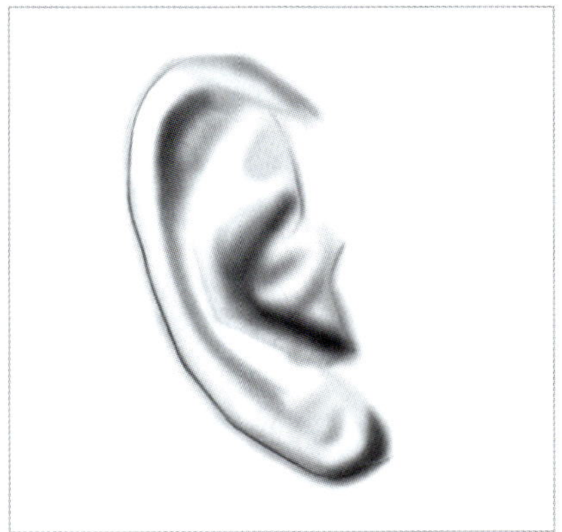

Grab your smudger and blend the lines that you just laid down. Doing so keeps the lower value of the line while making it more realistic.

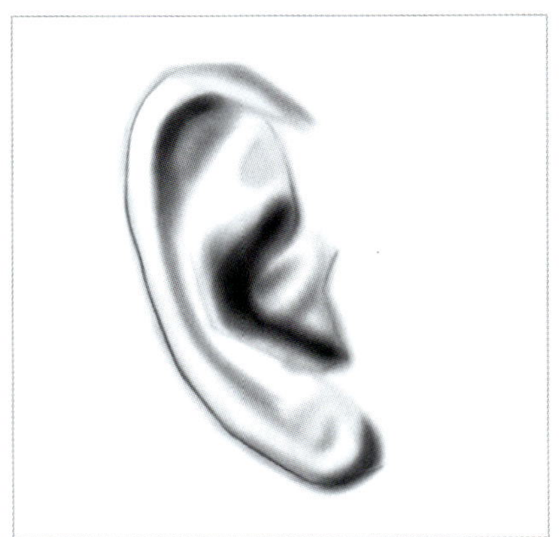

Time to focus heavily on where your low values appear in your reference. Use your smudger and soft charcoal powder to build up these lower values so your drawing pops.

Best Practice: *Much like when you first hatched your Asaro planes, pay attention to the flow of the ear. Use the underlying form as a guide for which direction to push or pull your smudger.*

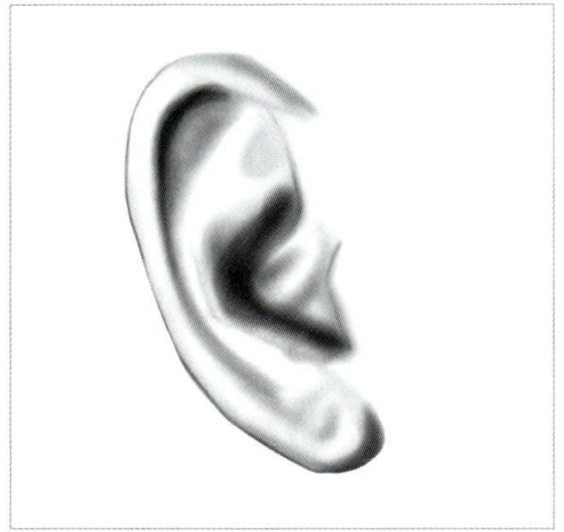

Retrieve high values as needed with your MONO Zero Eraser, then clean up around the edges of your drawing. Charcoal tends to get away from you if you let it! Tidying up will make the drawing's edges crisper and help it look sharper.

> **Best Practice:** *Make sure that your MONO Zero Eraser tip is clean before you start retrieving your high values. This will ensure that your high values are as sharp as possible.*

Project 10: Draw Three Sets of Ears

For **Project 10**, draw three sets of Asaro ears using the techniques and best practices you learned. If you need a more fluid explanation of the Asaro method or ear planes in particular, simply scan the QR code to watch **How to Easily Draw Ears | Understanding the Asaro Method**.

Conclusion

Remember, the most important part of drawing ears is your initial outline. Although the Asaro method is not the only way to draw ears, it is widely regarded as one of the best and simplest approaches. Once you learn how to see and draw the planes of the ears, you will be able to create the most dynamic outline possible. This, in turn, will give you a realistic drawing that you can be proud of.

How *to* Draw Hair

"For me, the working of hair is architecture with a human element."
—Vidal Sassoon

Up until this point, the Asaro method has guided us through our subjects' features. Hair, however, is where Asaro leaves us to our own devices—but water can help! Think about it. Water does not particularly enjoy being told what to do. It is in a constant state of flux. Hair behaves very much the same way. It tends to do what it likes, regardless of what the individual who wears it prefers. So, when you think about drawing hair, follow its flow and apply a relaxed approach to the portrait. This approach may sound counterintuitive after the very structured Loomis and Asaro methods, but you will soon see how going with the flow works.

Outlining the Hair Flow

Unlike the eyes, noses, and ears, there is no one common, basic shape for hair. Hair flows differently depending on your subject. As you study your reference, consider the basic two-dimensional shape of the outer edge of the hair and the inner shape of the hair. To create a pleasing aesthetic, focus on the outlines, both of the outer edge of your subject's hair and the various segments of hair that comprise the whole thing. For example, the bangs or fringe of someone's hair are just one segment or section of the whole.

Here we have our three references with their unique hairstyles. Notice how the segments of hair vary widely.

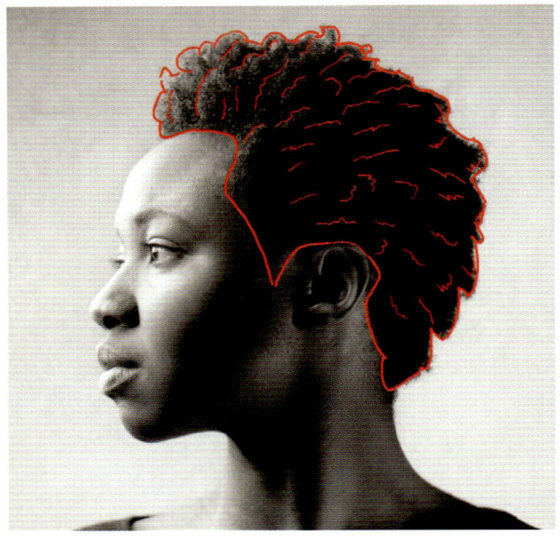

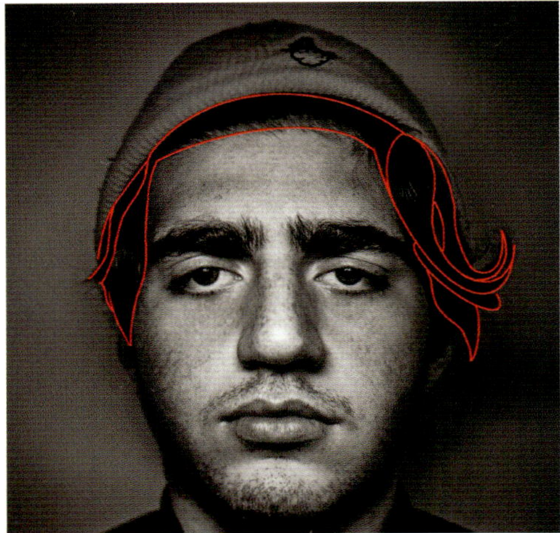

In the profile reference, the hair segments are smaller and not as complete. They very much tie into the other, which gives this drawing more of a single mass of various segments than the other two.

The straight-on subject's hair is mostly covered by a hat, but the sections tend to flow down the face in larger separate segments.

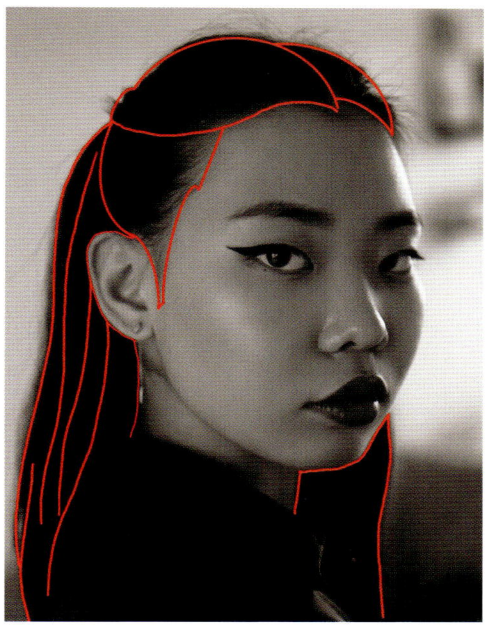

In the three-quarter-turn reference, the subject's hair clearly flows in very large segments across the top of her head and down her face and neck. On all the subjects, the red outlines are meant to help you see the outer outline and the inner segment outlines of the hair flow. We will use these as the guide in the drawing examples that follow.

Drawing Hair

Now, let's take a closer look at the drawing flow for hair in the three most common portrait angles. Remember, splitting hair into designated sections will help you to understand the flow of the hair and thus its underlying form. The form in hair is just as important as the form for a portrait's face. As with the features of the face, once you frame the drawing with its basic outline the rest falls into place.

The Profile Angle

Now it is important to understand that not only will hair vary in shape and volume across the different subjects that you draw, but their texture will as well. Pay attention to how the different segments of hair are brought out. Different textures require slightly different techniques.

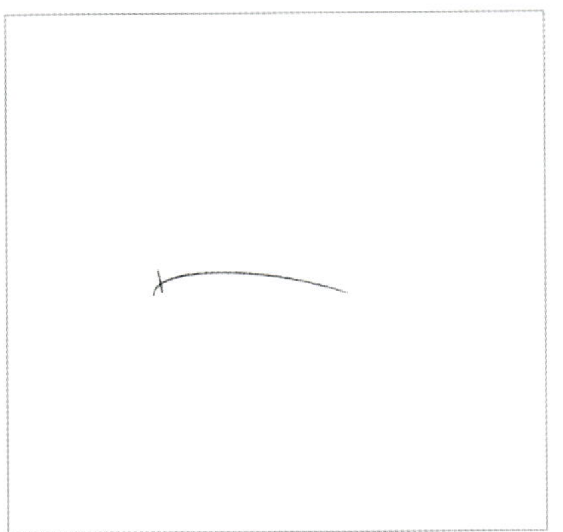

First, using a soft charcoal pencil draw an arch from left to right and then draw a vertical line at a slight angle to represent the center of the nose bridge. This line is the brow line, and it will help you to draw in the ear and the basic shape of the hair.

Best Practice: *Use a very light pressure to make adjustments with your eraser more easily.*

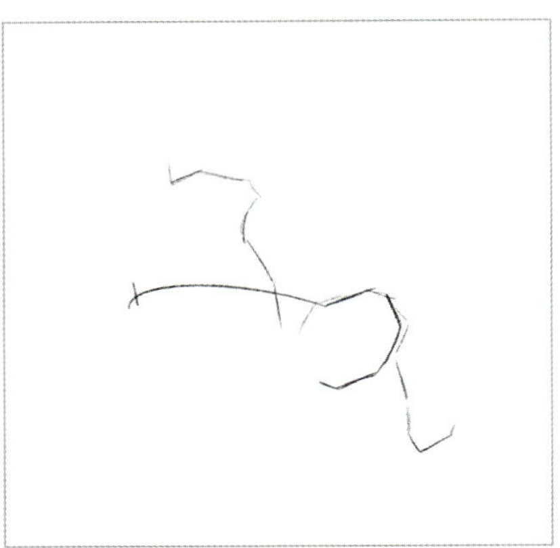

Starting from the end of the arch, sketch in a basic outline for your subject's ear. This is a placeholder so you can get an accurate outline of the hair stemming off the back of the ear. Next, sketch the sideburn and the front hairline. Remember to sketch with nice light, short pulls.

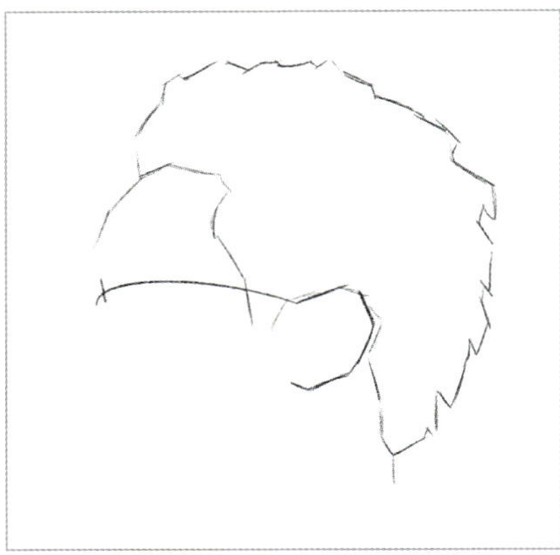

Continue to sketch the outer edge of your subject's hair. From the top of the front hairline, draw the outline over and down to the back of the head, connecting the hair to the bottom of the neck line.

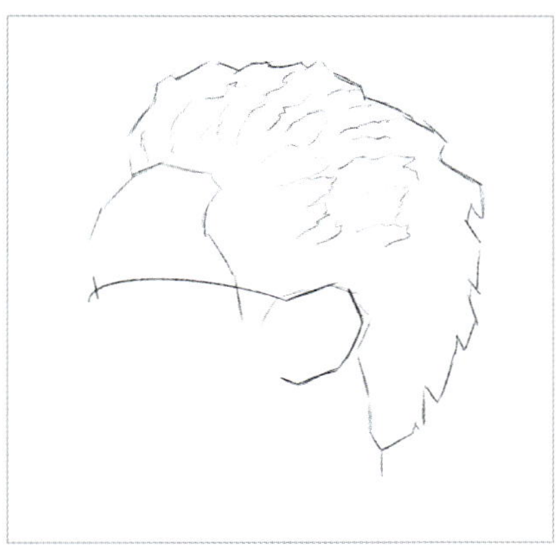

Start drawing the outlines of your inner hair segments. These are essentially where the hair clumps together and are very important for the flow of your hair.

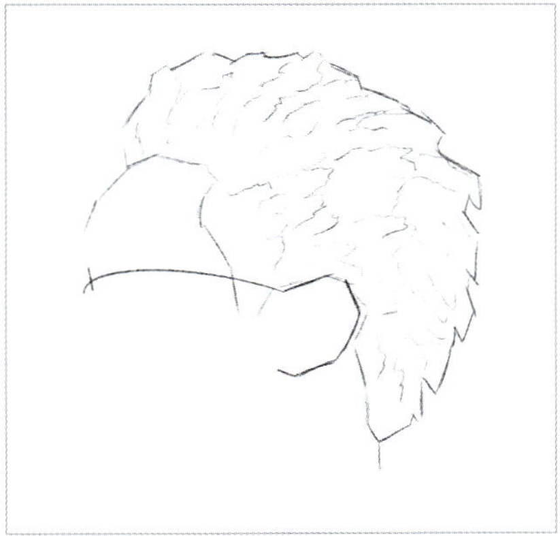

Continue filling in your outline segments until the whole of the head is outlined. Stay focused on the direction that the clumps of hair are flowing. These will be very important when it comes time to lower your values.

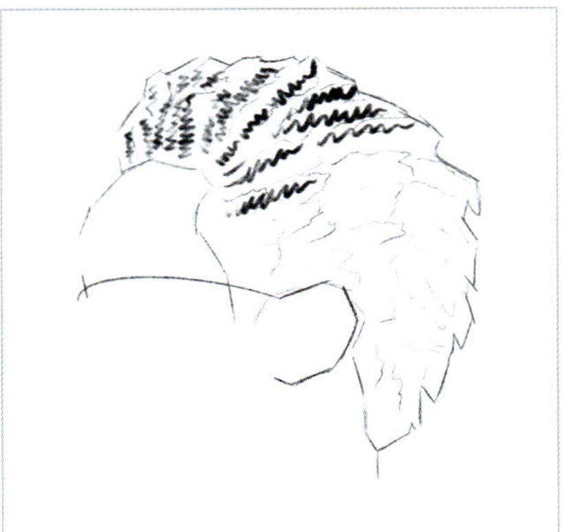

Holding a soft charcoal pencil in an overhand grip, press the side of the pencil tip on the paper and follow the outlined framework of your hair segments in a zigzag motion.

Best Practice: *Be sure to use a medium pressure for the zigzags. Do not use the pencil point, as you will risk scratching the paper.*

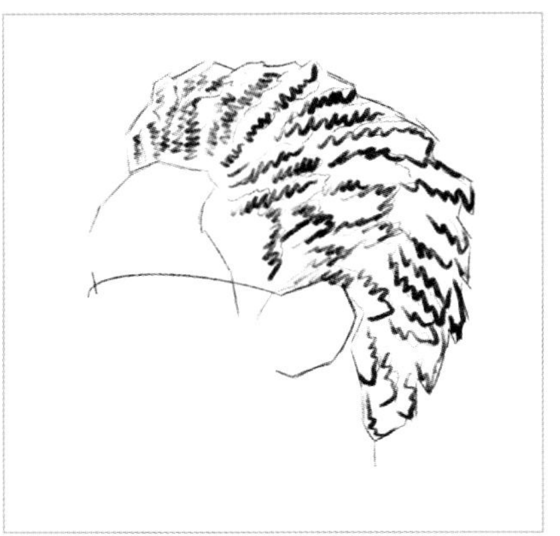

Continue to lay down lower values with your soft charcoal pencil throughout the drawing until the whole of the hair is filled in.

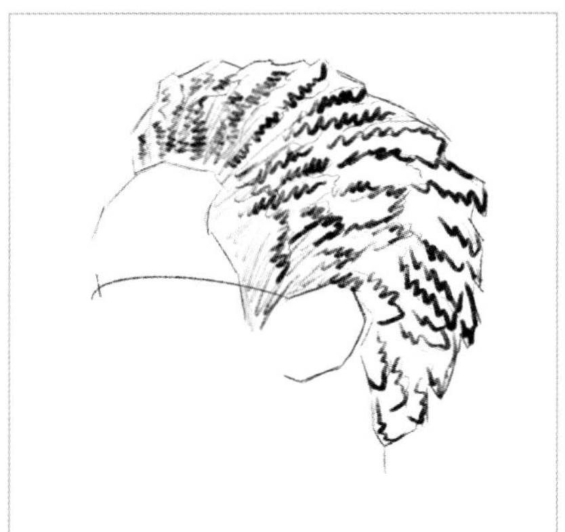

Now use the point of the soft charcoal pencil to lightly fill in between the low values and the segment outlines. Make sure to follow the same hair flow as before. This will help to convey to the viewer's eye the overall flow on the hair.

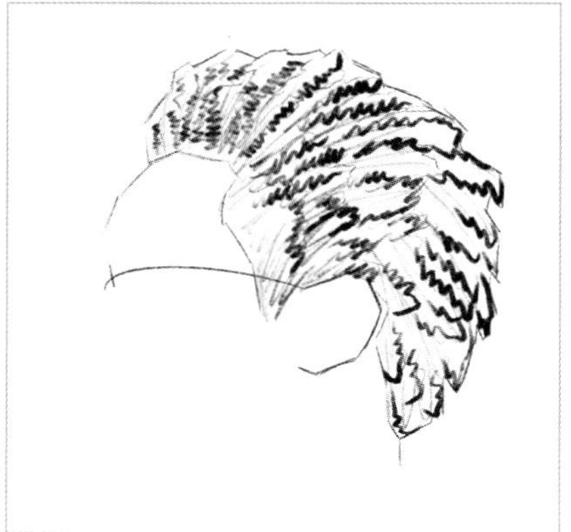

Continue to fill in the drawing until all of the hair is covered.

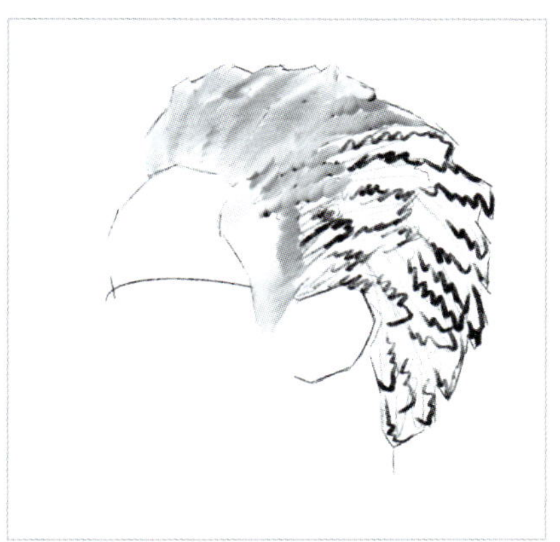

Switch to your smudger, and start blending your zigzags and marks, following the same flow as you did earlier.

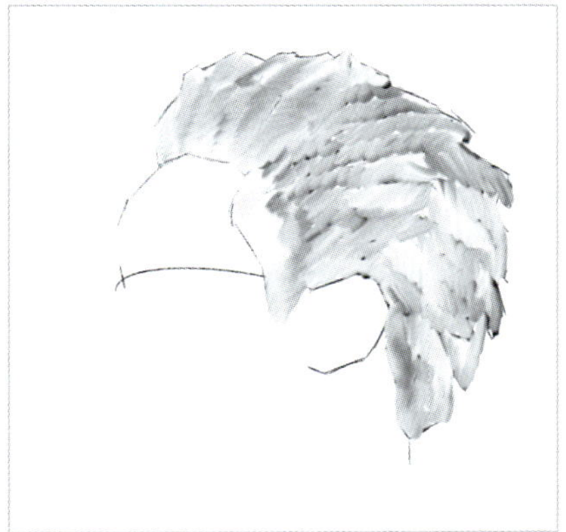

Continue smudging until the whole of the hair is blended.

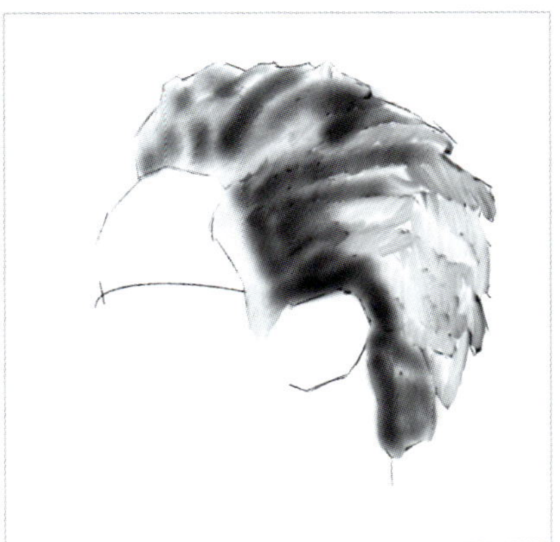

Grab your brush and load it up with ground soft charcoal. If clumps of charcoal should fall off onto the scratch paper when you check the tone, the brush is fully loaded and will convey the lowest value upon your initial strikes. Lower the values throughout the drawing.

Best Practice: *Dab the paper with your loaded brush to keep the integrity of your initial outlined segments while achieving a nice soft blend.*

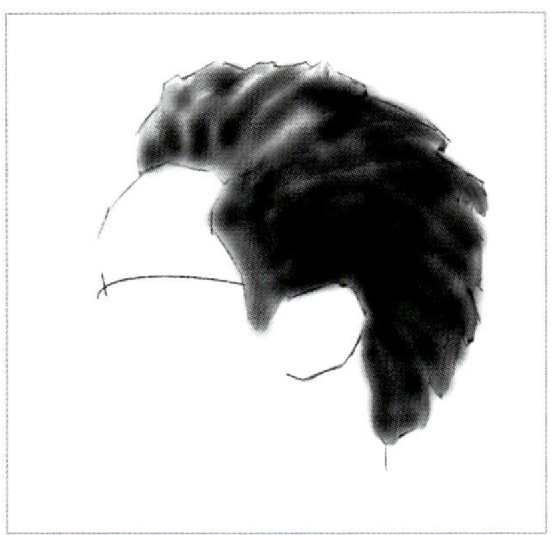

Continue to lower values throughout the hair, reloading your brush with more charcoal as needed. Even a fully loaded brush transmits less and less charcoal onto the paper as you continue to dab it.

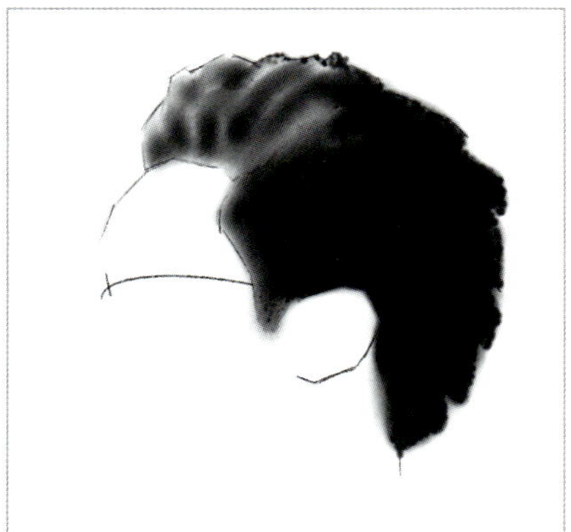

Switch to your smudger, and dip it in the soft charcoal powder. Stand the smudger on end and press it onto the paper to give the hair texture like the subject's and make it look softer.

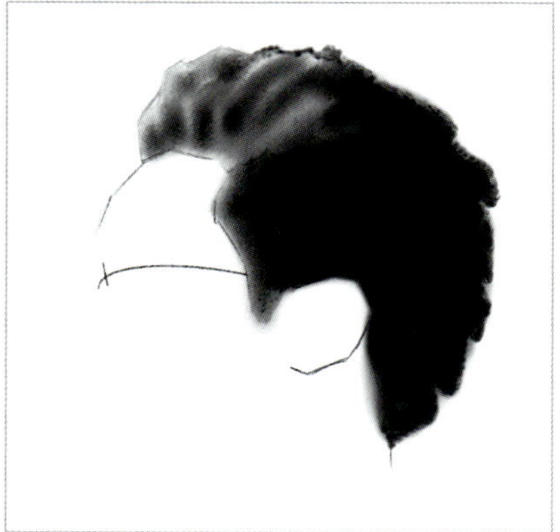

With a MONO Zero Eraser and very light pressure, make nice, tight circles and zigzags to retrieve the high value in the reference. This will add another layer of texture to your hair.

Best Practice: *Use the MONO Zero Eraser for this step as it is perfect for detail work.*

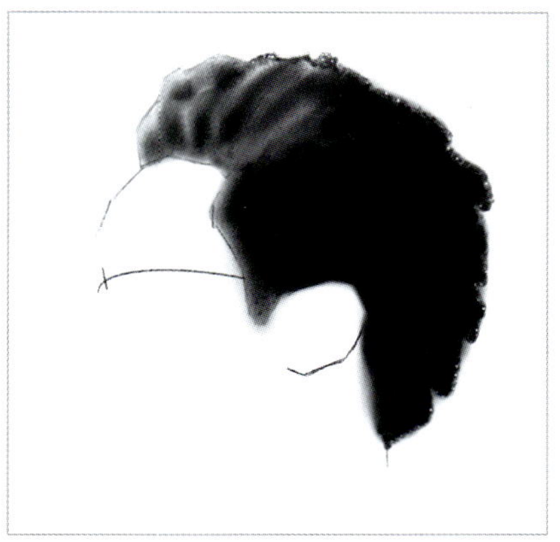

With an electric eraser, retrieve little circles of high values along the edges of the hair. This is another way you can add depth of texture to your drawing for this subject.

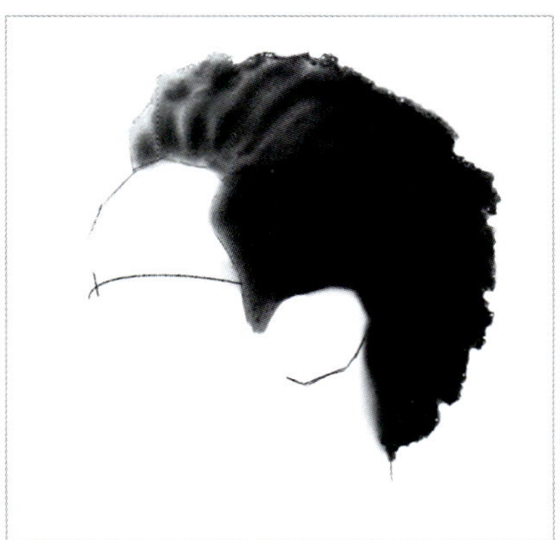

Clean up the outside edges of your hair with a MONO Zero or Pentel Clic Eraser. This sharpens the drawing and really sells the entirety of the texture that you are trying to convey. You can also use a kneaded eraser to lightly retrieve some lighter high values throughout the hair and bring out the segments that you initially outlined a bit more. To finish the drawing, add in flyaway hairs with a hard charcoal pencil.

The Straight-On Angle

Sometimes you will encounter a subject with a hat or headdress of some kind. This angle allows you to practice drawing hair with a hat on.

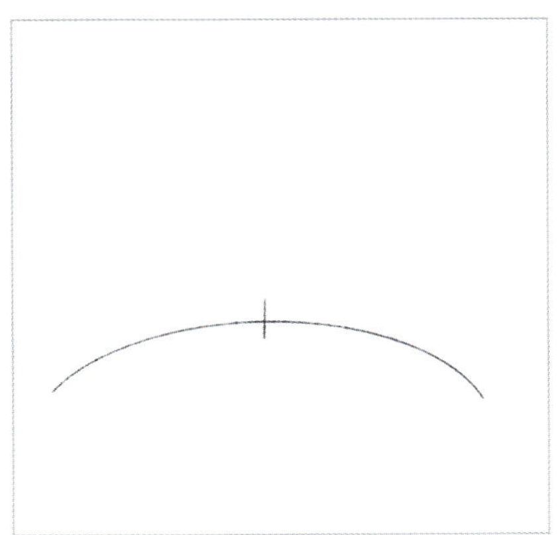

With a soft charcoal pencil, draw an arch from the top of the left ear to the top of the right ear. This will give you a basic structure to work from so you can keep a sense of proportion regarding the head beneath the hair.

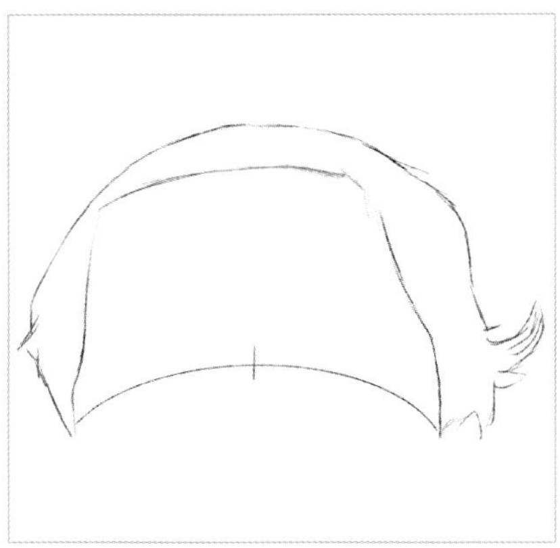

Draw the basic shape of the hair's outside edge only. Do not worry about the inner outline segments yet—those will come soon.

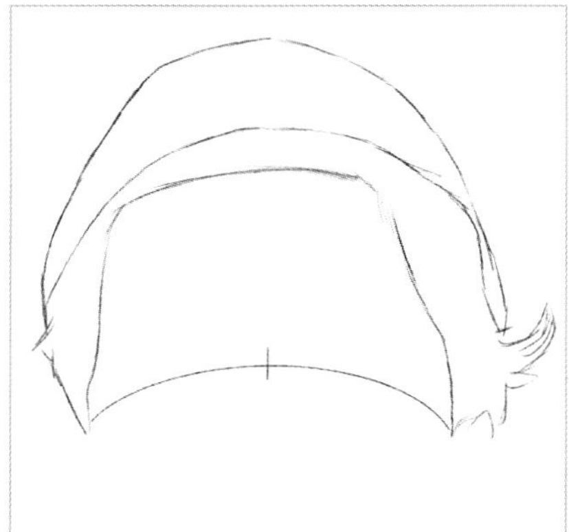

Draw the outline of your subject's hat.

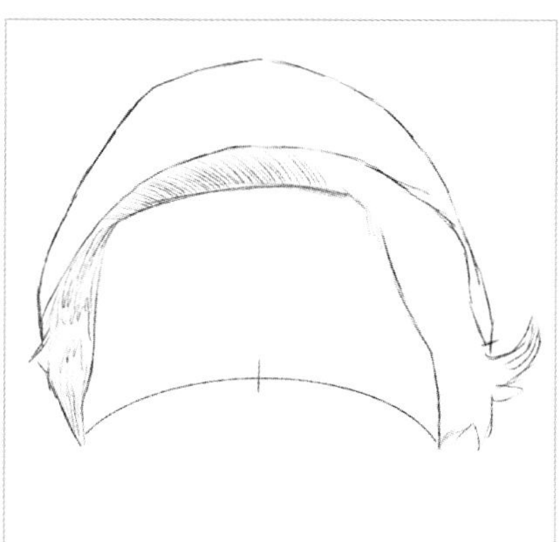

Start hatching your hair, being conscious of the flow of the hair and the segments. This is another way that you can draw hair and still achieve a realistic look. Remember that different types of hair will demand a slightly different approach.

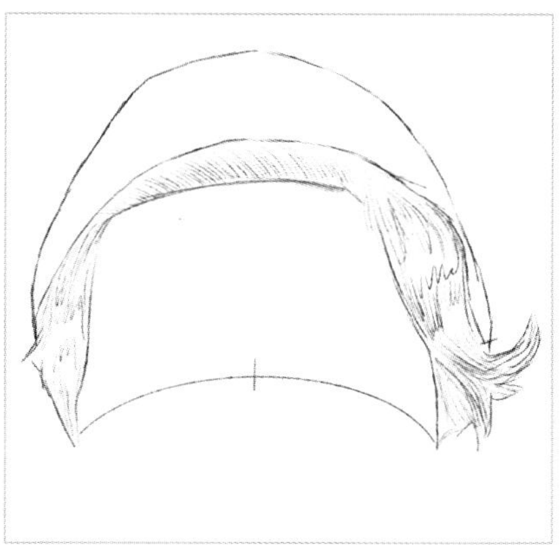

Continue to hatch until you have filled in the entire body of hair.

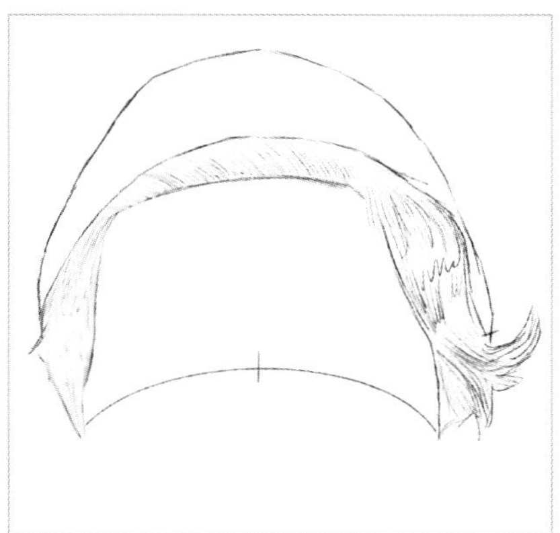

Switch to your smudger and start blending your hatch marks. Be sure to push or pull the smudger in the same general direction as the hatch marks.

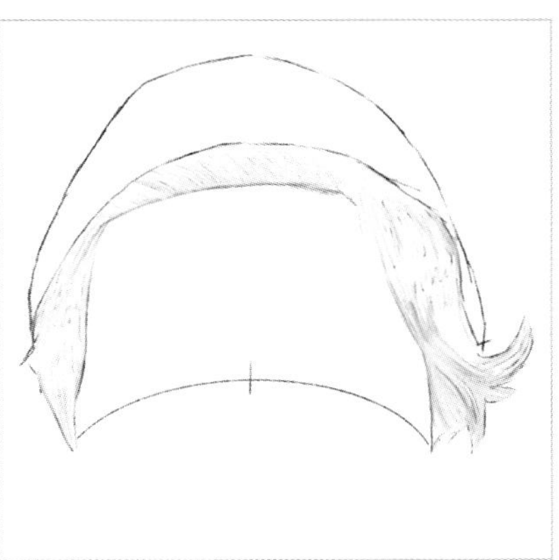

Continue to blend your hatch marks until the entire body of hair has been blended.

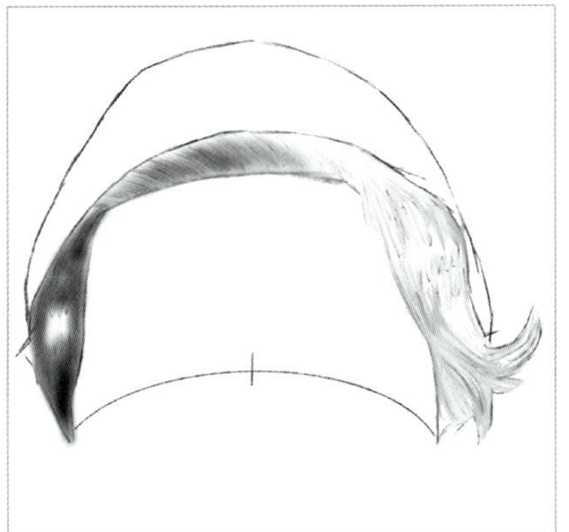

Switch to your brush, dip it in the ground soft charcoal, check that it is fully loaded, and start to build up your lower values.

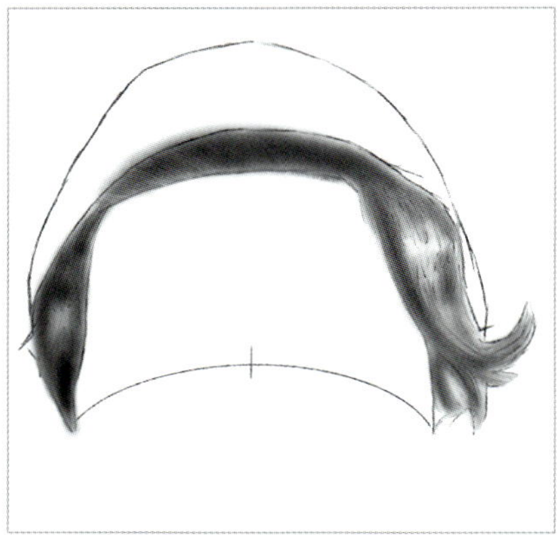

Continue using your brushwork to build up your lower values throughout the whole of the hair.

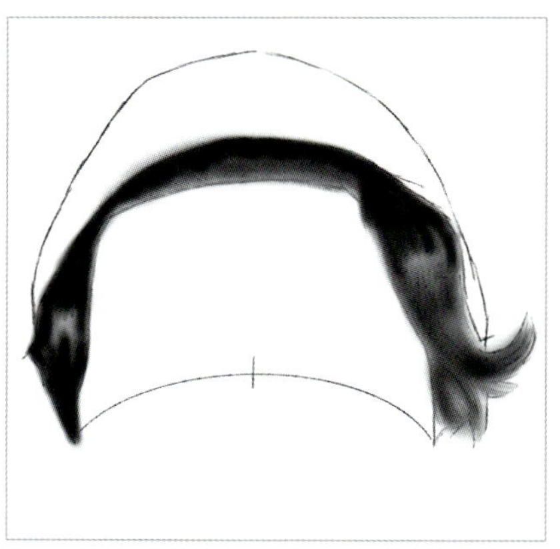

This is where you have some autonomy. You can continue using your brushwork to build up the lower values, or you can use light strokes with a medium charcoal pencil that follow the flow of your hatch marks to lower the value. The charcoal pencil offers more control than the brush but moves charcoal slower. The brush moves charcoal faster, but you sacrifice control.

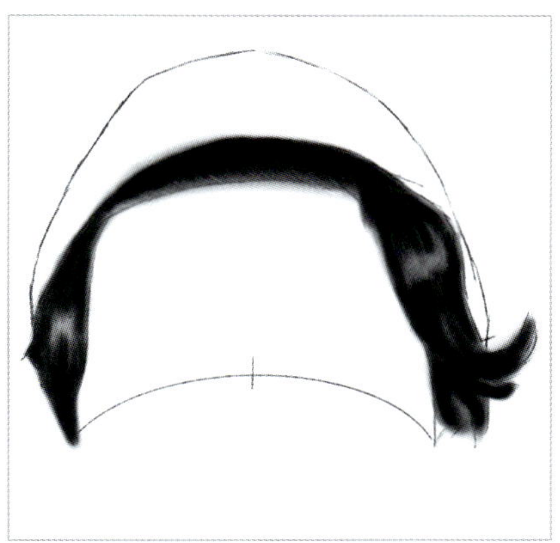

Continue to lower the value until the entire body of hair has been filled, then start retrieving high values with your MONO Zero Eraser. Use long and short pulls, making sure to follow the same flow.

> **Best Practice:** *The MONO Zero Eraser gives you more control when retrieving your high values for clumps of hair and hair texture.*

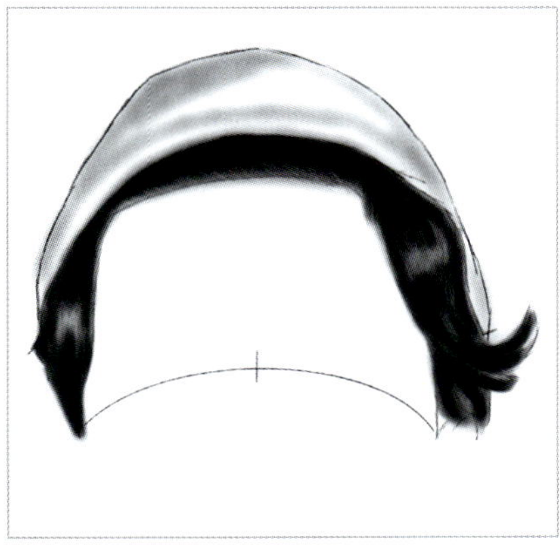

Switch to your brush, load up some soft charcoal powder, and start lowering the value for the front edge and backside of your subject's hat.

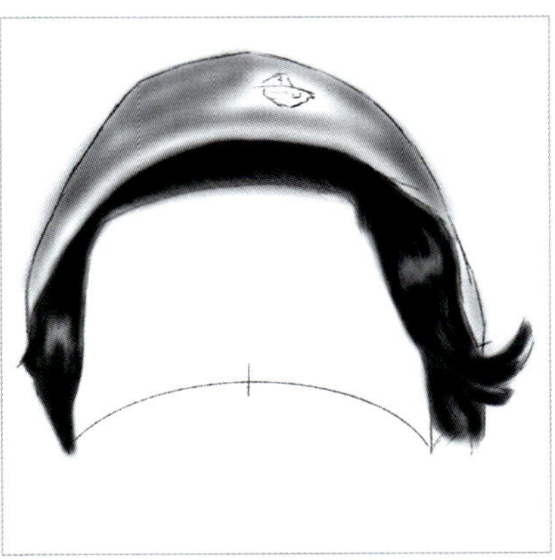

Continue lowering the value until you get a nice medium tone, then switch to a medium charcoal pencil to sketch the design on the hat.

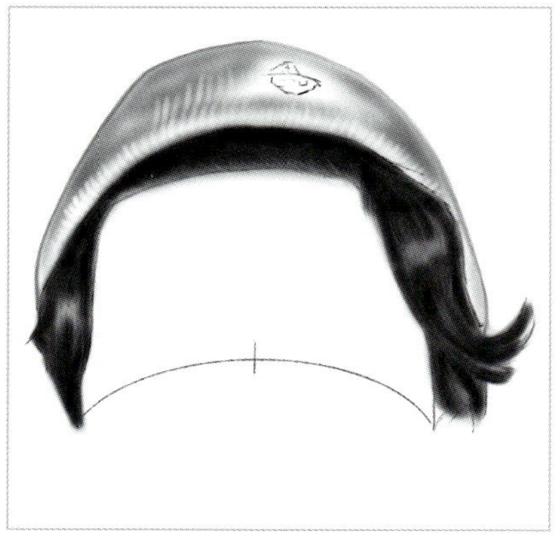

Retrieve the high values in the hat using a MONO Zero Eraser. Take your time with this step; really try to feel every pull of your eraser. This will bring out the stitching in the hat and make it look more realistic. To give the hat an overall softer look, blend its outline with a smudger.

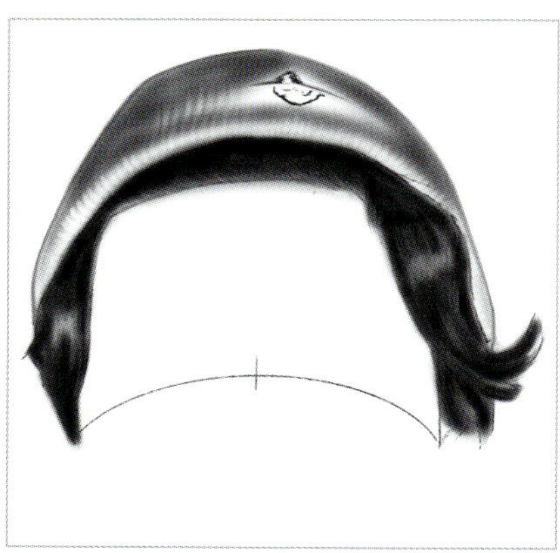

Now switch back to your brush and continue to lower the value on the hat so that you accentuate the value scale to its fullest potential to make your hair look more dynamic.

The Three-Quarter-Turn Angle

For this angle we are drawing a smoother texture, but smoother does not always mean simpler. In this one, make sure to take your time and draw in the different segments of hair. Really stay attentive to your technique when retrieving your high values to bring out that sheen and overall texture.

Draw an arch from left to right with a soft charcoal pencil, and then place a small vertical line to signify the nose bridge. This will help you locate the center of the face, which in turn will help you with the placement of the hair outline.

Draw an ear stemming from the end of the arch up, and then pull it over and down. Lightly place the line for your sideburn and keep pulling up until you get to the hairline. Bring the hairline over, then establish the side of the forehead with a line leading down to the arch. Pull your line up and over to bring out the top of the hair.

> **Best Practice:** *The overhand grip works the best for drawing these lines.*

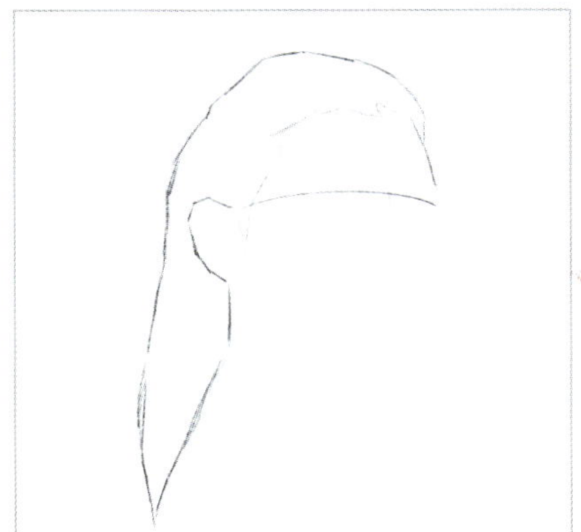

Continue to bring that line down using short light pulls, then come back up to establish the neckline of your subject.

> **Best Practice:** *Shorter line pulls enable you to assess your proportion as you go. This way you can see any adjustments that need to be made earlier rather than later.*

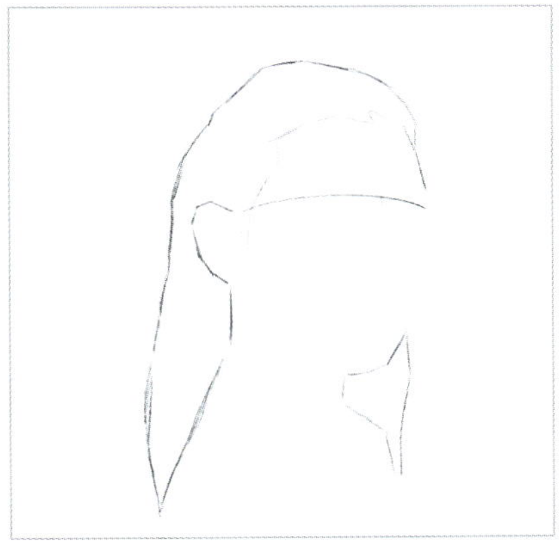

Use the slight bend in the line that showcases the back of the neck as an anchor point and bring your pencil straight over to the right to draw your line for the chin. Pull your line down and over to the right and then down again. Next, bring your hairline up and over to connect it with the far side of the chin.

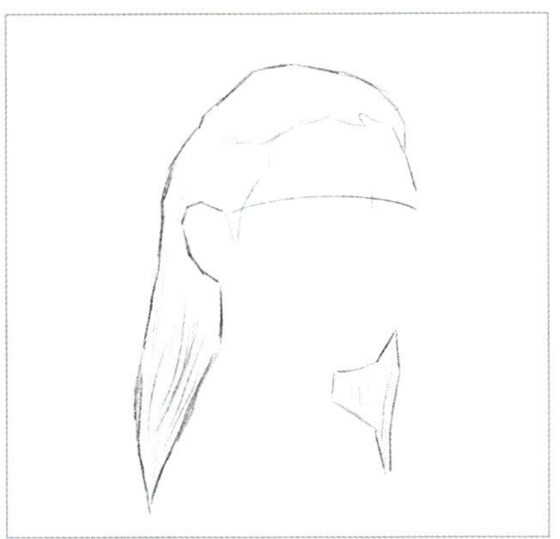

Start hatching your hair, following the flow. Look closely to identify the different segments of hair throughout the reference. Use these as your guide for your hatch marks. Remember, these hair segments are the flow that you want to follow.

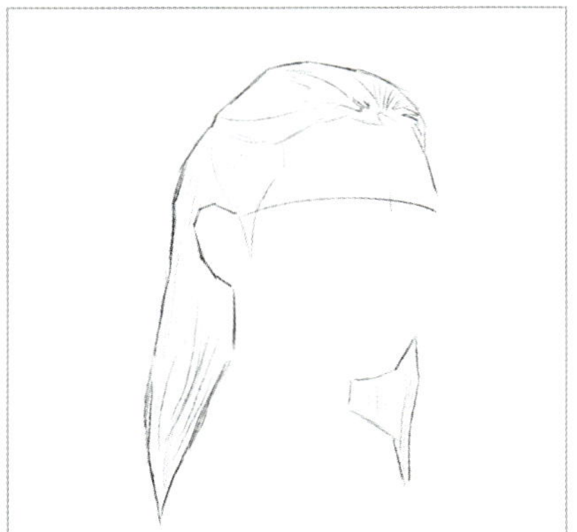

Continue to hatch the inner hair segments so that the overall flow of the whole head of hair comes out.

Best Practice: *You can use different line qualities to emphasize different segments of hair. This will help your drawing look more dynamic even after it has been blended.*

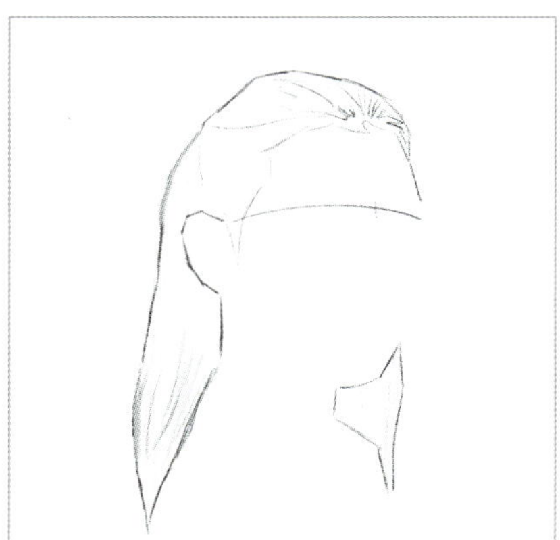

Switch to your smudger and begin blending the hatch marks while still adhering to the same direction.

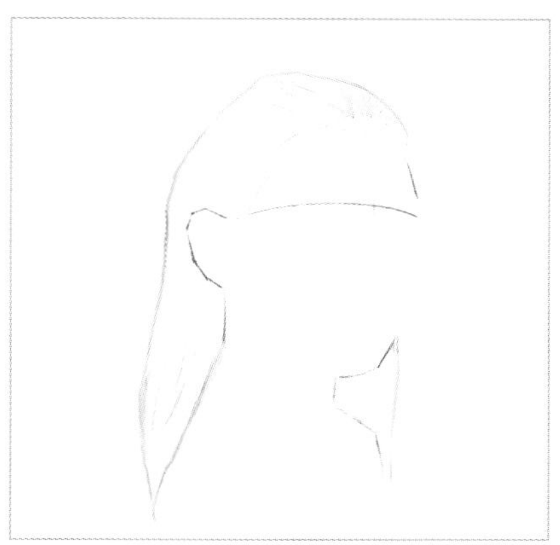

Continue to blend your hatch marks until the whole of the hair has been completely blended.

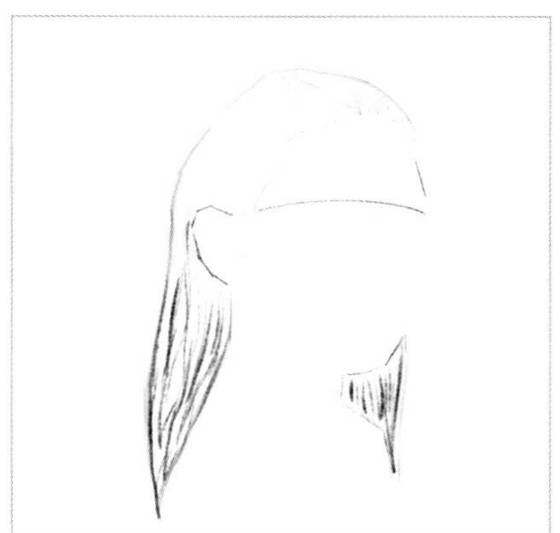

As with the profile angle, hold your soft charcoal pencil in the overhand grip, lay the pencil tip on its side, and emphasize the low values of each segment of hair. This will help the different sections show through when you hit the drawing with your brushwork and really start lowering the values with the smudger.

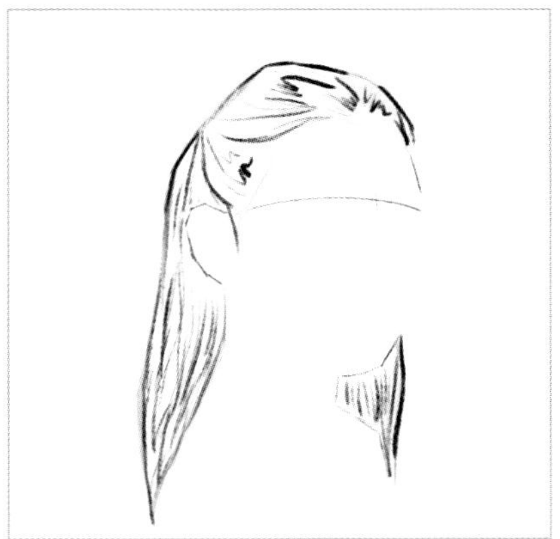

Continue to bring out the individual segments of hair until the entire head of hair is covered.

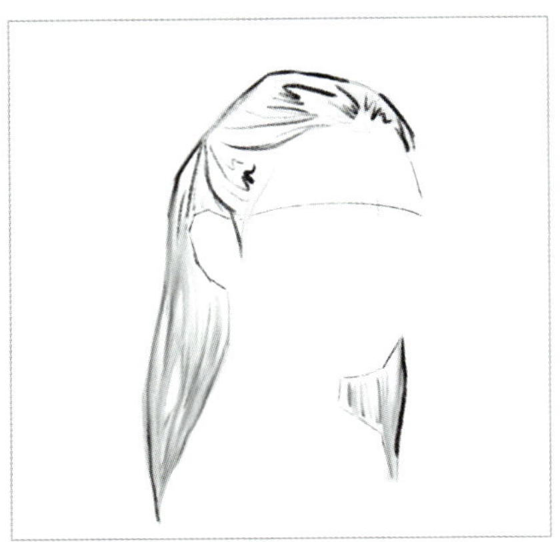

Switch to your smudger and start blending the thicker hatch marks as you did for the profile angle.

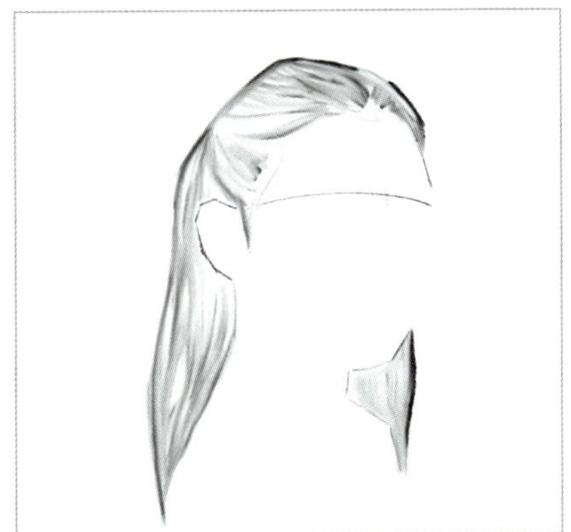

Continue to smudge all your hatch marks until the whole of the hair is blended.

Best Practice: *Leave different values in place during this step in the drawing process. When you start lowering your values, these variations will show through if only slightly.*

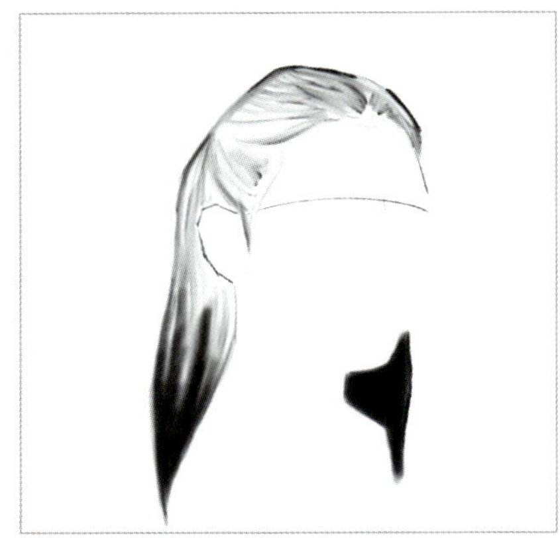

Study your reference, focusing on where the low values are. Much like for the straight-on portrait's subject, you can either build your low values with a brush and charcoal powder or with a medium charcoal pencil. Remember the medium charcoal pencil gives you more control but moves charcoal slower, whereas the brush moves charcoal quicker but gives you less control.

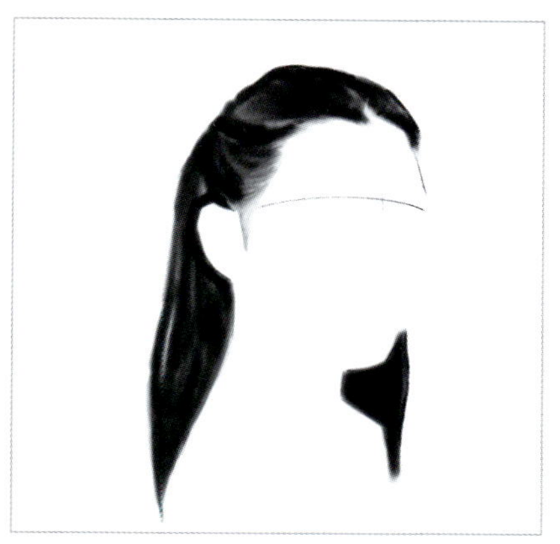

Continue to build up your lower values while following the flow of the various hair segments. Remember to leave some mid tones while you do this so that you make the hair as dynamic as possible.

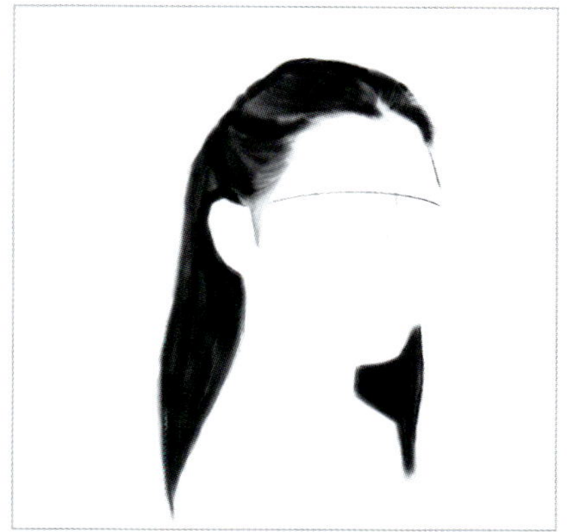

Now switch to your MONO Zero Eraser and start retrieving your high values throughout the entire head of hair. To give the hair an extra layer of texture, mimic the original hatch marks with the eraser.

Best Practice: *Vary your pressure control as you go to bring out different tones in your drawing.*

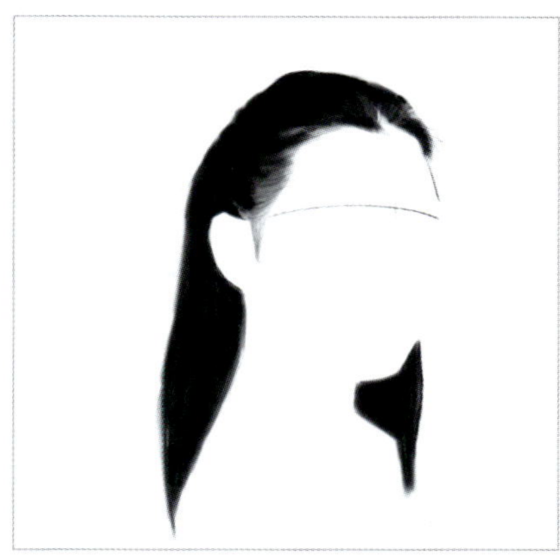

To bring out a soft gradation and help the hair look as realistic as possible, load your brush with ground soft charcoal and go over the entire head of hair. Add in flyaway hairs around the top and back of the head as desired with a hard charcoal pencil.

Project 11: Draw Hair for Each of the Three Angles

For **Project 11**, draw the three angles of hair using the techniques and best practices you learned. If you need a more fluid explanation of the Asaro method or hair in particular, simply scan the QR code to watch **How to Easily Draw Hair | Understanding Segments & Flows**. Each video features a real-time drawing flow and covers drawing hair at one of the three most common portrait angles.

Conclusion: Let It Flow

Hair is fairly simple to draw, because it tends to frame itself thanks to its natural movement. Remember, hair likes to flow much like water. While it's tempting to dive right in, first analyze the hair in your reference so you can pinpoint exactly where the various segments of hair live. Keep that movement in mind, and let it guide your drawing.

CHAPTER 9

Understanding

Feature Placement

and Flow

"Every block of stone has a statue inside it, and it is the task of the sculptor to discover it."
—Michelangelo

As you remember from Chapter 2, the Loomis method gives you a foundation on which you can lay down the features of your portrait with considerable accuracy. But by itself, a foundation is only that: a base on which to build. To help you construct your final vision, you need another tool, which is where the Asaro method comes in. Using the Asaro planes, you can construct your subject's facial features while placing them on your Loomis head. In this chapter, I'll show you how to fuse these two great methods to work in tandem. You'll learn how the Loomis method frames the face of your portrait, how and why it splits the face into three equal sections, and how to use the Loomis method's guidelines to tie in the facial features you'll draw using the

Asaro method. Even though these methods are simple, everything about them has a purpose. You can draw every portrait regardless of angle or lighting situation using the exact approach you'll learn here. This drawing flow is your ace in the hole for any portrait that you may draw in your art career.

How the Loomis Method Frames Your Proportions

While Chapter 2 walked you through the theory of the Loomis method, this time I'll demonstrate the method based on the three references you'll use for Chapter 10's final project. We'll also dive deeper into how the Loomis head's guidelines and use of the Rule of Thirds will help you accurately place facial features. With enough practice, this drawing flow will become second nature for you.

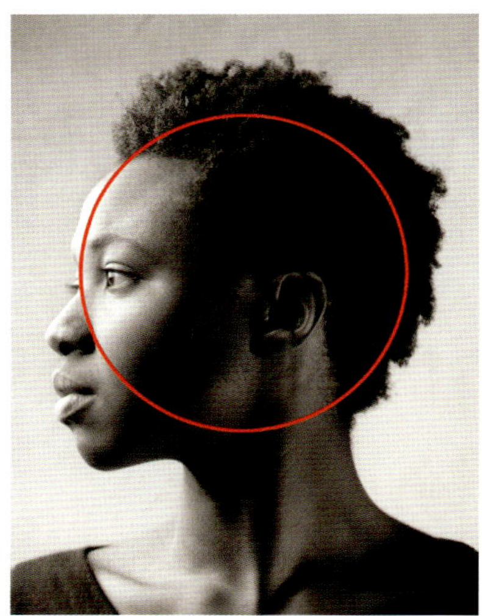 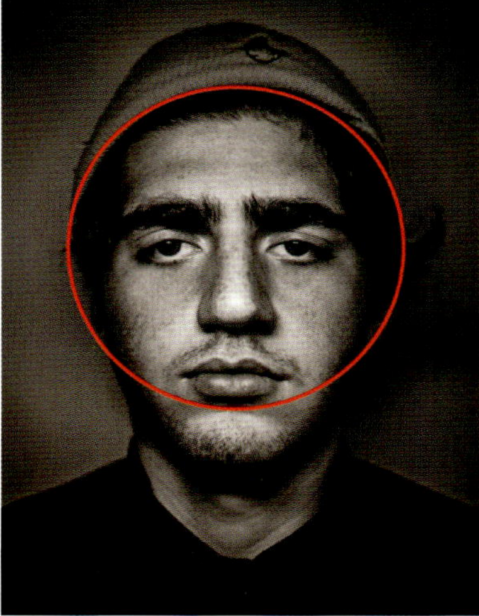 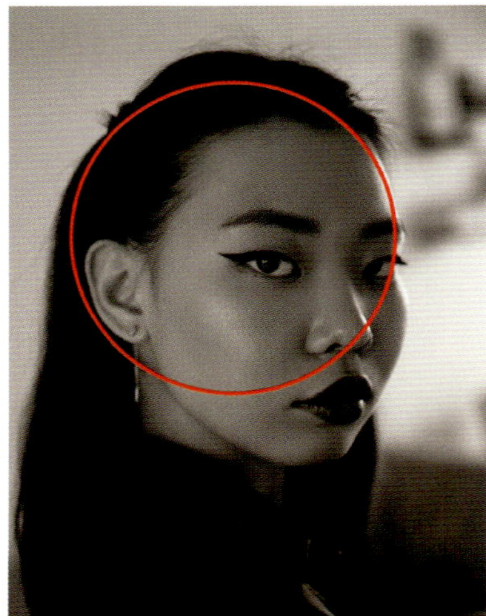

When you start a portrait with the Loomis method, first draw a circle to symbolize the cranium.

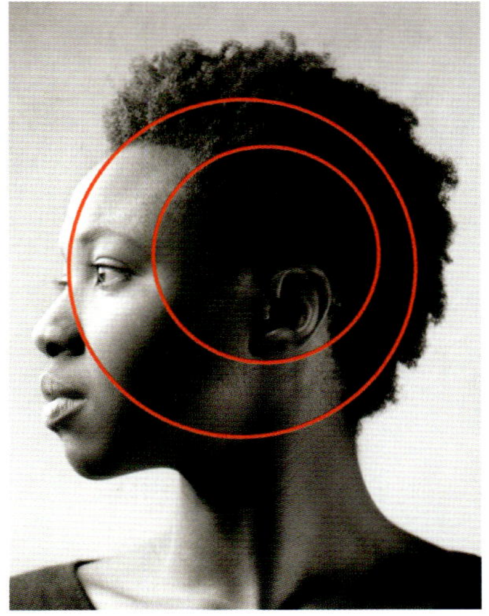 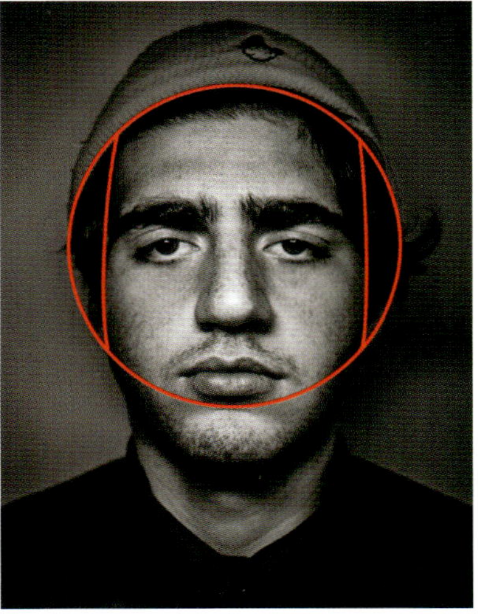 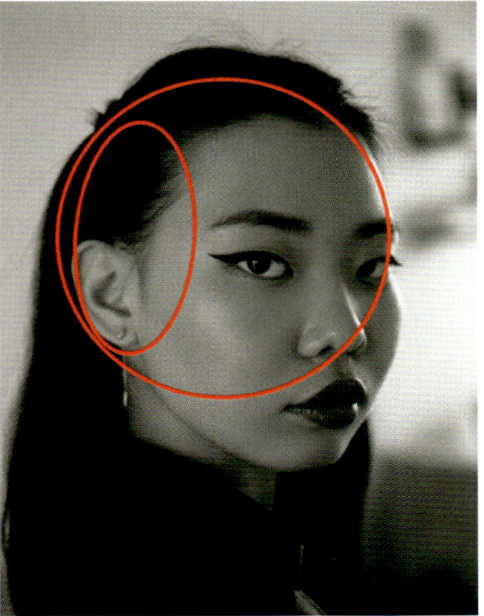

Next, draw an oval to represent the side plane of the head. Remember to align the top of the oval with your subject's hairline and the bottom with the bottom of your subject's nose.

> *Just like with the Asaro method, the actual approach will always be the same when drawing a Loomis head. The only thing that will vary across your subjects will be the proportion.*

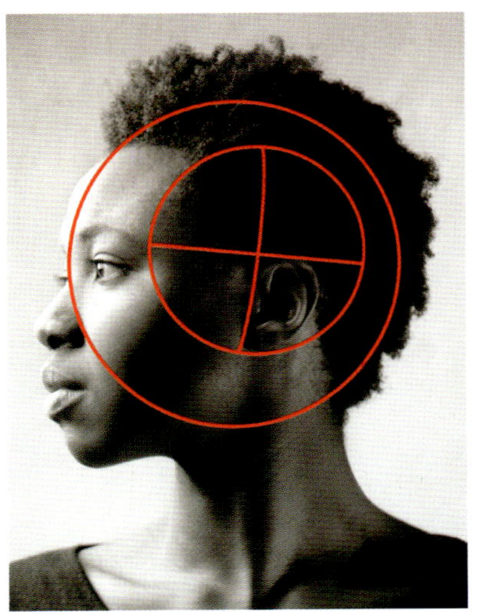 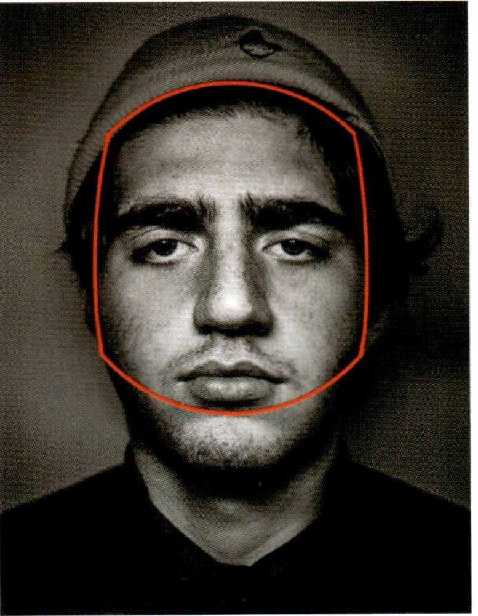 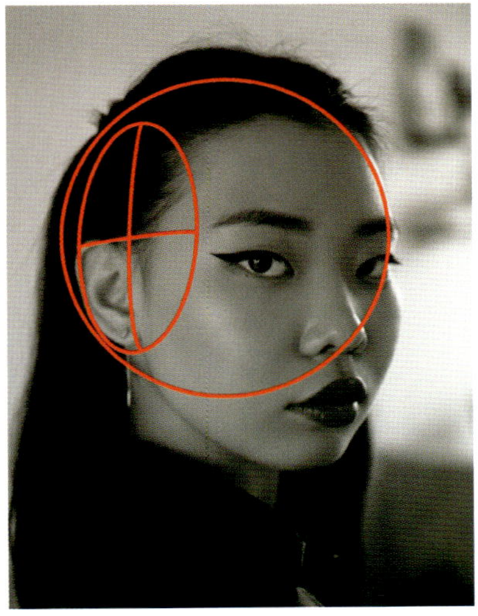

Now add the vertical and horizontal axes of your subject's head. Draw a vertical line just in front of your subject's ear and inside the oval. Draw the horizontal axis line just above the ear and aligned with the direction of the eyes.

For straight-on angles, you don't have to worry about this step. Instead, you just need to elongate the cranium by showing the side planes.

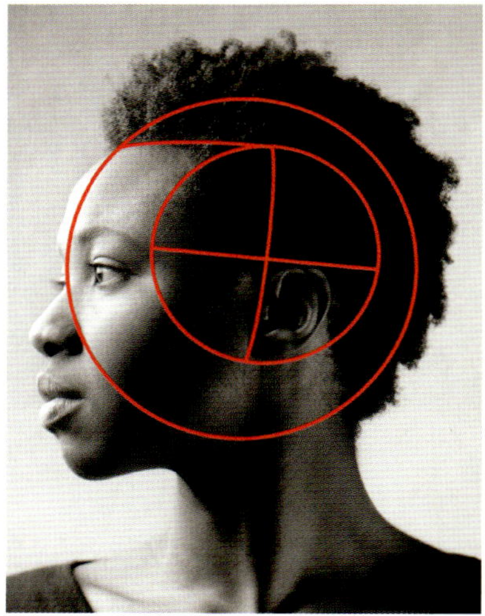
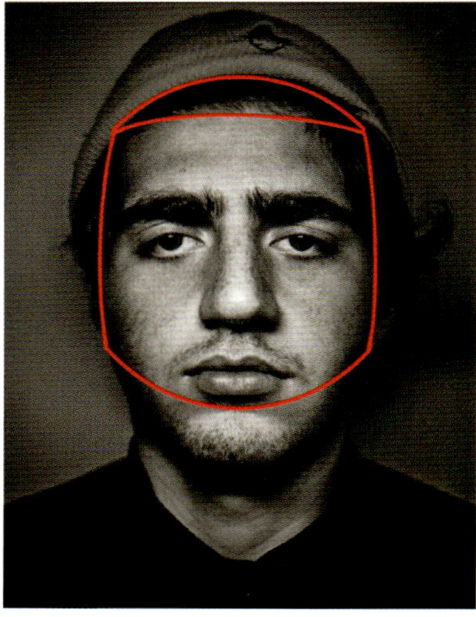
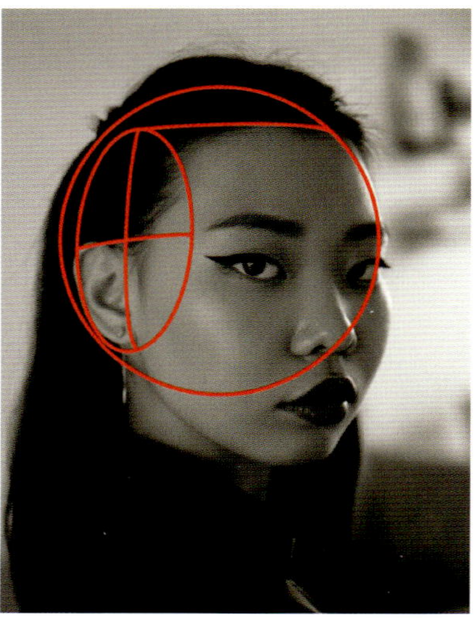

To help you place your subject's hairline, pull a line from the top of your oval across to roughly the other side of the circle.

Best Practice: *Use light pressure. Remember, the Loomis head is not absolute. It's meant to be a general framework and guide for feature placement. If you need to erase and adjust, by all means do so.*

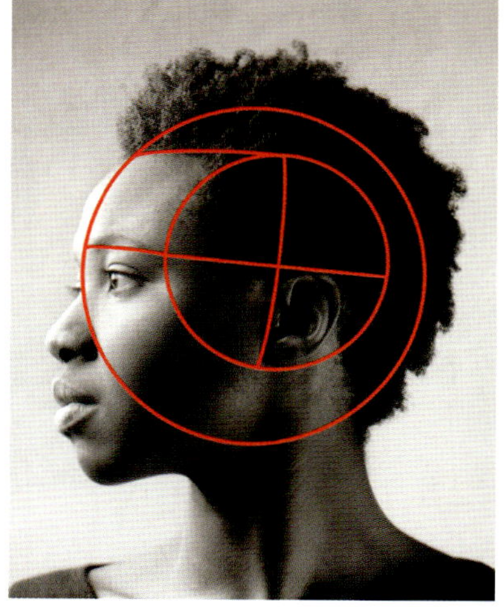
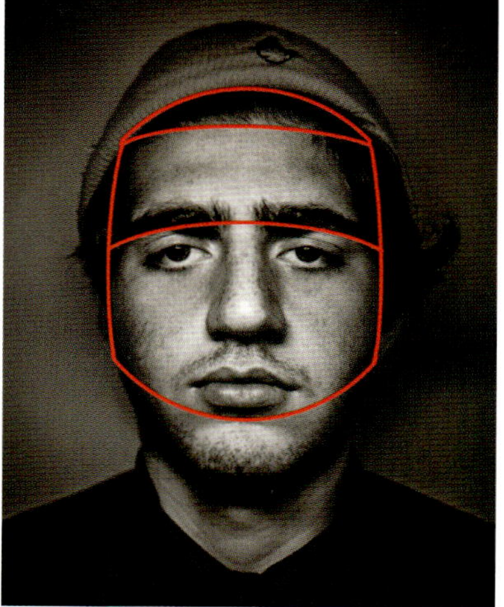
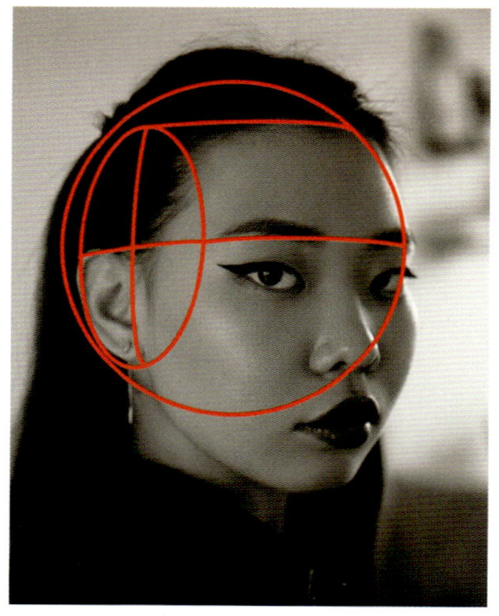

Draw a line that extends the horizontal axis line from the side plane over to the other side of the circle. Called the brow line, this line should fall roughly in line with your subjects' eyebrows and is meant to help you place the eyes.

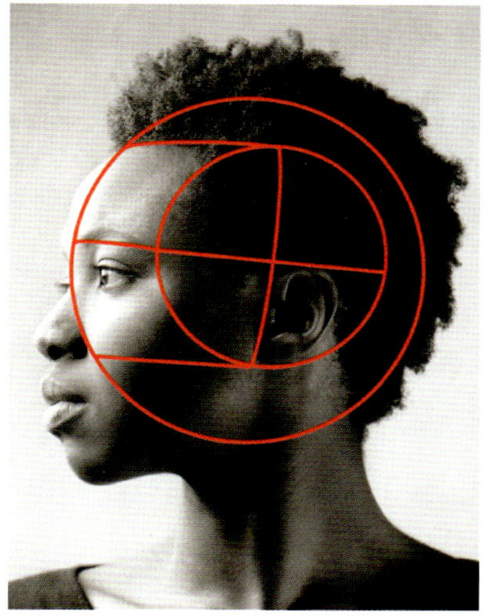
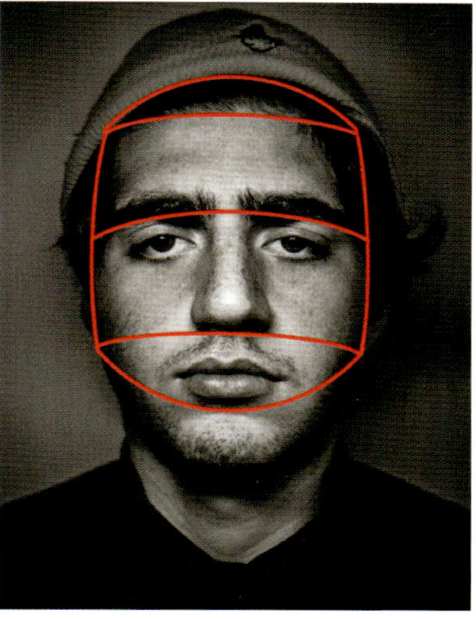
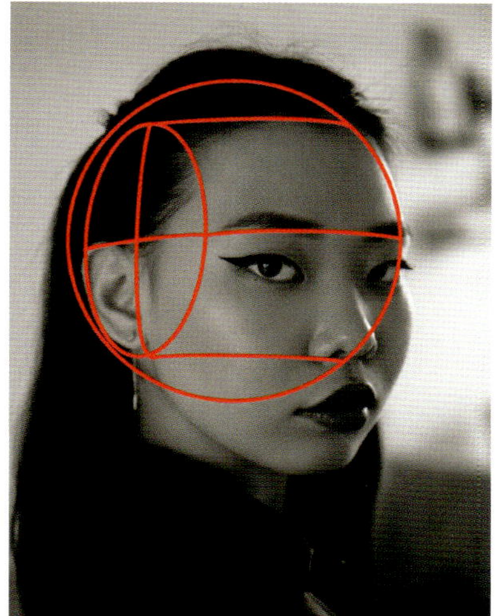

Draw a line from the bottom of the oval over to the other side of the circle. This line is meant to help you place the nose and should run just under the bottom of your subject's nose.

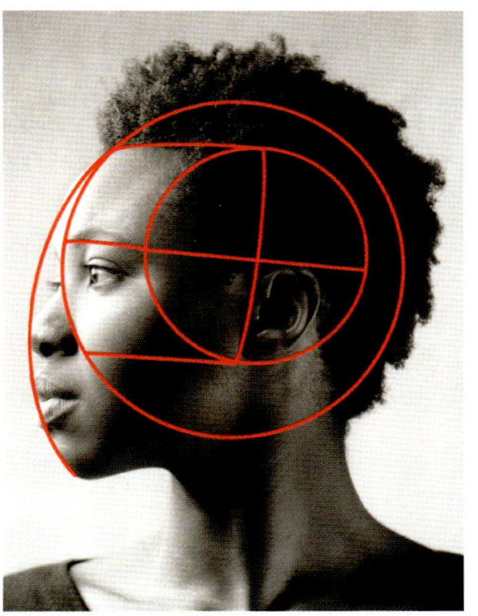
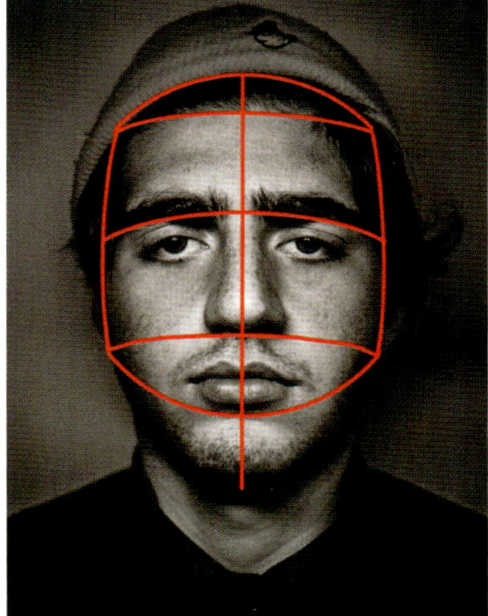
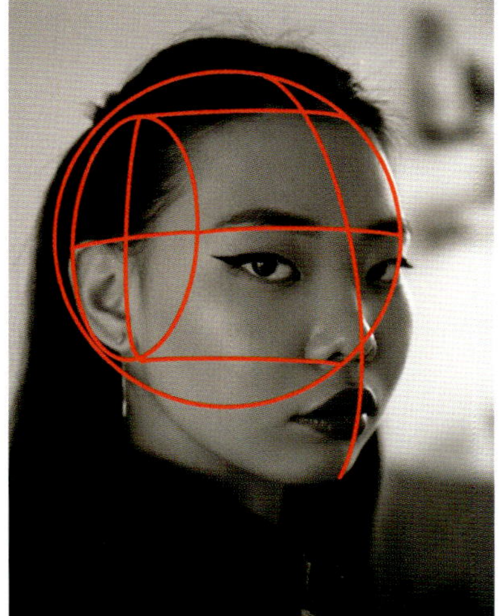

Draw a line down from the top of the initial circle, running the full length of the face to roughly the subject's chin. Called the center line, this line will help you gauge where to place the nose bridge, which will become the center point of your eyes and thus the face. You will also use it to align the center of the nose and the lips.

> **Best Practice:** *To gauge the position of the chin, as well as where to end the center line, use your pencil as a measuring tape. Place your pencil pointing vertically on the face of your Loomis head with the tip in line with the hairline and pinch the pencil where the brow line crosses under it. Without moving your pinched fingers, slide the pencil tip down to the nose line. Your pinched fingers now mark roughly where you should draw the short horizontal line to signify the bottom of the chin. Extend the center line all the way to this point.*

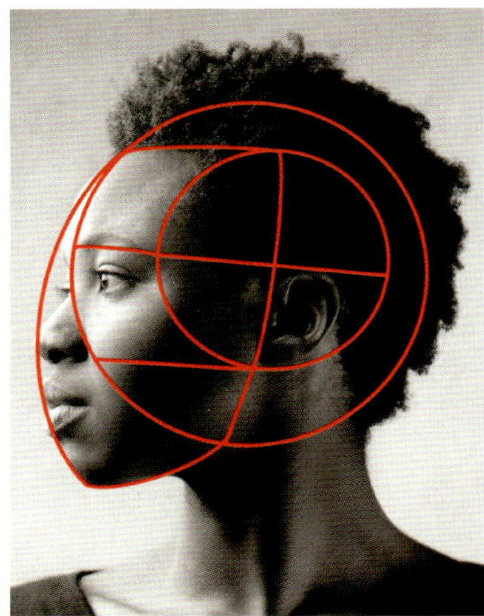
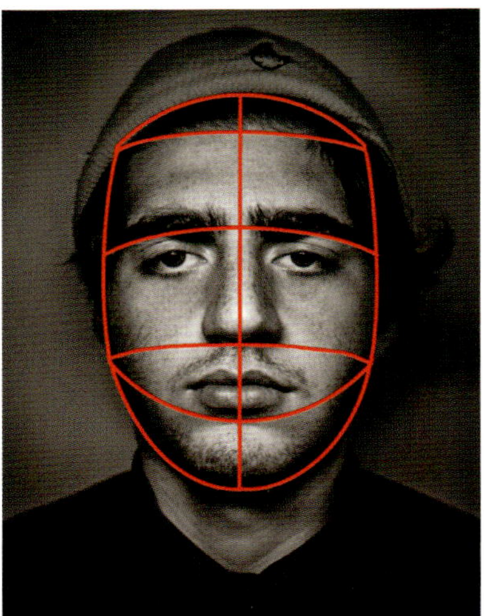
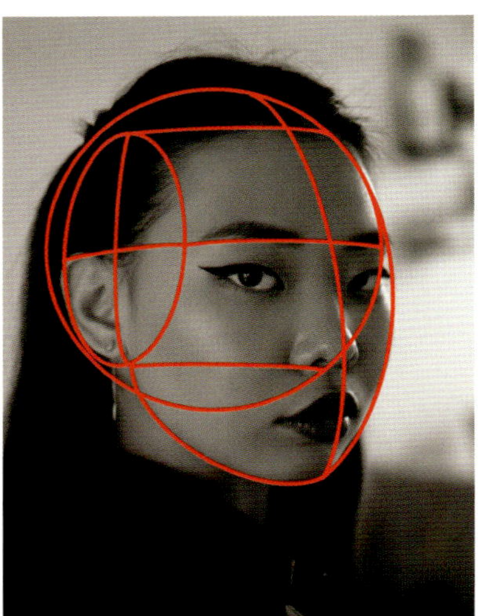

To add a generic jaw line, draw a line that extends down from the vertical axis, then connect this line to the chin line. Next, run a line up from the other side of your chin line, slightly sloping it into the far side of the circle. This second jaw line will vary depending on the angle that you are working with.

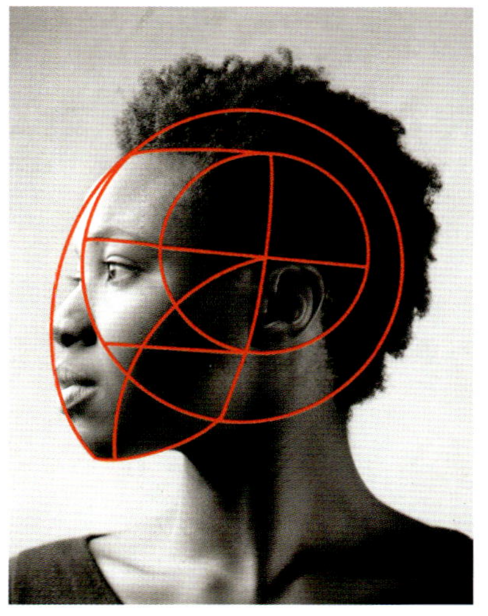
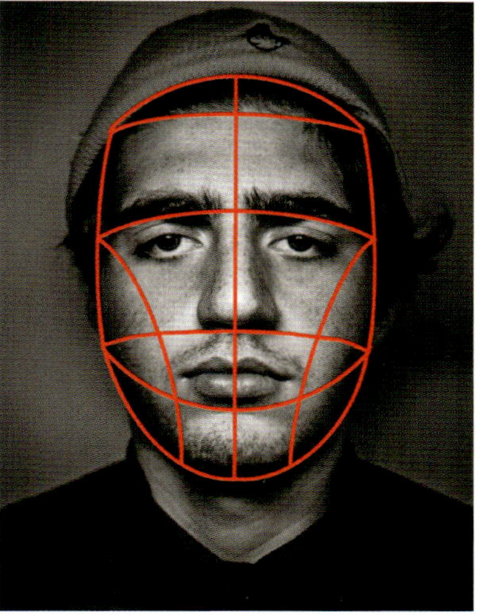
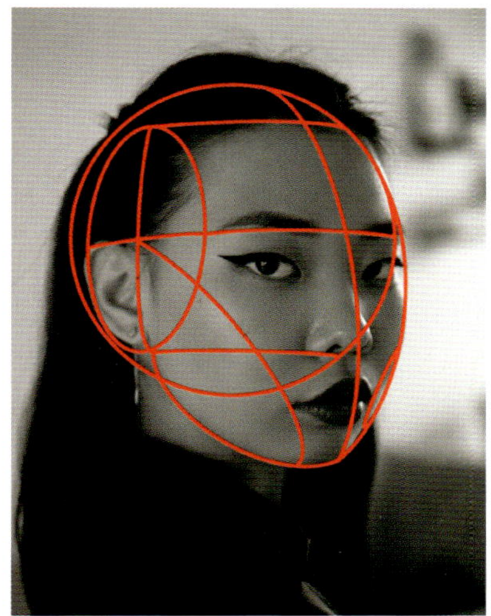

Now, place a line to identify your cheek plane (you'll add a line for each cheek for the straight-on angle): Start from the center of the vertical and horizontal axes and pull a line in an arching motion down past the corner of the mouth to the chin line. Aim the line just outside the corner of the mouth, but don't worry too much because the exact closeness is not a huge deal. The line (or lines for the straight-on angle) is meant to help you gauge the shading of the cheek more than the placement of the mouth.

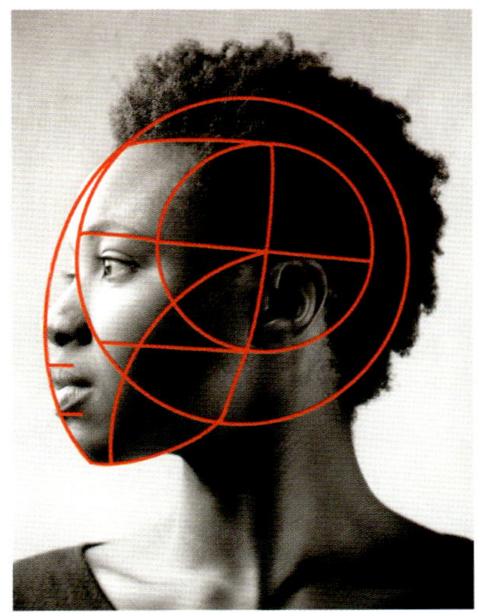
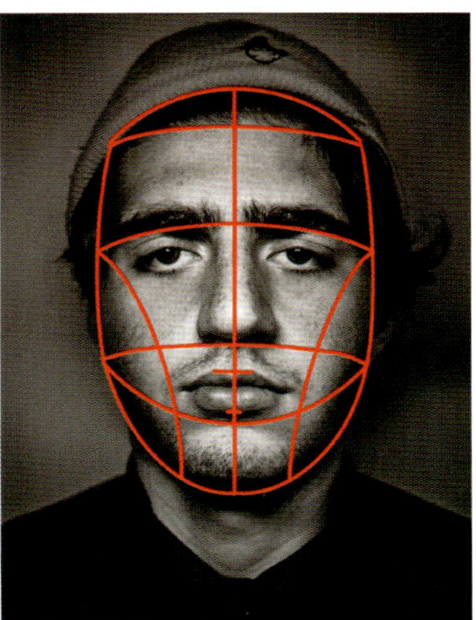
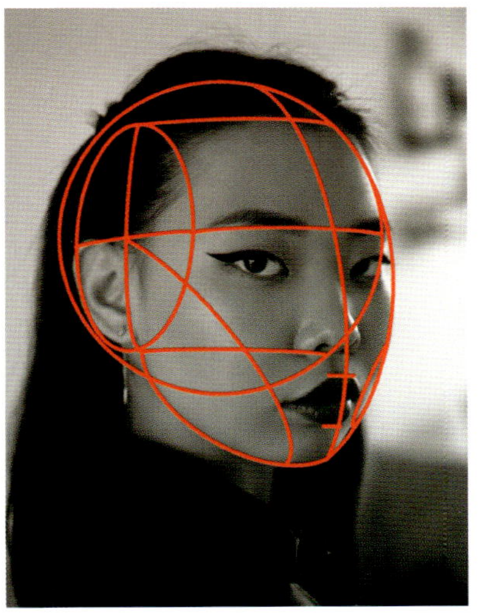

In the final step, draw anchor points for the top of the upper lip and the bottom of the lower lip. Just like the area from the hairline to the chin is divided in thirds, you want to split the nose-to-chin section roughly into thirds as well. The top mark will represent the top of the upper lip, while the bottom mark will represent the bottom of the lower lip. (You can use the same pencil-as-measuring-tape method you used to figure out where to place your chin line.)

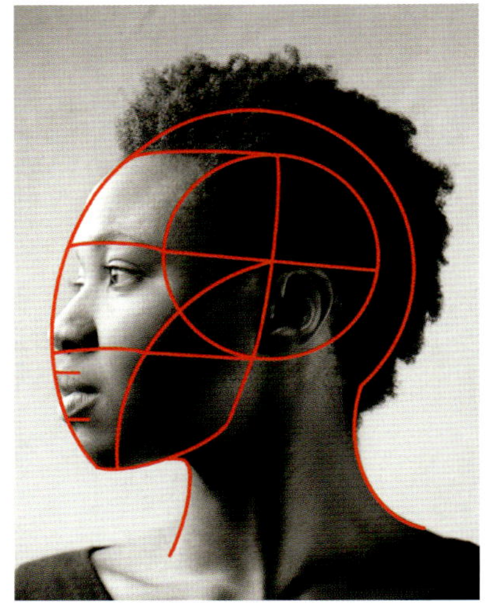 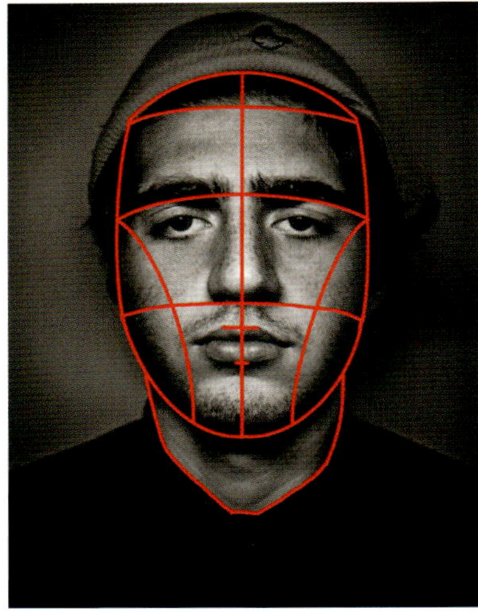 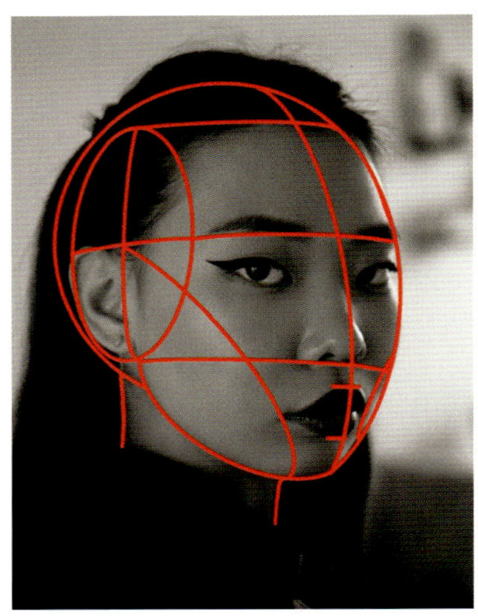

The basic framework of your portrait is now complete, and you can sketch in shoulders and attach your Loomis head to the neck.

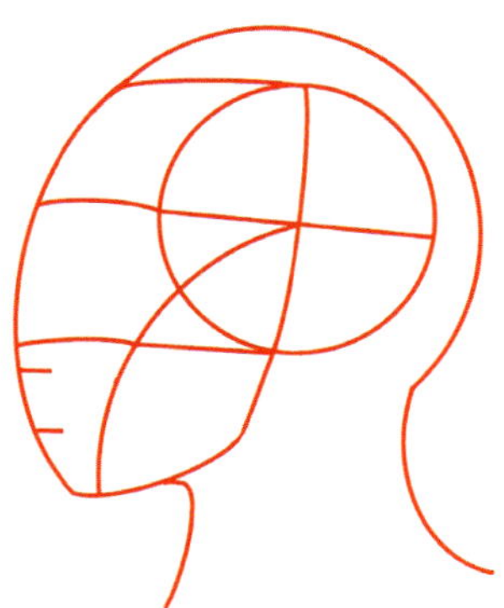 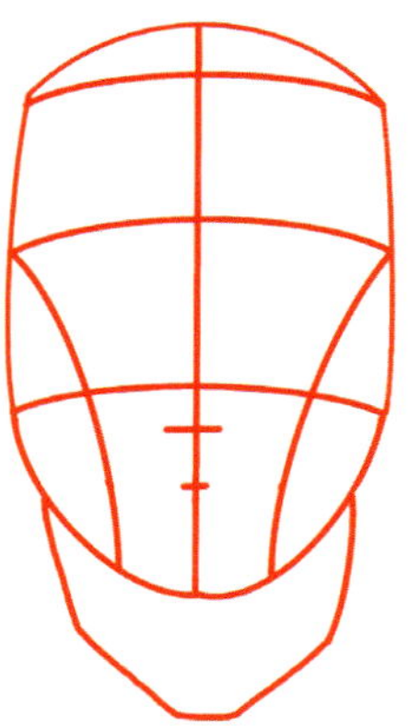 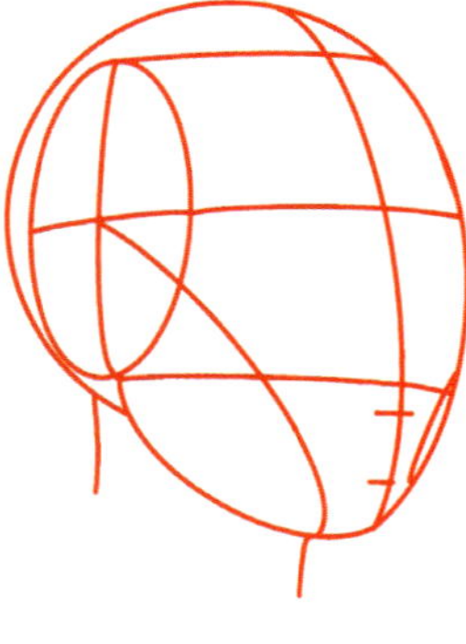

Your Loomis heads are complete! You may not think so right now, but you have everything you need to have accurate proportions as you draw in your portrait's features. Everything you draw moving forward will plug into these Loomis heads.

Remember to take it slow and enjoy every stroke, smudge, blend, and adjustment.

Placing the Features on the Loomis Head

Now I am going to show you the drawing flow for placing facial features on a Loomis head for profile, straight-on, and three-quarter-turn portraits. Personally, I have found over the years that placing the ear first helps me to gauge the other aspects of the portrait, so we'll start the examples there. Regardless of your portrait's angle, always place the ear in the lower quadrant of the side plane that is positioned away from the front of the subject's face. Let's get started!

Remember that this example flow is not absolute. If you feel more comfortable drawing the nose first instead of the ear, then you should follow your intuition. Whichever facial feature you start with, use a graphite pencil for sketching it so that you can easily erase and adjust as needed.

The Profile Angle

Here I am showing you step by step exactly where the features are placed in relation to the Loomis head in a profile angle. Pay attention to the underlying Loomis head's lines as they are the guides for where the Asaro features will live.

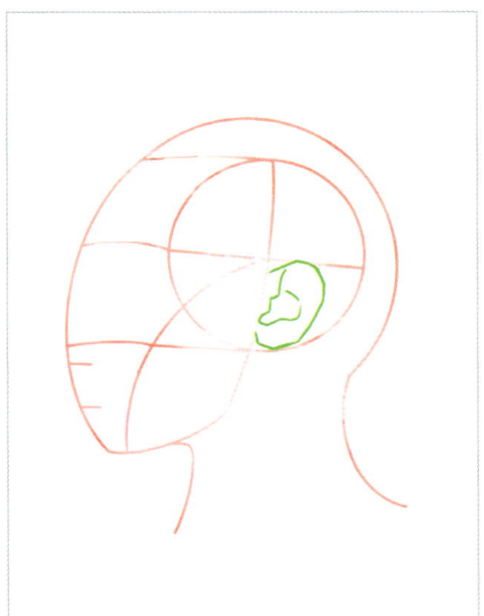

Now I am going to show you the drawing flow for using the Asaro method to place facial features. To place an ear on your Loomis head, locate the lower quadrant of the side plane that is away from the front of the face. If the subject is looking to your left, then the section that will house the ear will be the bottom right. If your subject is looking off to your right, then the section that will house the ear will be the bottom left. Use very light pressure to draw in the ear, so you can easily erase and adjust without permanently marking your paper.

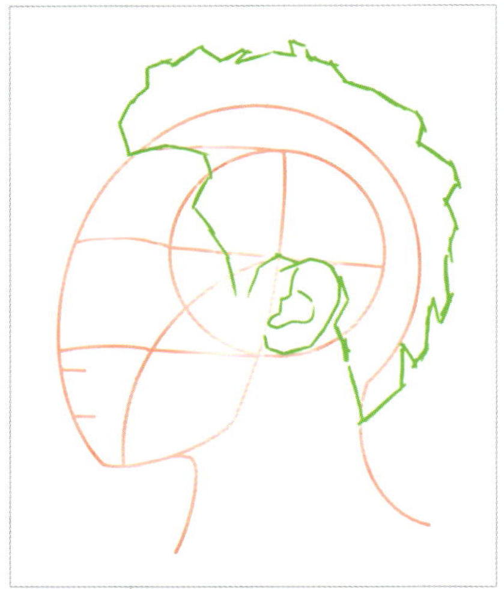

Use the ear and the underlying structure of the Loomis head to lay down line work for the basic outline of your subjects' hair.

Best Practice: *If your Loomis head was drawn properly, the hairline is a great place to start drawing your hair's outline.*

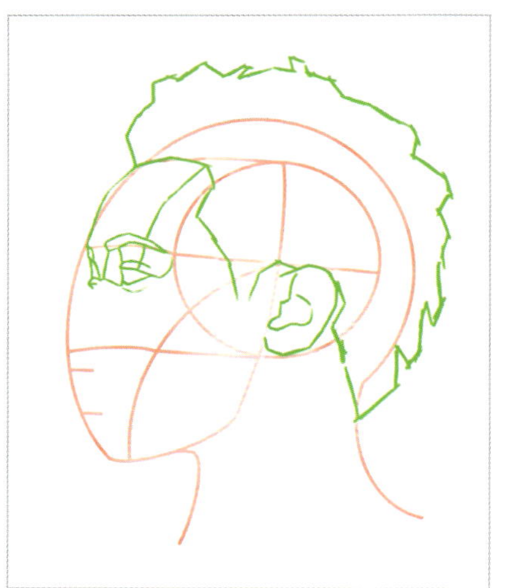

Using the brow line of the underlying Loomis head, sketch in the nose bridge and eyebrow lines. Next, pull down three frame lines and connect them to form the eyes. The brow line will give you proportions for eye placement.

Best Practice: *Draw the outer outline of the far forehead to help give you some more structure before you commit your pencil to sketching your nose bridge. This will help with proper placement of the eyes.*

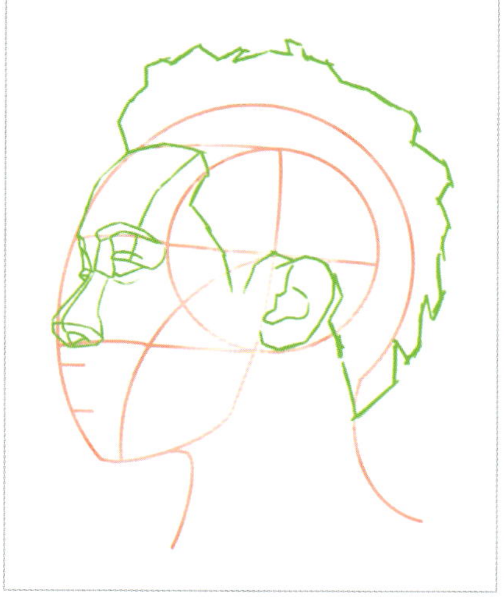

Now start sketching in the nose from the nose line up. After you draw the bottom Asaro plane, simply pull the ridge plane up and connect it to the nose bridge. Sketch in your slope plane for the nose.

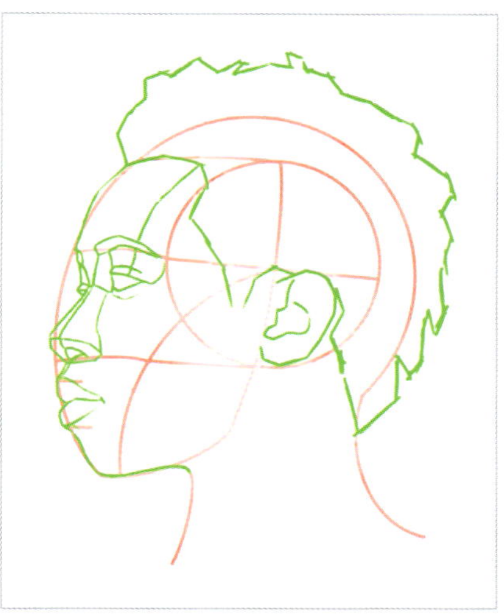

Pull the philtrum plane down to the anchor point for the upper lip. From there, sketch in the upper and lower lip. Remember the lower lip should extend down only to where you placed your lower anchor point.

> **Best Practice:** *Mark the corner of the mouth to help you gauge the size of the lips. The corner of the mouth typically resides just outside of a subject's outer nostril.*

The Straight-On Angle

The straight-on angle is a little tricky to start because you cannot see the ovals that represent the side planes of the head. However, the principal structure remains the same. For example, the ears start on the nose line just like the other angles.

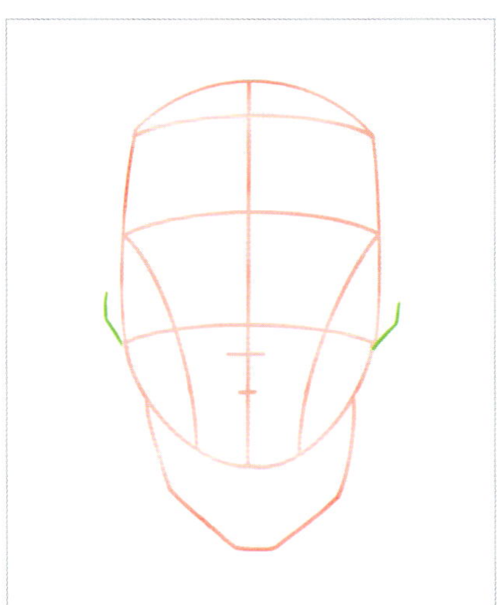

Use the nose line as your basis for where the ears start. Refer to the profile and three-quarter-turn examples and notice that the bottom of the ear aligns nicely with the nose line as it stems off the bottom of the oval. With this in mind, draw ears up from the nose line on both sides.

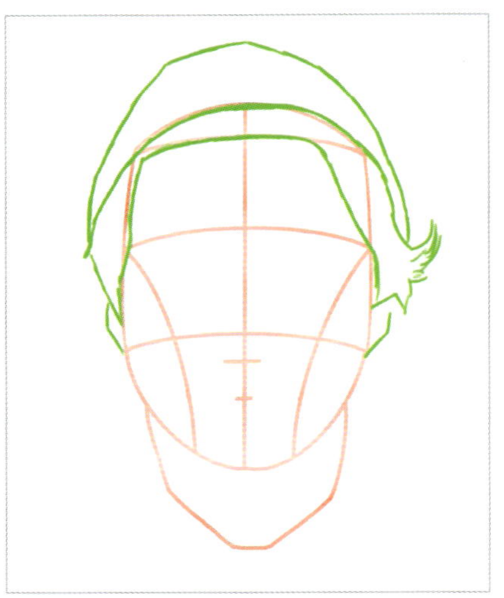

Sketch in the outline of the hair and hat. Remember to use the underlying Loomis head structure to help guide your proportions through this step.

Best Practice: *Start drawing the hair from the hairline of your Loomis head.*

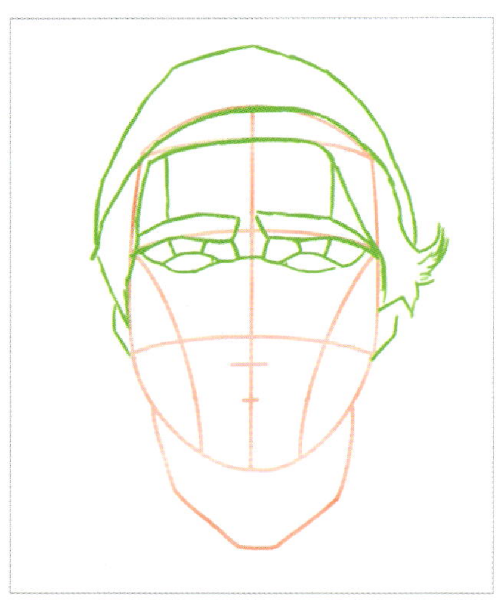

Draw the nose bridge, which is the center of the eyes according to the Asaro method. Next, draw the outline of the eyebrows, which stem from the top of the nose bridge, and then draw your three frame lines. Remember the second frame line should align with the temple plane lines. Connect the frame lines to create the outline of your subject's eyes.

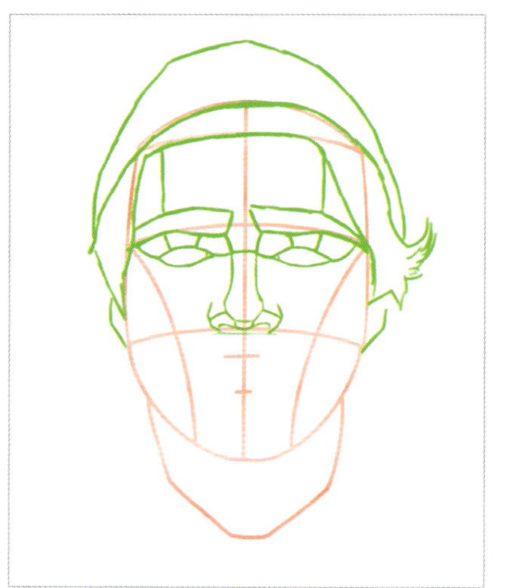

Sketch in the bottom plane of the nose so that the nostrils are sitting on the Loomis nose line, then draw the nose up from there. After you establish the bottom of the nose planes, draw your nose ridge plane and extend it up to connect with the nose bridge plane.

Best Practice: *Draw the nose from the bottom up versus from the top down. Everyone is different, but I find that drawing the nose this way leads to better results with fewer adjustments needed along the way.*

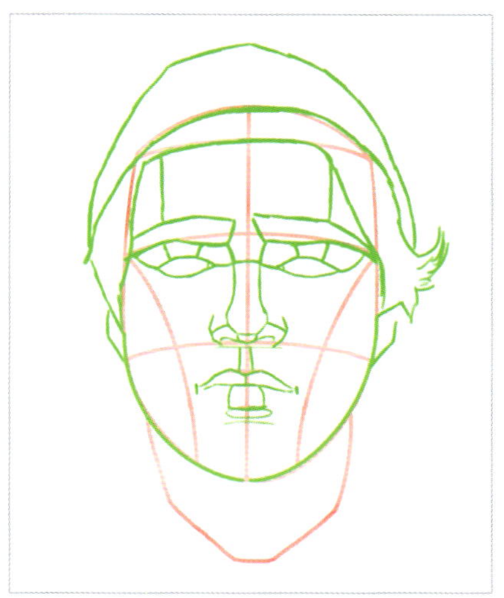

You're almost done. Draw in the philtrum lines so that they meet the anchor point of the top lip. Next, identify the corners of the mouth to help you to draw accurately sized lips. Connect the corner of the mouth with the anchor point for the top and bottom lips, then draw in your Asaro planes. Remember the upper lip has two planes and the bottom lip has three planes.

The Three-Quarter-Turn Angle

This angle has its own sets of challenges when it comes to drawing in proportion. For example, when drawing the eyes, they are not symmetrical. The far side of the face needs to be foreshortened in order to achieve accurate feature placement.

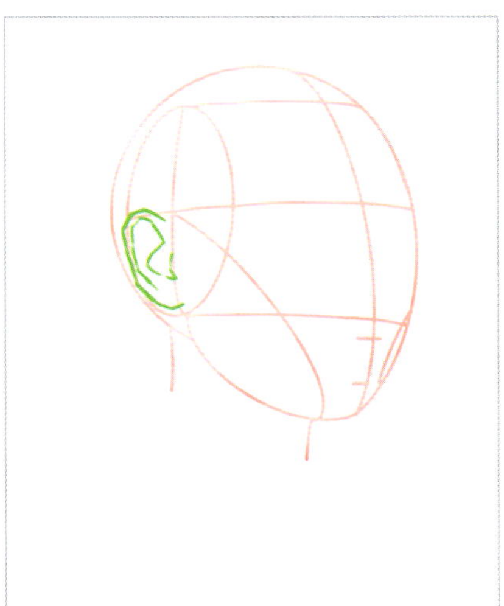

As with the profile angle, draw the ear in the bottom-rear quadrant of the oval (the lower section of the side plane positioned away from the front of the face).

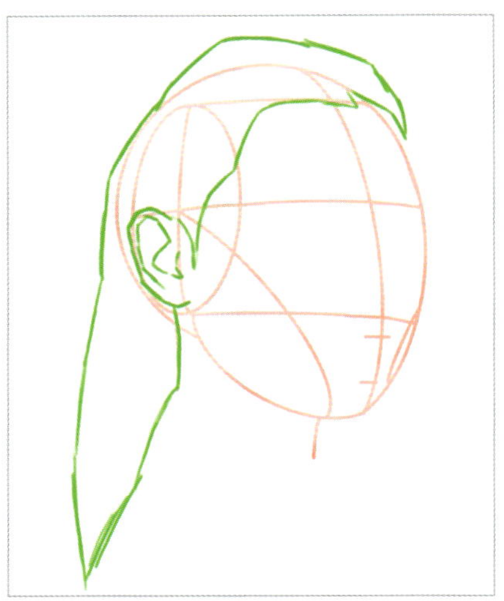

Start at the Loomis hairline and draw the outline of the subject's hair. Remember, by starting with the hairline you give yourself the best chance of accurately drawing your proportions for the hair.

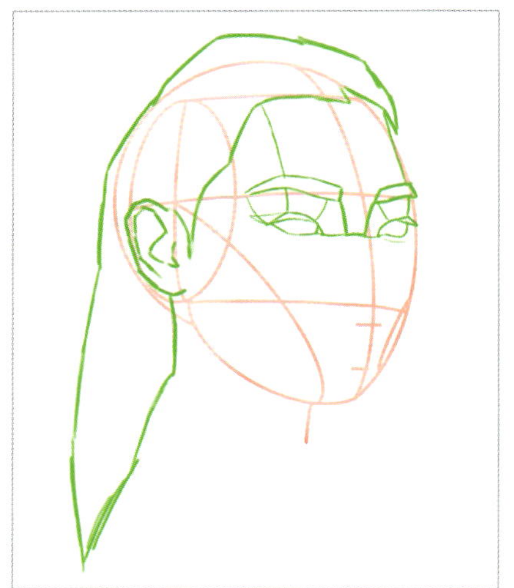

Draw the nose bridge (two parallel lines angled slightly away from each other), then draw the basic shape of the eyebrows stemming off the corner of the bridge's two lines. Next, draw in the frame lines for the eyes. Remember, the temple plane line aligns with the second frame line for the eye, giving your portrait more structure for when shading comes. After that, simply connect your frame lines to bring out the whole outline of your subject's eyes.

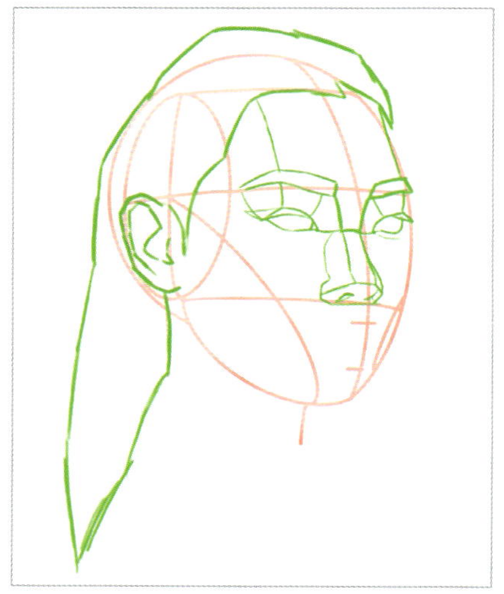

Draw the bottom nose plane on the Loomis head's nose line, then draw in the nostrils as well as the nose ridge plane. Extend the nose ridge plane up, connect it to the nose bridge, and then draw in the slope plane.

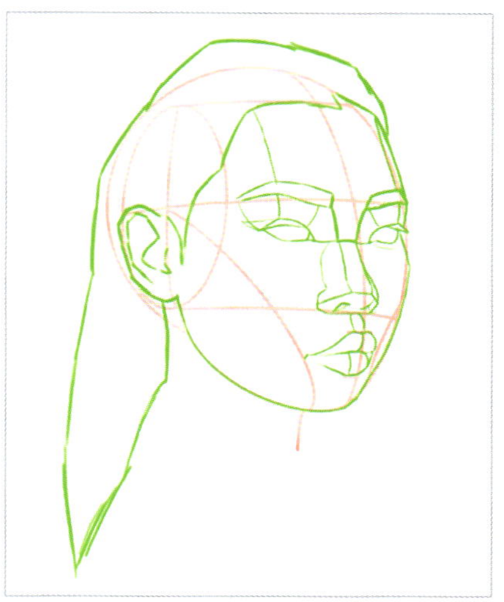

Time for the lips: Draw two philtrum lines, pulling them down until they meet the upper lip's anchor point. Mark a small hatch mark where the corner of the mouth lives, then connect that corner mark with the anchor point of both the upper and the lower lip. Finally, add Asaro lines to split the upper lip into two planes and the bottom lip into three planes.

Project 12: Draw Three Loomis Heads with Features

For **Project 12**, draw a profile, straight-on, and three-quarter-turn Loomis head with features using the techniques and best practices you learned. If you need a more fluid explanation of adding features to a Loomis head, simply scan the QR code to watch **How to Place Facial Features on a Loomis Head | A Beginners Guide**. Each of the three videos covers a specific angle.

Build from Your Foundation

Of all the methods that have been conceived for easily drawing the human head, Andrew Loomis created one of the simplest yet most accurate approaches. Coupling the Loomis method with John Asaro's facial planes approach makes for the ultimate fusion of simplicity and accuracy. Of course, the methods can only guide you, they cannot draw portraits for you. This is where the "art" of creation comes into play—and practice. When practiced enough, these two methods will become second nature and enable you to yield optimal results and create portraits with a very pleasing aesthetic. If you still need more guidance during your feature placement practice, be sure to scan the chapter's QR code and draw along with me on YouTube.

CHAPTER 10

Drawing
Your
Final Portraits

"The artist who aims at perfection in everything achieves it in nothing."
—*Eugene Delacroix*

All builders must follow specific steps in a certain logistical order to construct a sturdy house, but an appreciation of the importance of a solid foundation coupled with an intimate understanding of the entire construction process is the mark of a true professional. Art is no different: An artist who is well read in their given medium, who understands its foundational concepts and methods, will be able to practice their craft and produce results at a higher level than their contemporaries. In this final chapter, I will walk you through the entire drawing flow—from the Loomis heads to Asaro planes to the final details—for portraits of our references at the three main angles. Everything that we have covered up until this point has been in preparation for this.

You now have all the knowledge needed to draw your portraits in a complete and holistic way. One last piece of advice before we begin: Remember always to have fun!

Drawing the Profile Angle

Follow along for one last practice session with the profile subject.

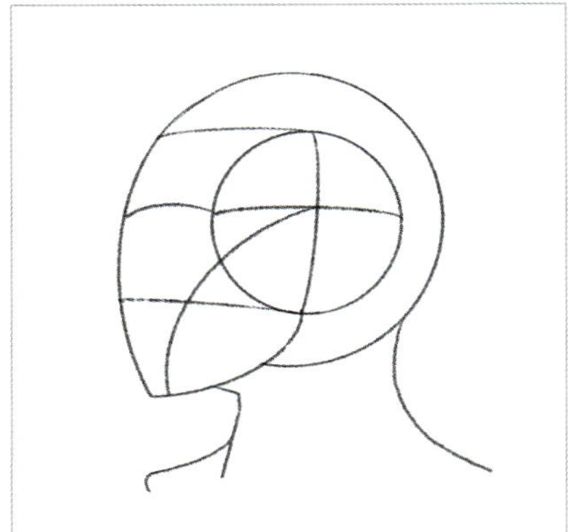

To start the process, draw a Loomis head. Make sure to use a graphite pencil with a light pressure in case you need to erase and adjust.

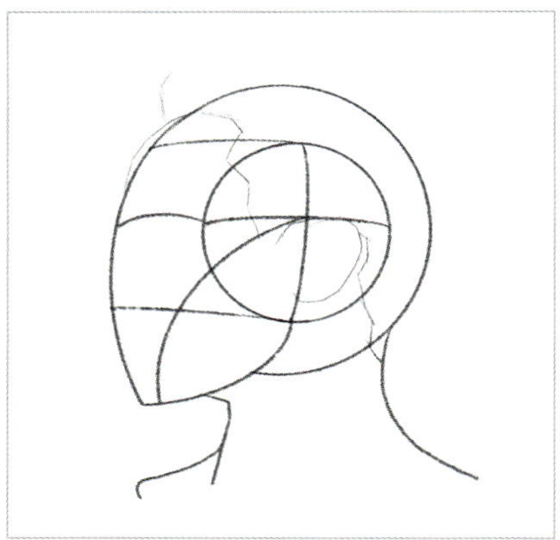

Begin sketching the basic outline of the ear and hair. Remember, the ear sits in the bottom-rear quadrant of the side plane.

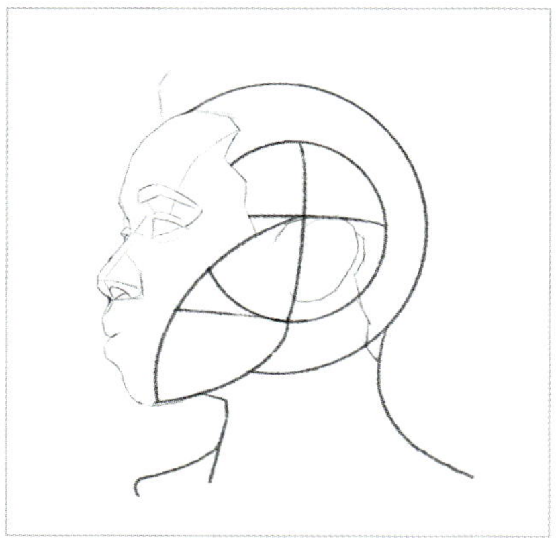

Place the eyes and nose while also establishing the outer edge of your subject's face. Remember, the eyes should follow the brow line, while the nose should sit on the nose line of the underlying Loomis head.

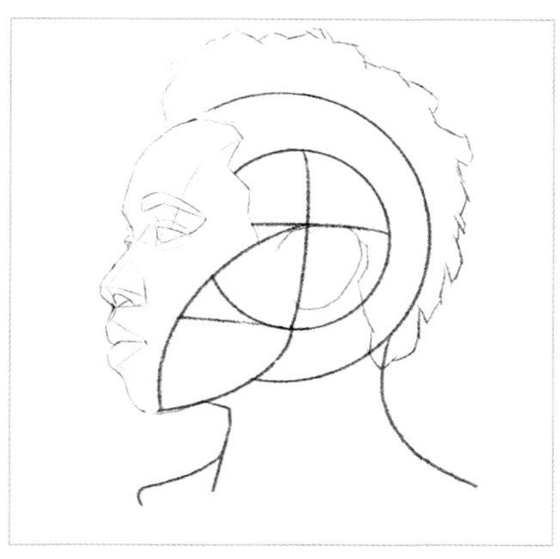

Sketch in the basic shape of the mouth and finish drawing the outline of the hair.

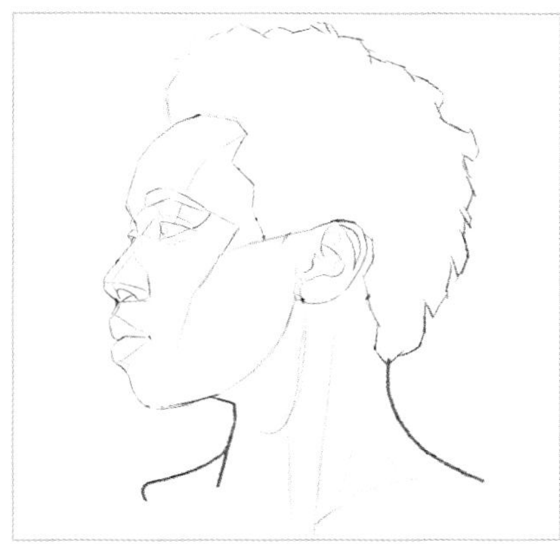

Now that you have the basic two-dimensional shape of your portrait drawn, it is time to erase your Loomis lines. You can erase them completely or keep them slightly visible. Next, draw in Asaro planes for the cheek and neck to help guide your shading.

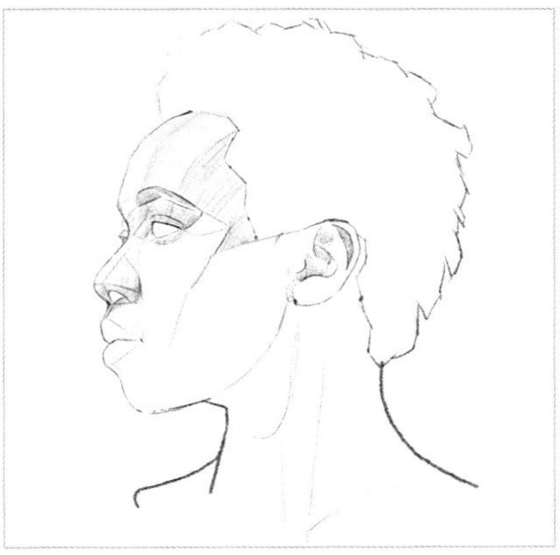

Switch to a soft charcoal pencil and begin to shade the individual planes of the face and ear. The most important thing is to follow the underlying form with every push and pull of your pencil.

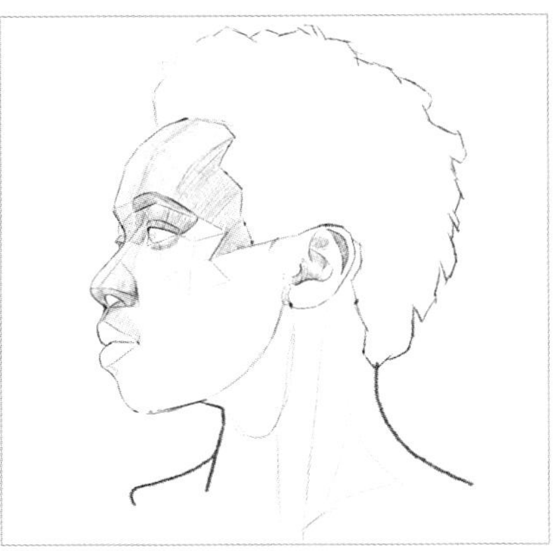

If you need more structure for your shading, go ahead and add more Asaro planes. This is the adaptability of the Asaro method in action.

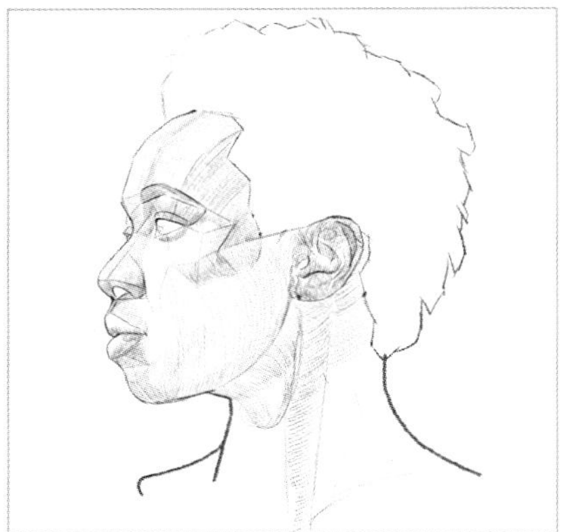

Continue hatching all the individual planes throughout the portrait.

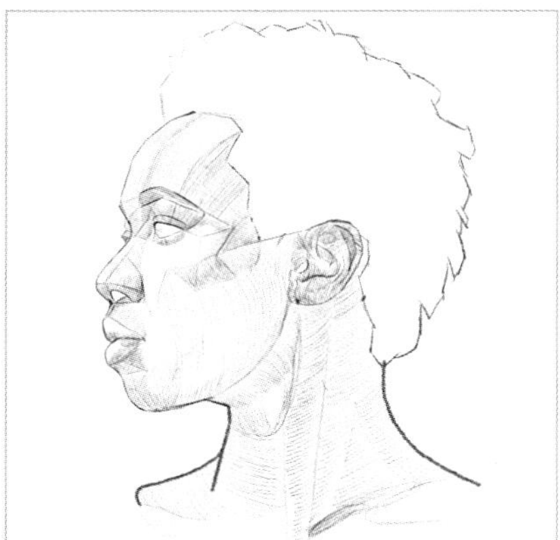

Do not shade the front of the cheeks or under the eyes for this reference. This way you can convey a very high value in these areas without having to retrieve much after you have blended all your hatch marks.

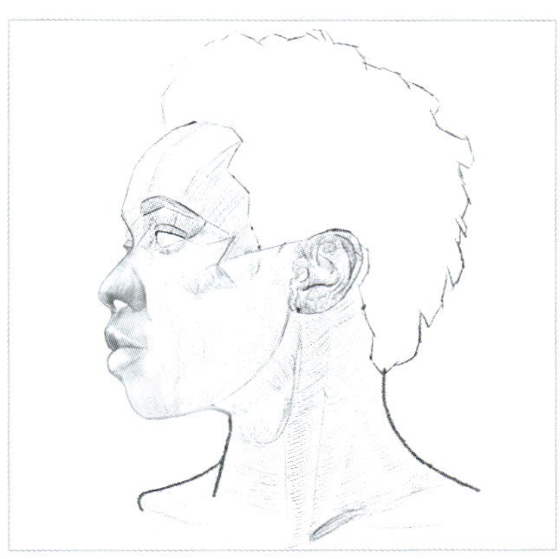

Switch to your smudger and start blending your hatch marks. Be sure to follow their general direction and flow so you do not lose the underlying form.

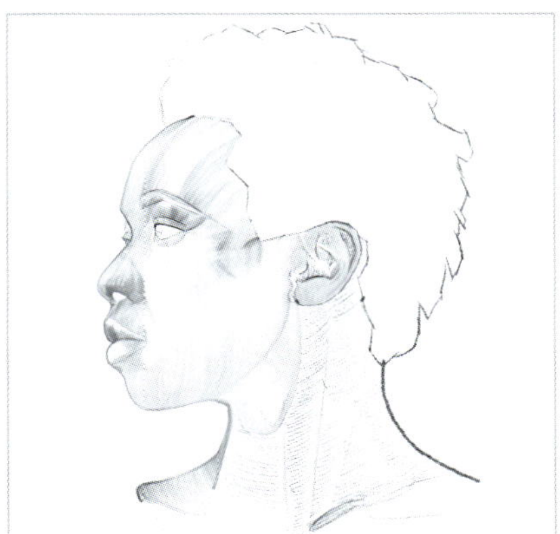

Continue smudging your hatch marks throughout the drawing.

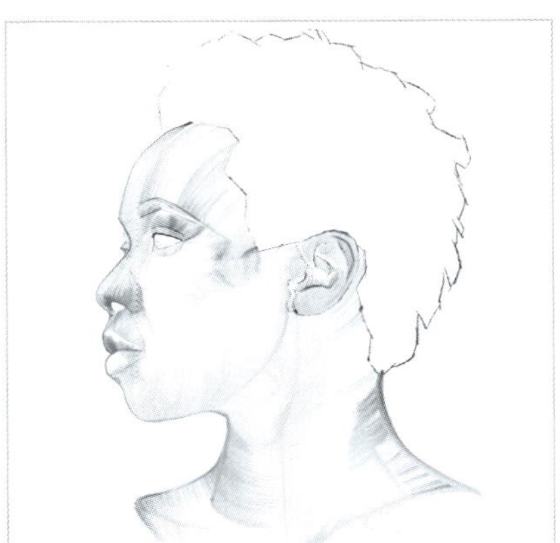

Smudge all the planes of the face, ear, and neck until the whole of the portrait has been blended.

Best Practice: *An easy way to ensure that you are blending your hatch marks in the proper direction is to follow the direction of the hatch marks themselves.*

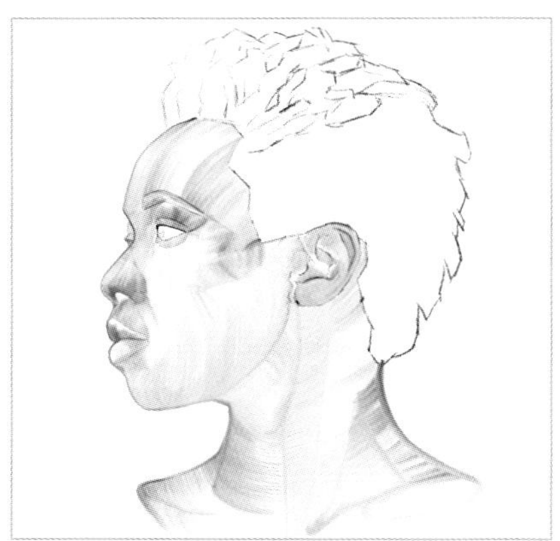

With a soft charcoal pencil, start sketching in the outlines of the various hair segments. Remember, the individual segments of hair help you to bring out the flow of the subject's hair.

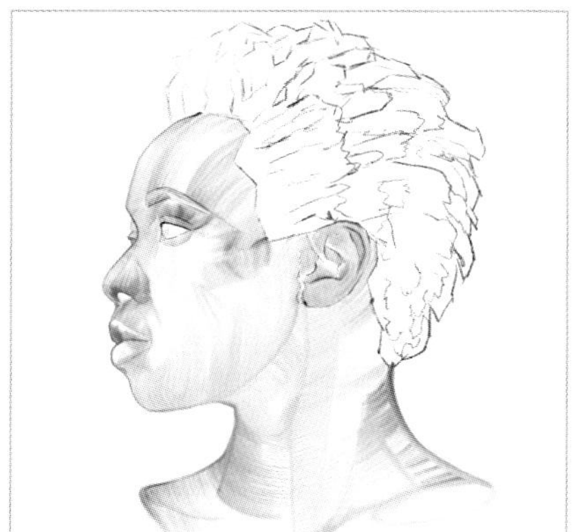

Continue sketching hair segments until the whole of the head is covered.

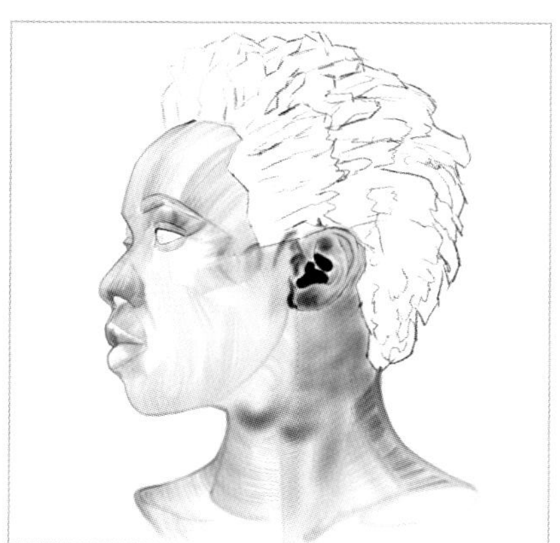

With a medium charcoal pencil, fill in the low values in the subject's ear. Switch to your brush, dip it in the ground soft charcoal, and start lowering the value of the neck and ear.

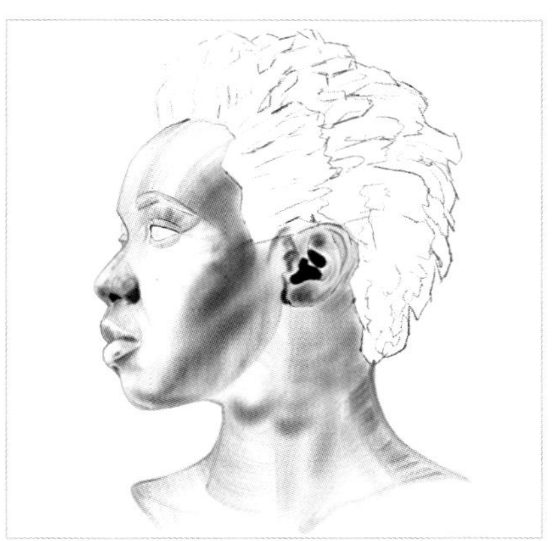

For the darkest areas, such as the nostril and inner ear, swap tools: Use your medium charcoal pencil, which will help you to achieve lower values with much more control. For the rest of your portrait's face, use your brush to help you more easily blend the drawing while producing a nice soft gradation across your values.

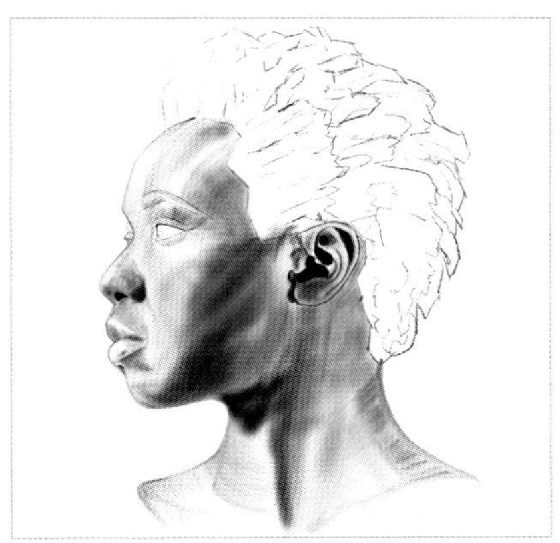

Continue to follow the underlying form and build up your lower values with your brushwork as you need to. Don't forget to repeatedly reload your brush with soft charcoal powder to keep conveying the low values you need.

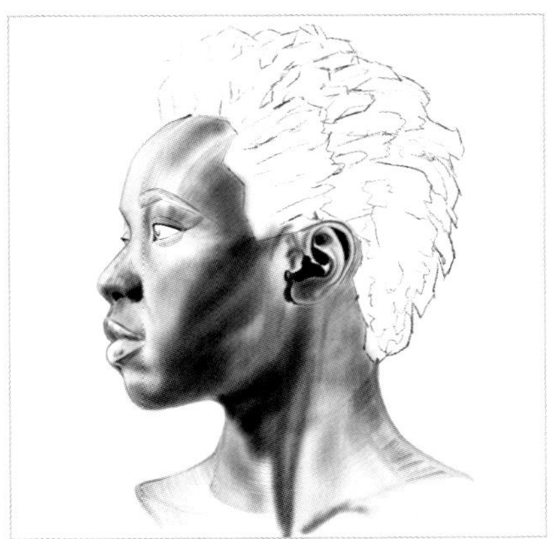

Remember, you can always switch to your smudger to blend and lower the value in a specific area.

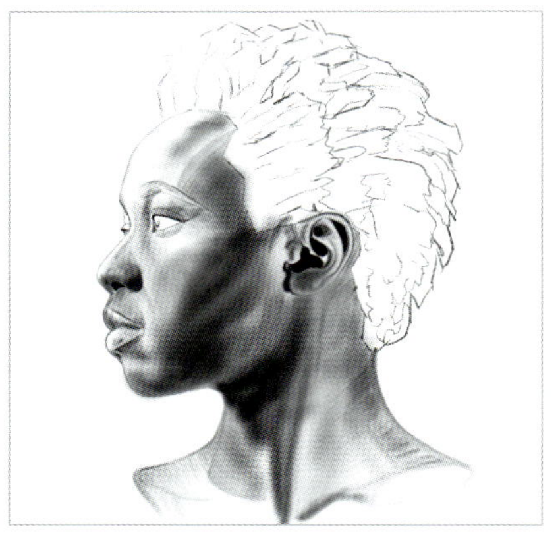

With a kneaded eraser, start retrieving high values in areas such as the forehead, eye lids, and ridge of the nose.

> **Best Practice:** *A kneaded eraser will be your best eraser for this step as it retrieves and blends the contrast between your values in those specific areas at the same time.*

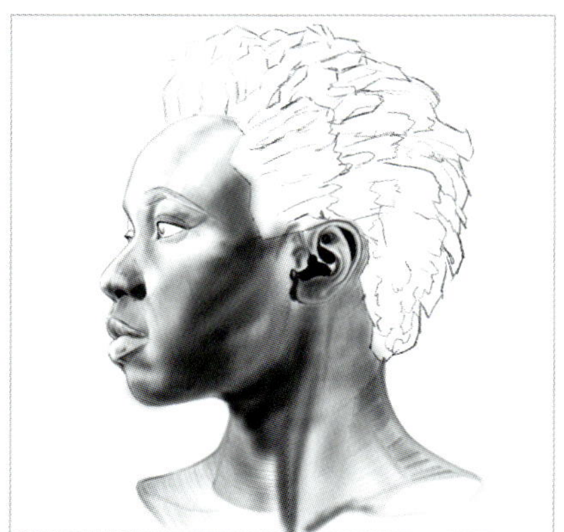

Continue retrieving your high values around the forehead, eyes, and nose.

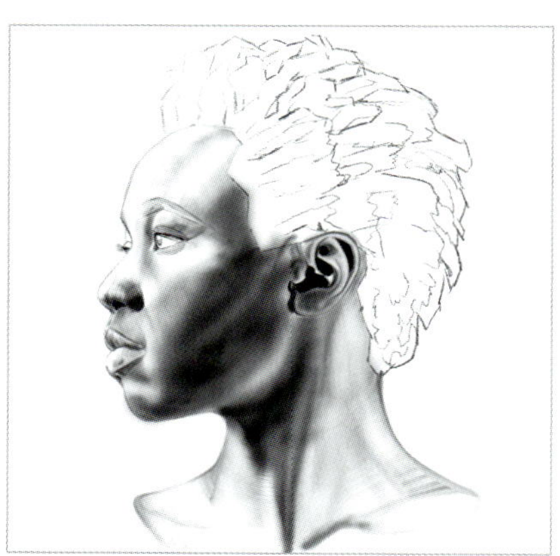

Retrieve your higher values throughout the neck and jaw line, then trade your eraser for a hard charcoal pencil and draw in the eye lashes.

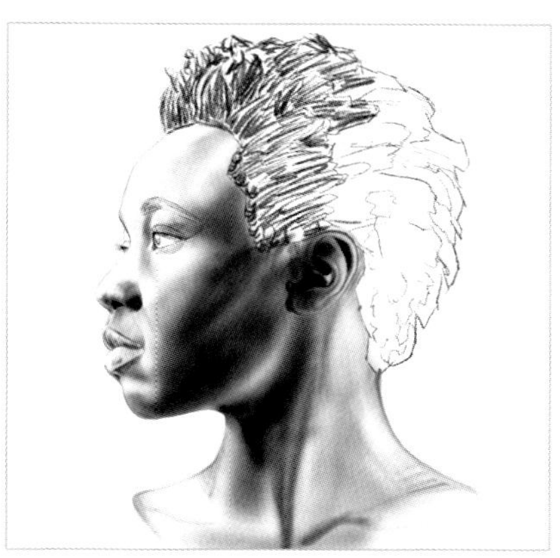

Using an overhand grip and the side of a soft charcoal pencil, start filling in the outlines of the hair segments.

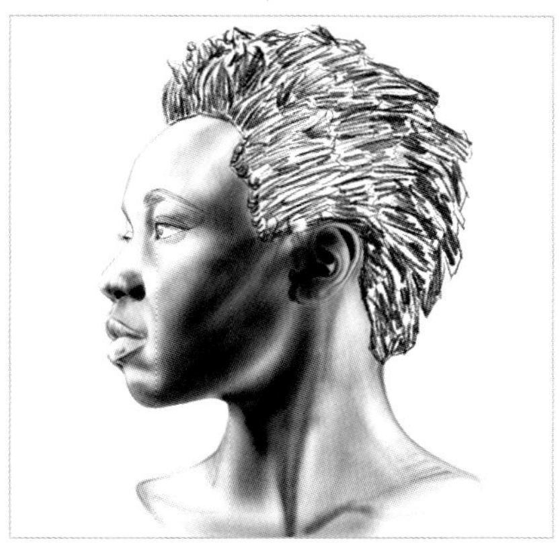

Continue to draw hair segments, making sure to fill the segments more thoroughly towards the back of the head where light is cast the least.

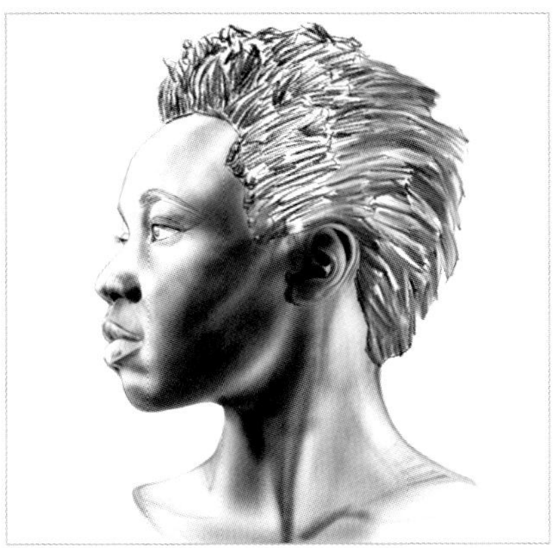

Switch back to your smudger and begin blending your hatch marks while keeping the hair's flow in mind.

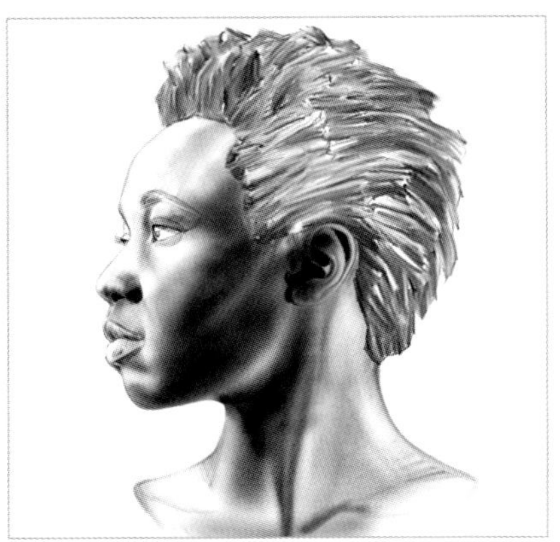

Continue to blend the hair segments until the whole of the hair is blended.

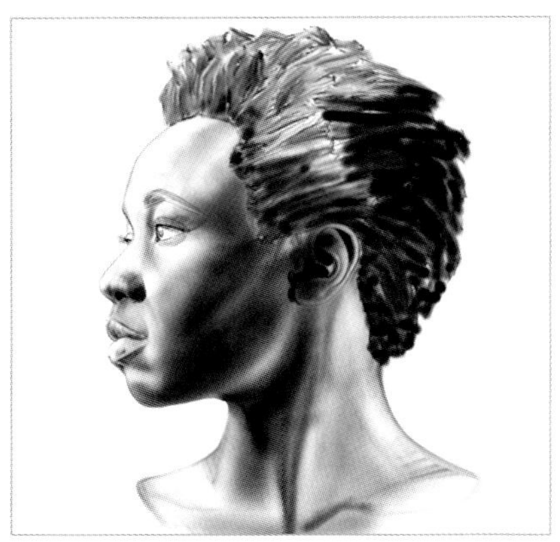

Dip your smudger into the soft charcoal powder, then push the smudger into the paper to begin lowering the value for your hair segments.

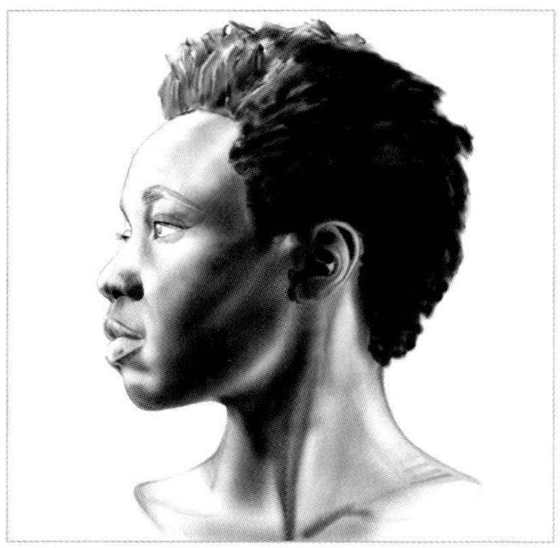

Continue to blend your hair segments with your smudger until the whole of the hair's value has been lowered.

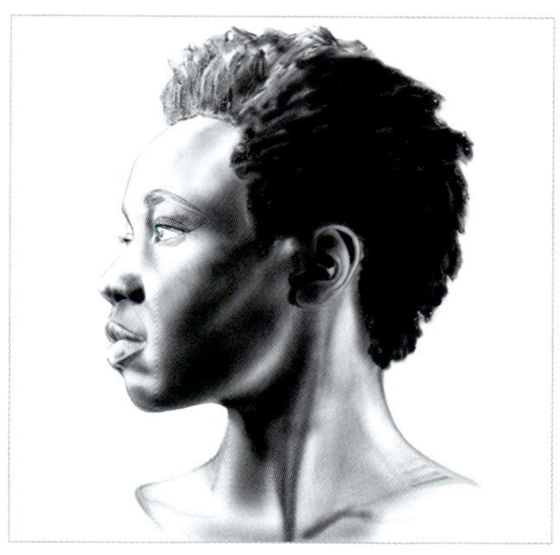

To bring out detail within the hair, retrieve high values throughout the hair with a MONO Zero Eraser.

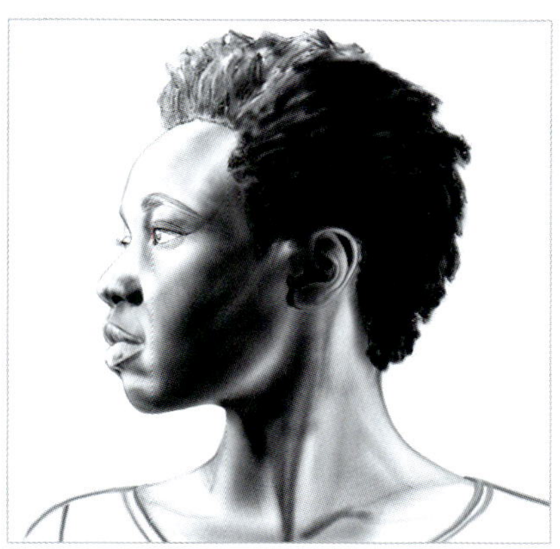

Continue to retrieve the hair's high values and texture. You can also use an unloaded brush and dab the paper to blend the hair and make it softer. Finally, add any desired detail work with a hard charcoal pencil. The hard charcoal will sit on top of the medium and soft charcoal very nicely.

Drawing the Straight-On Angle

The straight-on subject presents a few unique challenges, but you should be familiar with them by now.

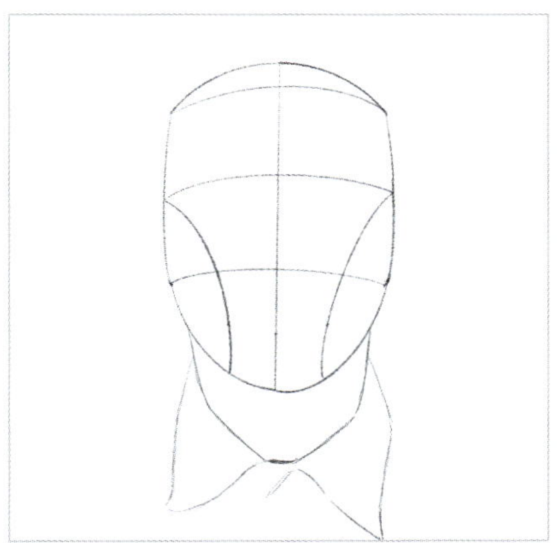

Draw a Loomis head with a graphite pencil. Be sure to use light pressure so you can easily erase and adjust if needed.

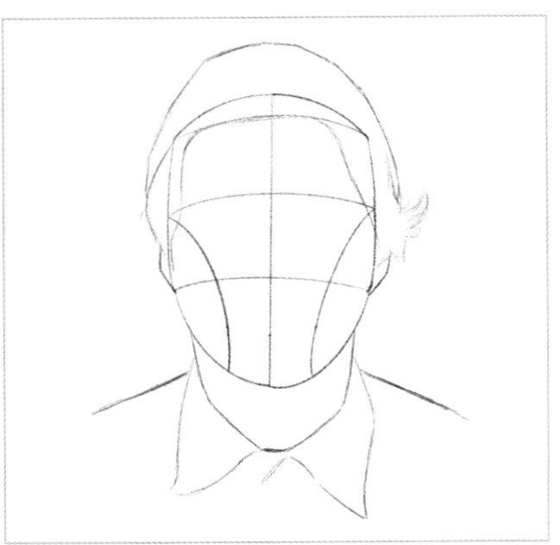

Draw in the outline of the hair, hat, and top of the shoulders. Next, sketch in the bottom of the ears, which should align with the nose line.

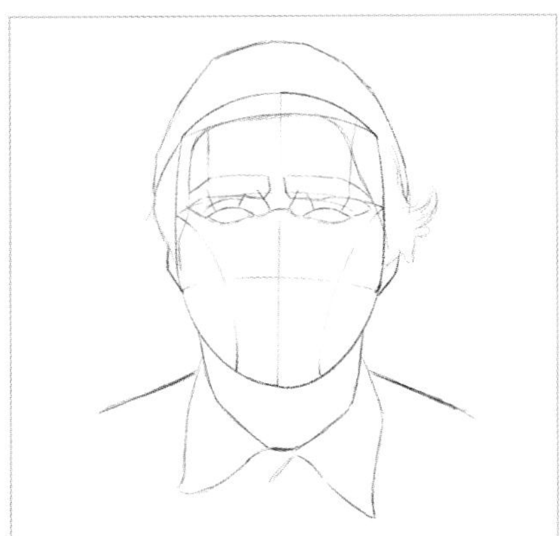

Using the brow line and the center line of the Loomis head as your guide, sketch in the nose bridge and then the outline for the eyebrows. Add the frame lines, then connect them to form your eyes.

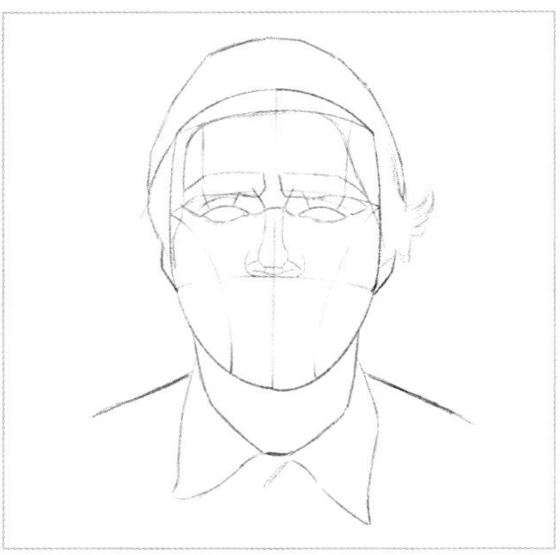

Using the nose line as your starting point, draw in the bottom plane of the nose. From there, draw the nose ridge plane; start from the bottom plane, then pull up and connect it to the nose bridge.

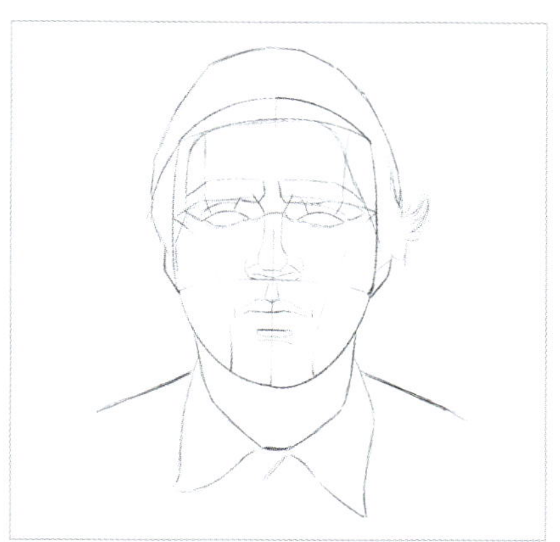

Draw the philtrum plane, pulling it down to roughly where the top lip begins. Next, roughly identify the corners of the mouth, connect the philtrum plane to the mouth's corners, and draw the center line of the lips. Sketch the bottom lip. To make it look more dynamic, do not connect the lower lip line to the corners of the mouth.

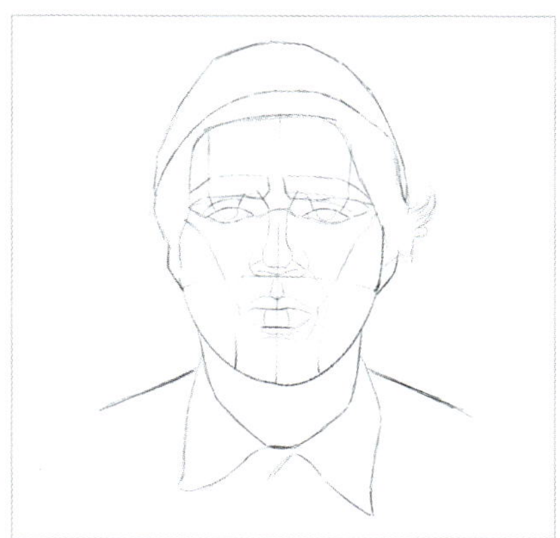

Add Asaro planes throughout the face. They will help you nail the underlying form while hatching and shading the face later. Remember, there is no absolute right or wrong way to draw them, and you can always add more planes later if you need tc.

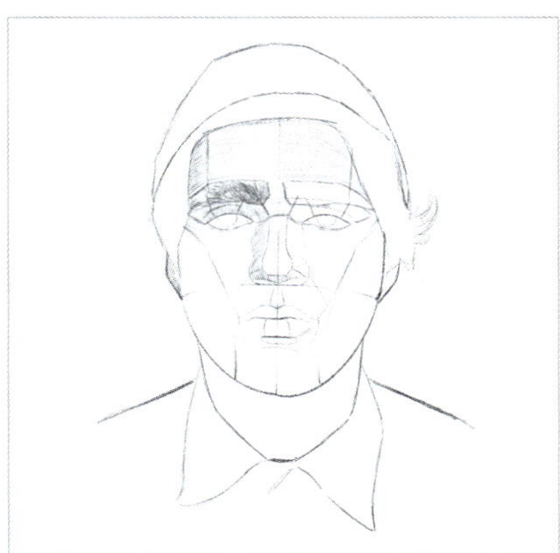

Switch to your soft charcoal pencil and start hatching the individual planes of your portrait. By hatching your planes this way, you start to make the drawing more dynamic even before you blend it.

> **Best Practice:** *Crosshatch in areas that will need a lower value. Once blended with the smudger, these crosshatched areas will already have a lower value, so you won't need to spend so much time lowering their value.*

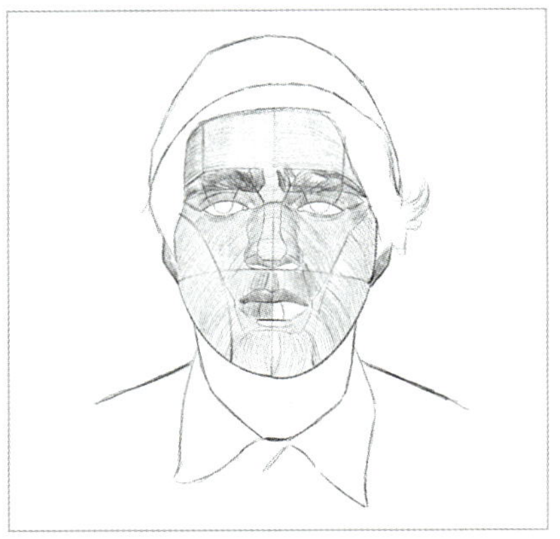

Continue hatching the face and facial features until the whole face is completely hatched.

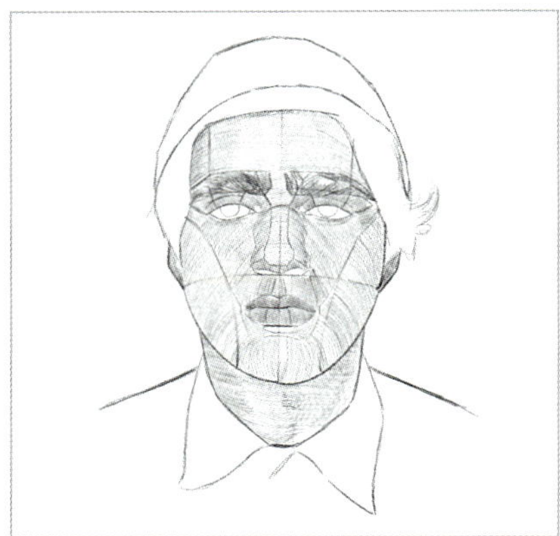

Now, hatch the entire neck of your subject.

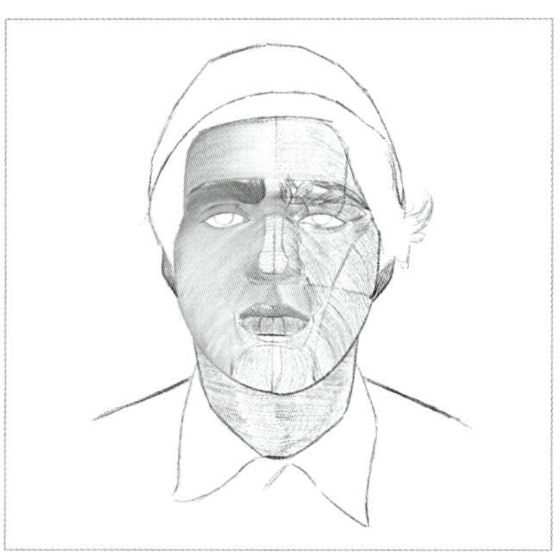

Switch to your smudger and begin blending your hatch marks. Make sure that you adhere to the planes and the direction of your original marks.

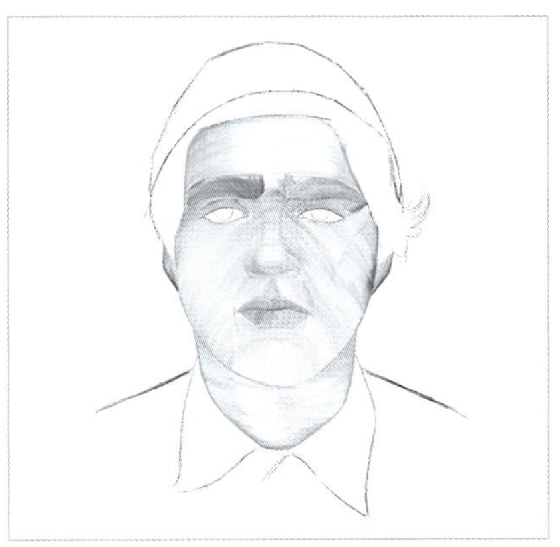

Continue to smudge your hatch marks until the whole of the face and neck are completely blended. If some hatch marks are still visible, that is totally fine. These will disappear with value building and more shading.

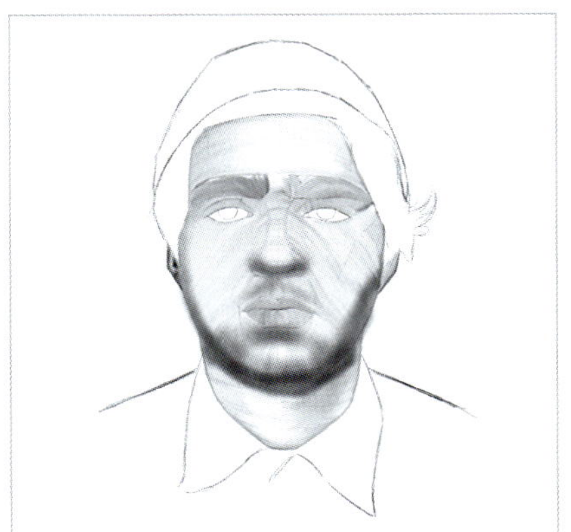

Dip a brush in soft charcoal powder, check your tone on scratch paper to ensure it will give you the lowest value possible, then begin to build up your lower values around the jaw line and under the nose.

> **Best Practice:** *To give you a better and more concentrated blend, try dabbing the paper with your brush instead of swiping.*

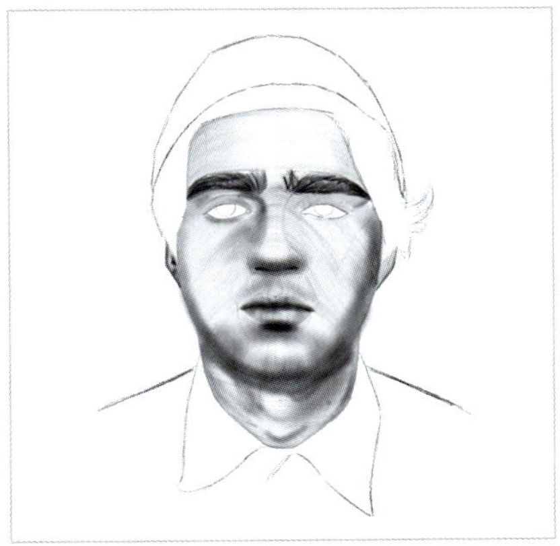

Continue to lower the value under the lower lip and the bottom of the upper lip with your brush, then switch to a medium charcoal pencil and fill in the flow of the eyebrows using soft strokes.

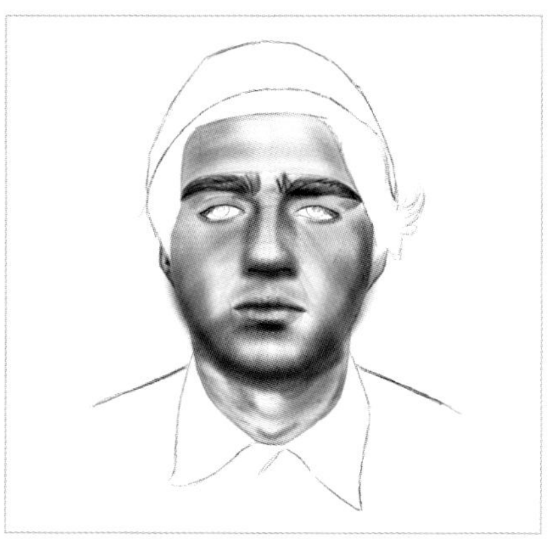

Make sure your medium charcoal pencil is very sharp, and then draw the irises, pupils, and eye lashes. Switch back to your brush and continue to lower the value throughout the portrait as needed.

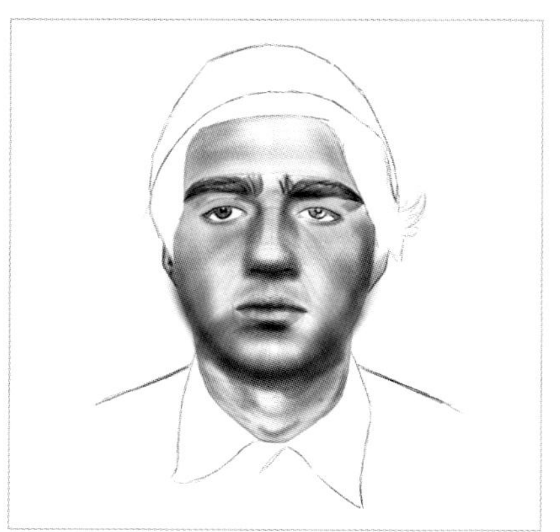

Take up your medium charcoal pencil again, fill in the pupils, and line the outside edge of the irises. Switch back to your smallest smudger and push the charcoal line around each iris towards the pupil. This will give your eyes greater detail and make them look realistic.

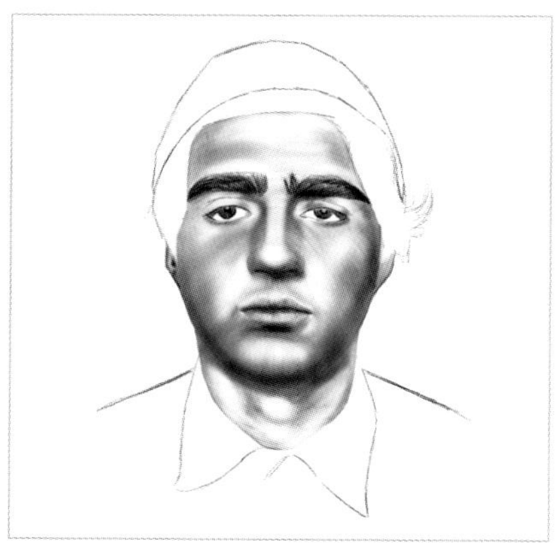

Charcoal tends to get away from you if you let it, so clean up the edges of your drawing with your Pentel Clic Eraser.

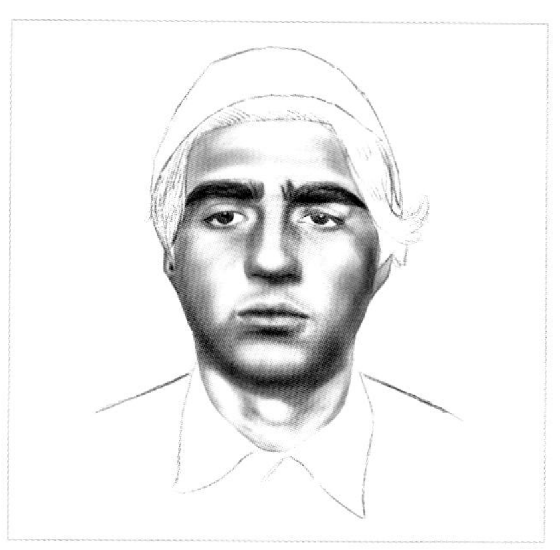

Now begin hatching your hair in the direction it flows. Make sure to bring out the segments of hair as well.

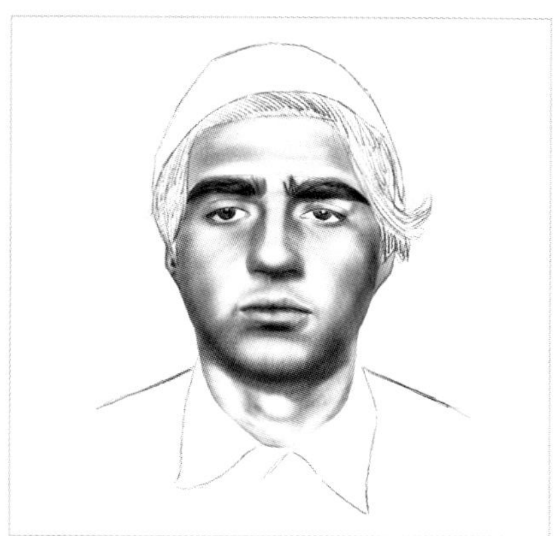

Continue to hatch the hair until all of it is covered.

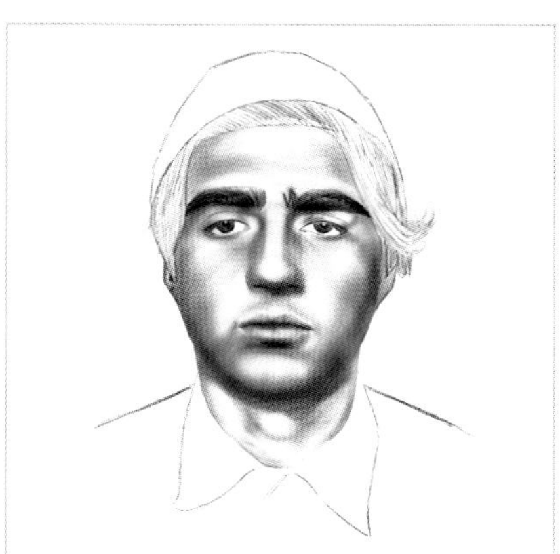

Switch to your smudger and blend the entire head of hair.

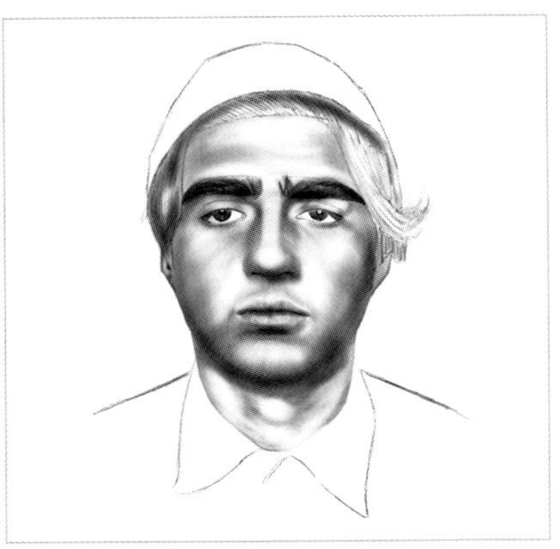

With your brush, begin to lower the value across the hair. Remember to dab the paper instead of swiping it to maintain the integrity of the hatch marks and, thus, the flow of the hair.

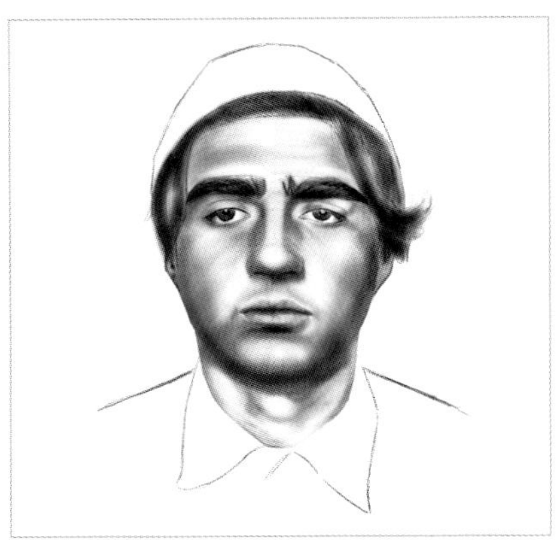

Continue with your brush until all the hair is blended.

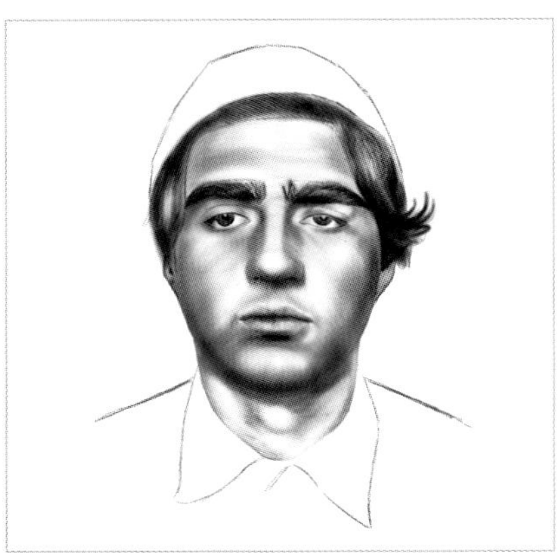

Switch to your MONO Zero Eraser and begin to retrieve the high values throughout the hair, adding texture to the drawing and making the hair's flow more apparent.

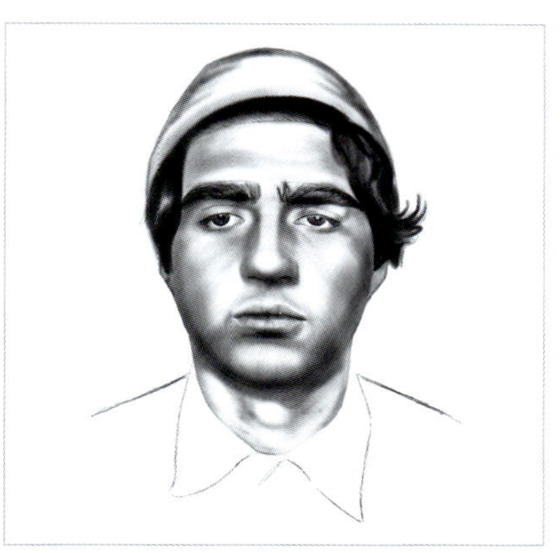

Return to your brush and begin lowering the value of the subject's hat. Make light strokes from the outer edge and work your way in.

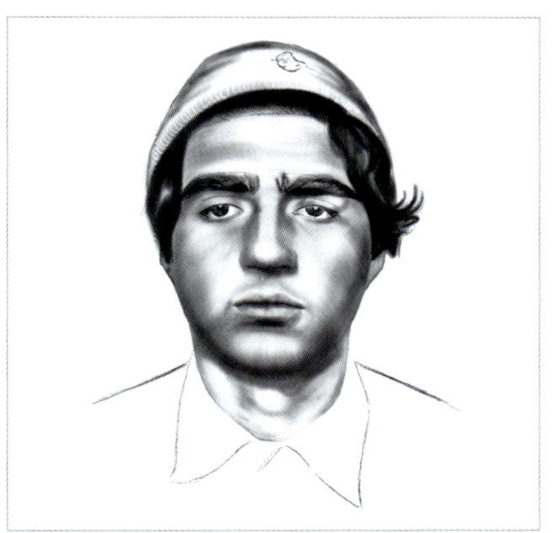

To bring out the hat's stitching, retrieve high values with a MONO Zero Eraser. Next, switch to your hard charcoal pencil to sketch the emblem on the hat.

Best Practice: *Take your time with the high value retrievals for the hat's stitching. The longer you take the better the stitching will look.*

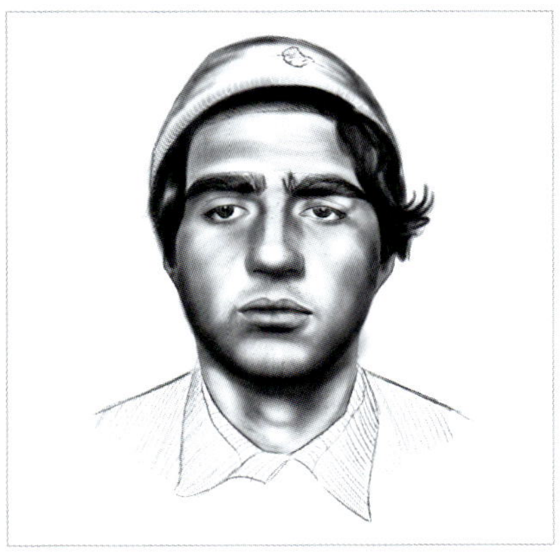

With a soft charcoal pencil, hatch the collar and the shoulders, then switch back to your brush and lower the value along the subject's chin line. This will make the face look like it's closer to the viewer and overall make the portrait look more dynamic.

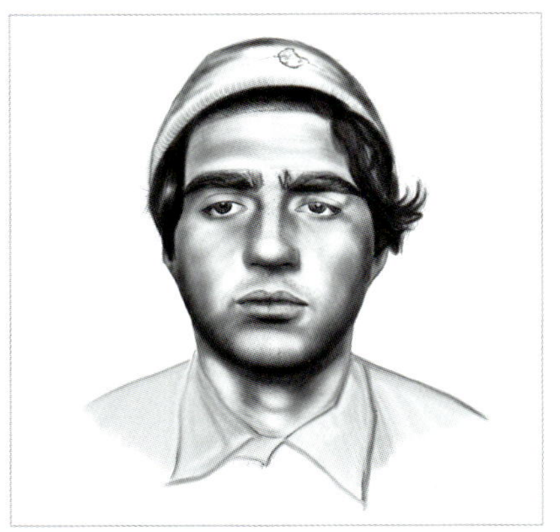

Time for the final details: Dip your smudger in soft charcoal powder, stand the smudger up on end, and very lightly dot freckles on your portrait. Next, add the short hairs for the beginnings of the subject's mustache with a hard charcoal pencil. Finally, go over your drawing with an empty brush to put a nice gradation across all your values.

Drawing the Three-Quarter-Turn Angle

With this one, make sure to focus on your hatch marks always with the underlying form in the back of your mind. Remember every pencil stroke needs to be made with intention and sincereness.

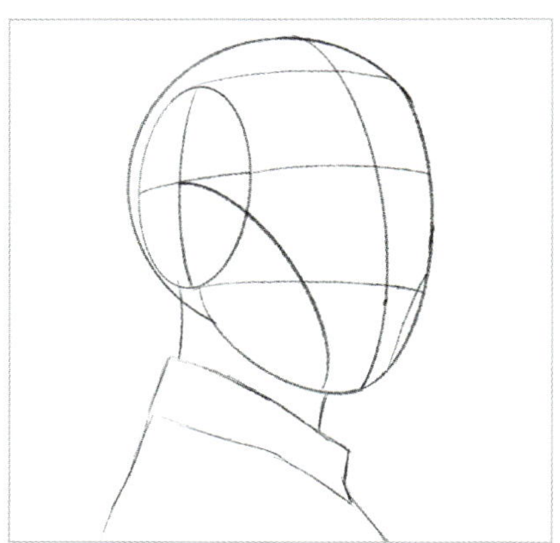

As with the other two angles, your first step is to draw a Loomis head with a graphite pencil and light pressure control.

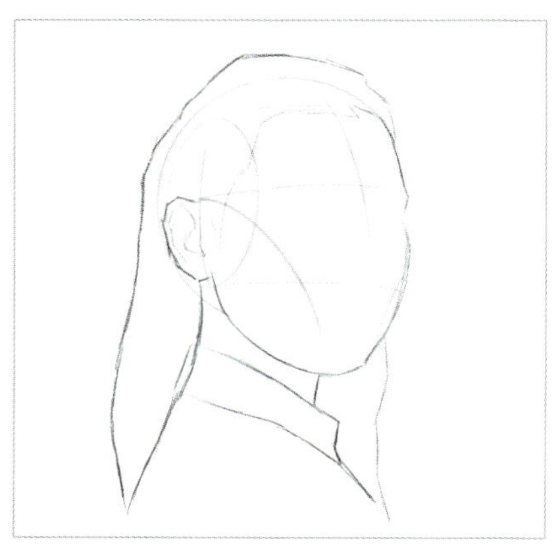

Sketch the basic shape of the ear in the bottom-rear quadrant on the side plane, then starting from the Loomis hairline, begin to draw the outline of the subject's hair. Use short pulls for the most control. (If you start going astray, you can also make adjustments sooner rather than later.)

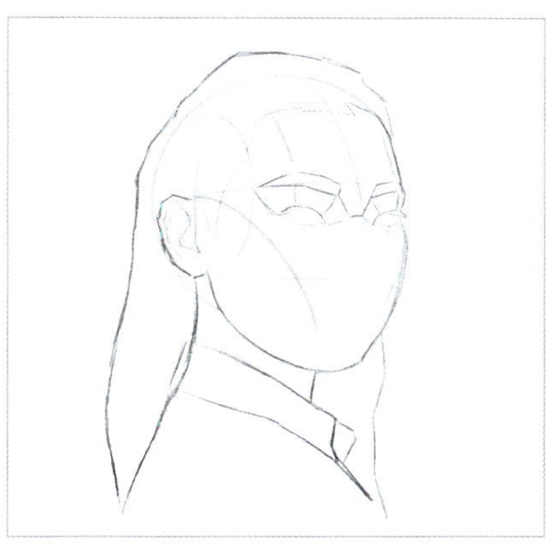

Using the Loomis brow line as your guide, draw the nose bridge plane and the eyebrows, which should connect to the top of the nose bridge lines. Next, draw the frame lines, then simply connect your frame lines to give you the basic shape of the eyes.

> **Best Practice:** *Remember, you also can sketch in the temple plane. That line will connect to your second frame line for the eyes.*

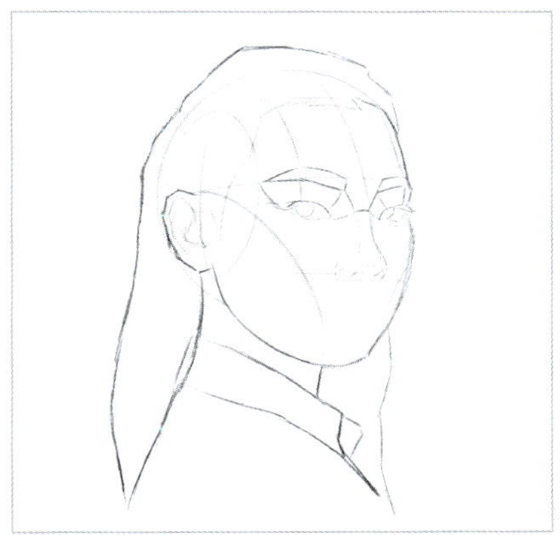

Using the Loomis nose line as the guide, draw the bottom plane of the nose followed by the nostrils and the edges of the bottom of the nose. Pull the nose ridge plane up and connect it with your nose bridge. It's also a good time to sketch in the nose slope planes.

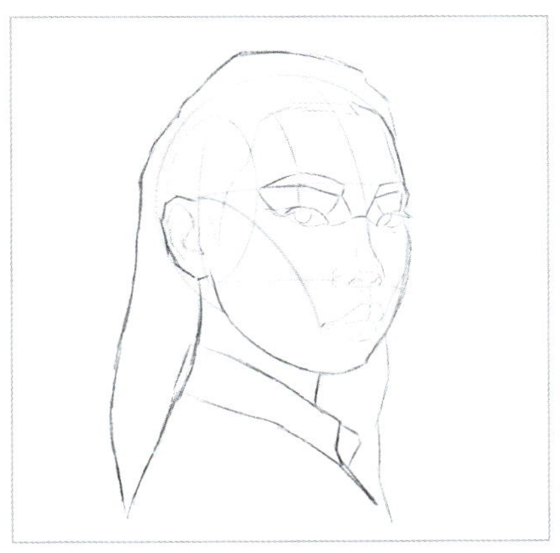

From the nose line, pull down two lines that represent the philtrum, draw in the corners of the mouth, and then connect them with the bottom of the philtrum. Sketch in the lower lip, draw the center line between the upper and lower lips, and then place the Asaro planes on the lips (two for the upper and three for the lower).

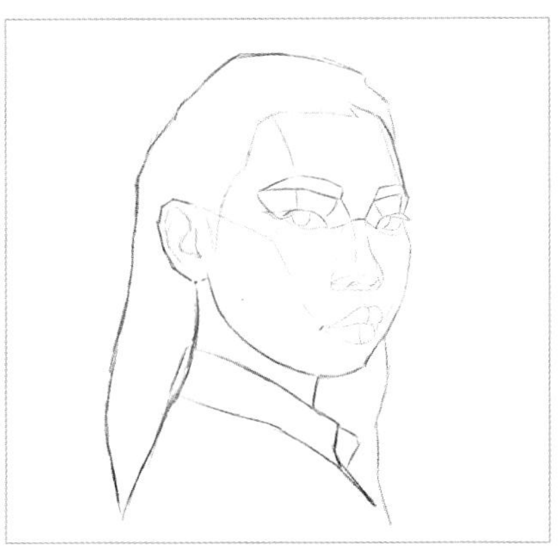

Now, begin to place the Asaro planes throughout the portrait. Remember that every face is different—you get to choose which planes to identify. For this angle, I decided to demonstrate a more reserved framing of the planes compared to the first two angles.

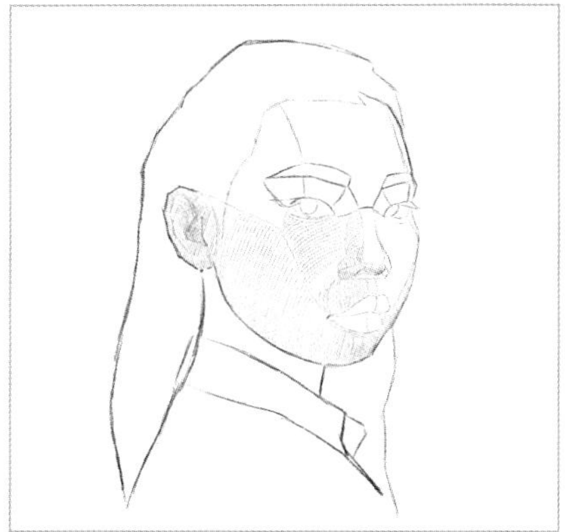

Start hatching the individual planes of the portrait, abiding by the underlying form of the subject's face.

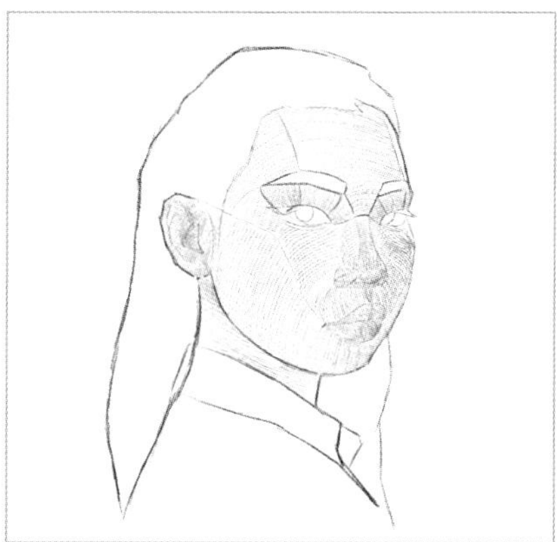

Continue to hatch until all the planes that comprise the face and neck have been completely covered.

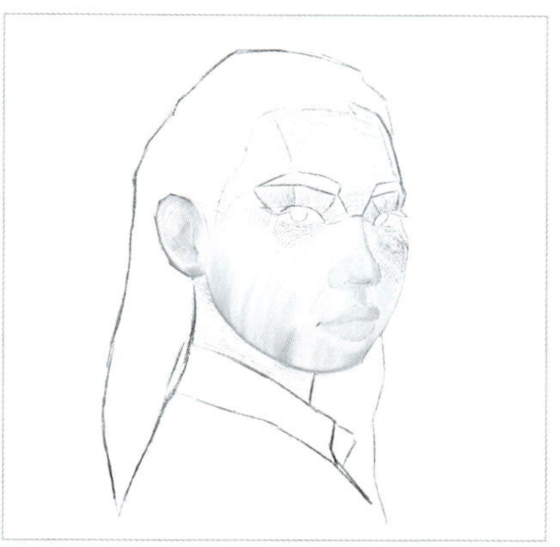

Switch to your smudger and begin to blend your hatch marks in the same direction you drew them.

> **Best Practice:** *Begin smudging from your subject's jaw line. After you've smudged the entire jaw line, pull up and then blend the jaw line itself. This will give the jaw a smooth look and round the face.*

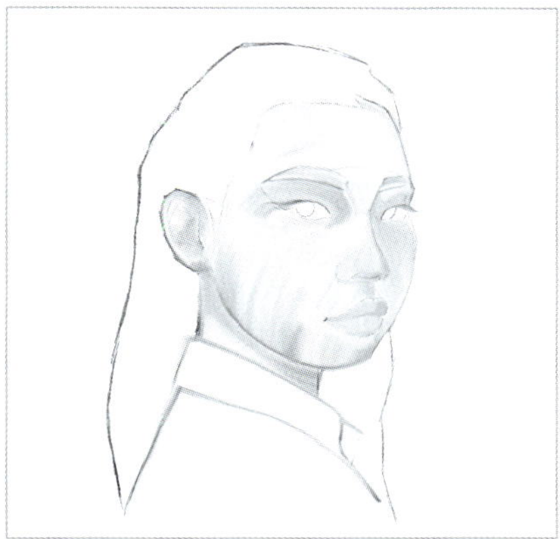

Continue to smudge your hatch marks until the whole drawing is blended, including the neck.

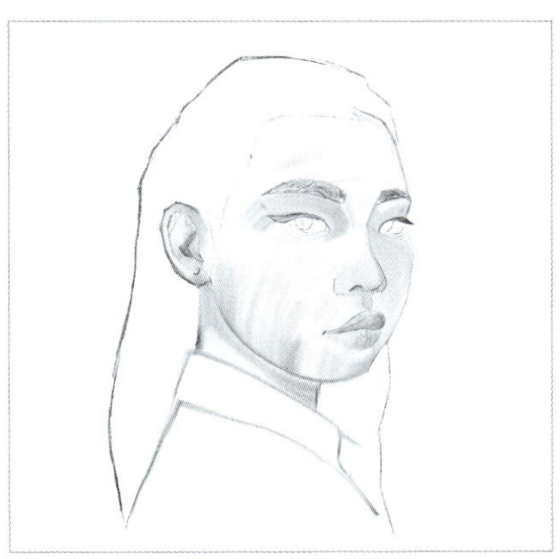

With a medium charcoal pencil, hatch another layer on top of the blended soft charcoal in the ear, eyebrows, eye lashes, and lips. This will help lower the value in those areas during the next round of blending.

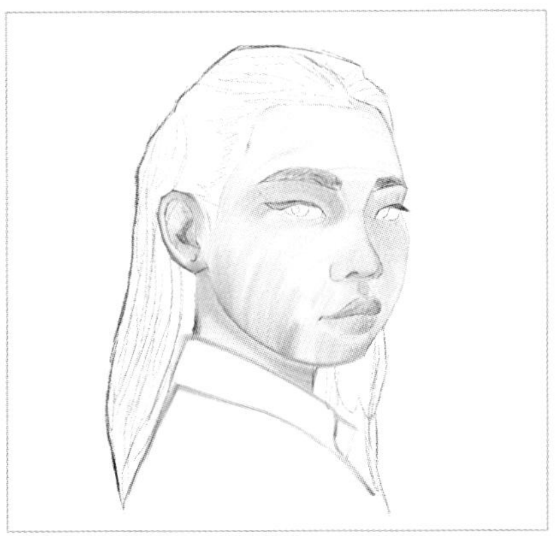

Return to your soft charcoal pencil, and sketch in the various segments of the subject's hair. Always pay attention to the flow of the hair!

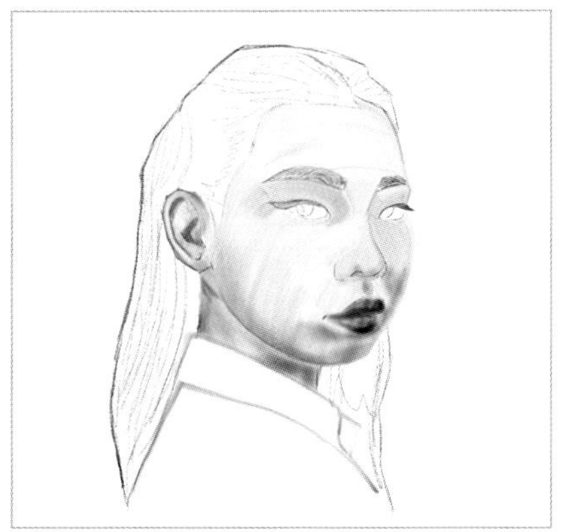

For smaller areas, such as the lips, use your smudger to blend. For areas that are more open, such as the chin and cheeks, use your brush to lower your values. Remember to use light pressure for both; you can always keep adding more charcoal to lower your values.

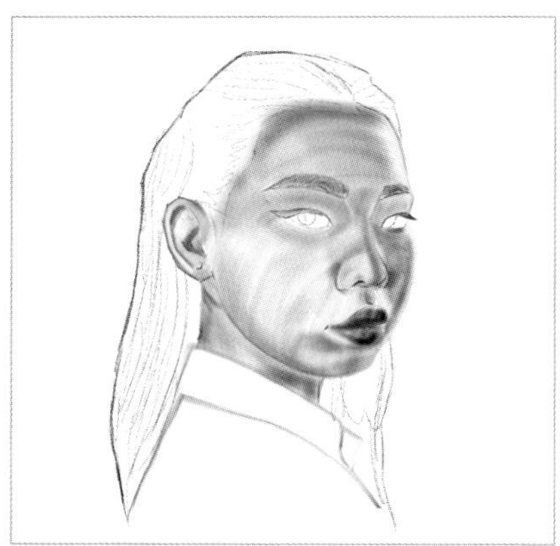

Continue to strategically lower your values in the areas that need more attention. The more you use the brush, the more gradation you will bring out and thus the smoother the drawing will become.

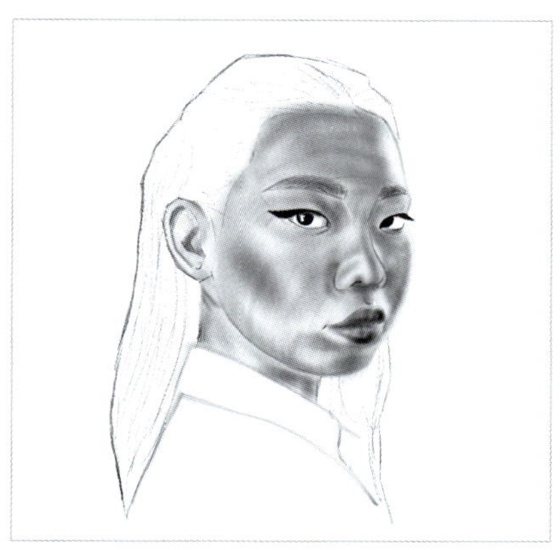

With a medium charcoal pencil, fill in the pupils and irises along with the eyeliner. Make sure to leave a small amount of light reflection in the subject's left eye. This will make her much more dynamic. Switch back to your brush and continue to strategically lower your values throughout the portrait.

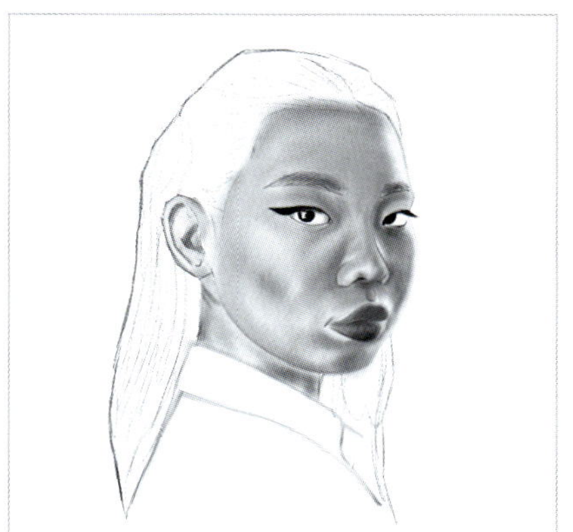

As you continue to brush that harshness will dissipate, and your portrait's skin will become smoother and smoother.

Best Practice: *If you want to blend the charcoal that you have on the paper but don't want to continue to lower the value, then simply blend with an empty brush.*

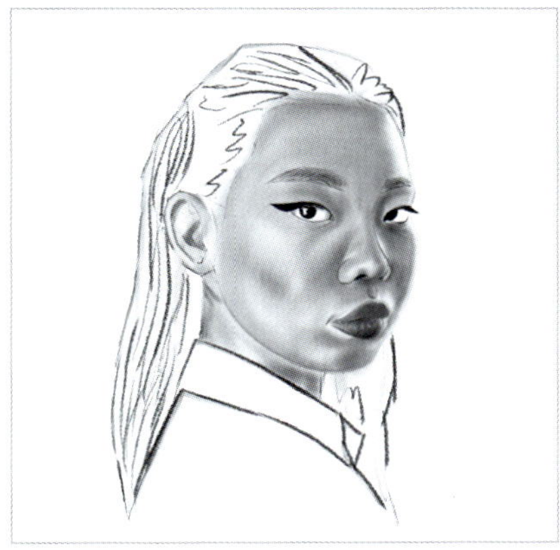

Using a soft charcoal pencil on its side in the overhand grip, start to draw in the hair segments. (I don't need to remind you to follow the flow of the hair again, do I?) This is also a great time to outline the collar and shoulder of the shirt.

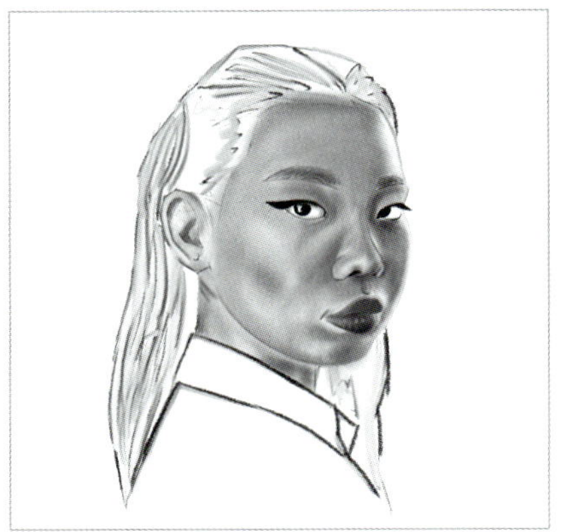

Switch to your smudger and begin blending the hair in the same direction you laid the charcoal down.

Best Practice: *Make sure to vary your pressure control throughout the hair. The variety of tonal values will make the hair more dynamic.*

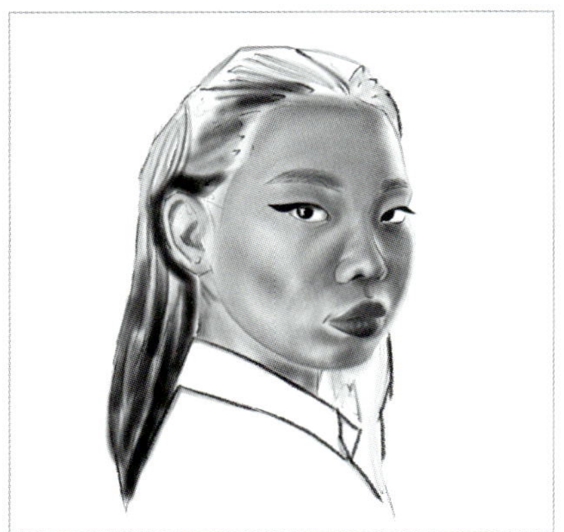

With your brush, lower the value within the hair. Depending on how low you want to go with your values, you could also use a medium charcoal pencil for this step. Just be sure to use light pressure so that you do not scratch the paper.

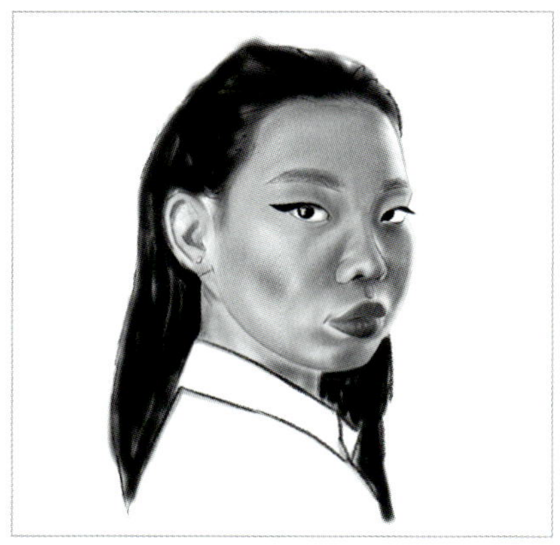

Continue to lower the value until all the hair is blended. You can also retrieve any high values throughout the hair with a kneaded eraser as you see fit. This will help your viewer's eye see the contrast in tones and the different segments of hair. Don't be afraid to leave some spots in the hair as mid-tones; they will help you accentuate the value scale and really bring out the hair's character.

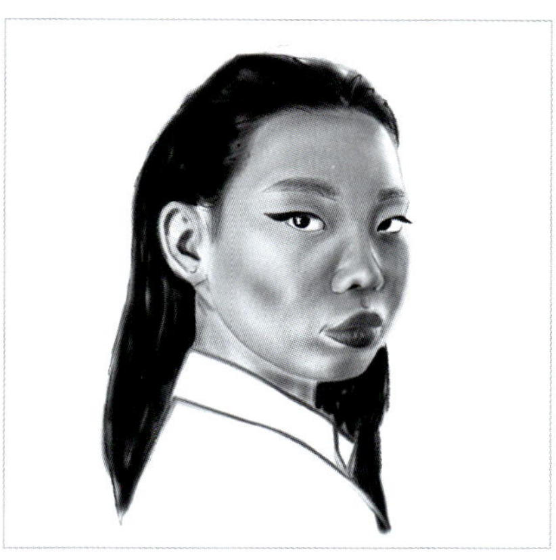

For the final step, go through the hair to retrieve any high values that you need to. You can also use a kneaded eraser for any high values or blends the face still needs.

> **Best Practice:** This is the perfect time to go through your drawing with a hard charcoal pencil, drawing in flyaway hairs, as well as details in the eyes, lips, and ears. Remember, the hard charcoal is your detail pencil for the three-layer method.

Project 13: Draw Three Final Portraits

Now it's your turn. For **Project 13**, draw a portrait of each reference subject. We've walked through the drawing flow of the three portrait angles so you could see the progression from start to finish, as well as how the Loomis and Asaro methods can be fused together to create something different, something simple, and something easy to apply. The next step is to practice, practice, practice. Immerse yourself in your art but remember that perfection is a myth.

If you still find yourself asking questions, scan the chapter's QR code to watch **How to Easily Draw a Portrait Part I, Part II, and Part III**, which offer real-time drawing flows of each angle. While you're on my YouTube channel, poke around my other videos. You'll find a massive library of step-by-step demonstrations, advice on charcoal drawing, and more to help you.

This book has been my pleasure to create for you, and I hope that it finds a special place in your home. Stay happy, stay healthy, and remember—never stop drawing!

Gallery

In this gallery you will see examples of portraits I have created over the years using the methods you have learned throughout this book. There are portraits created using the traditional mediums of charcoal and colored pencils, as well as ones created digitally using the Procreate app. What I want you to take away from this book is that the methods you have learned can be applied to any medium you wish. These principles are the foundation for creating a beautiful portrait, no matter if you are a traditional or digital artist. I highly encourage you to try both approaches if you can, and remember, never stop drawing.

Digital Portraits

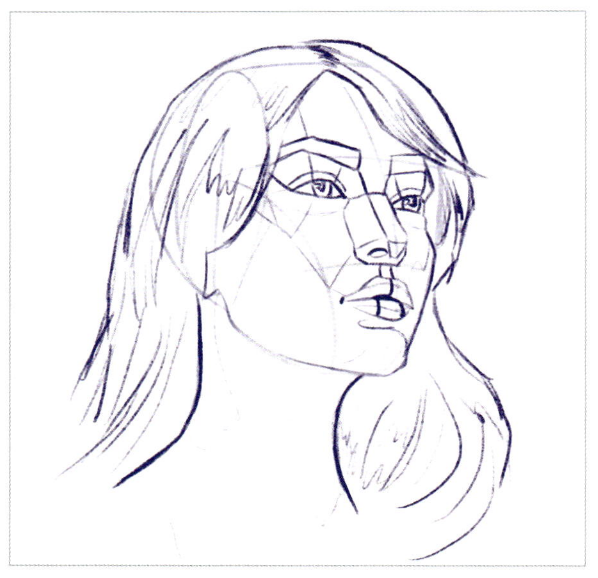

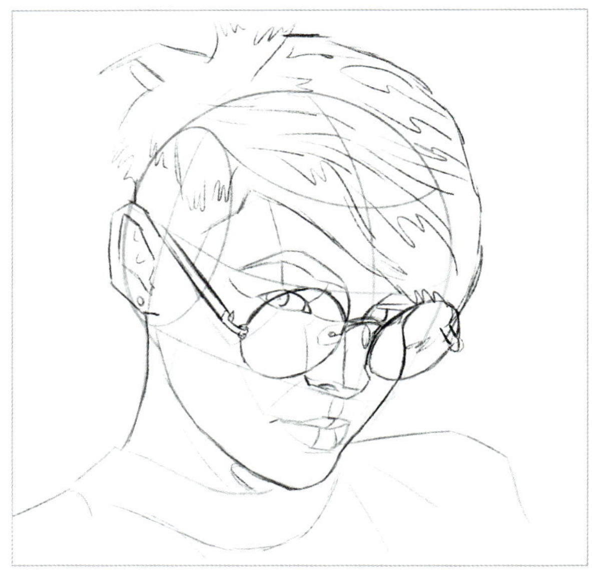

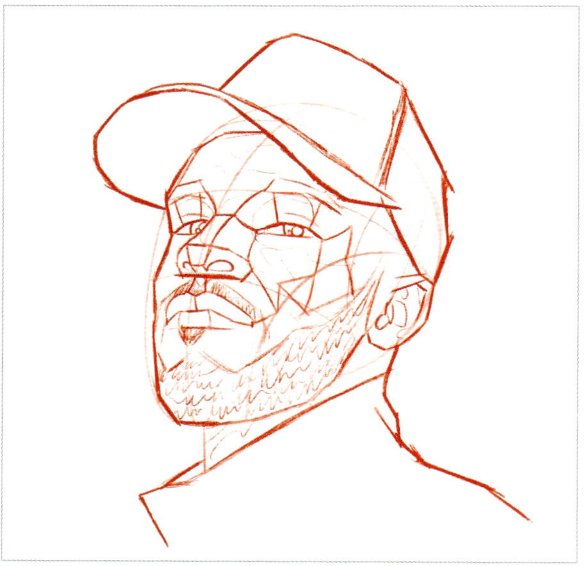

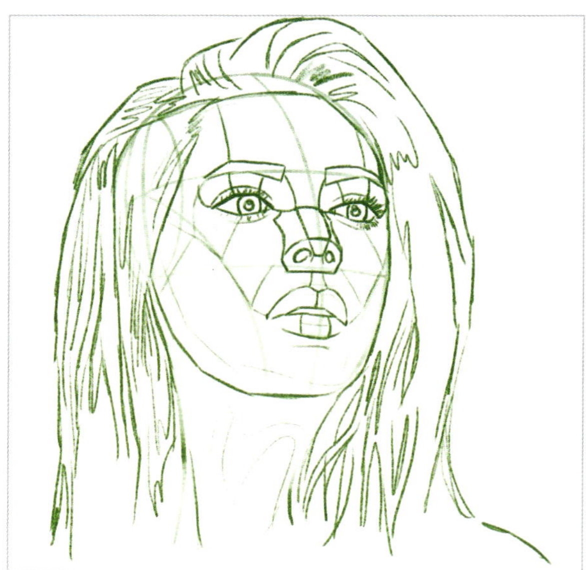

Traditional Portraits

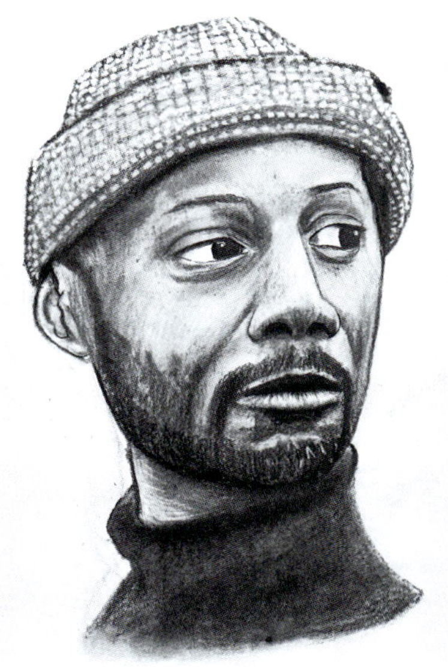

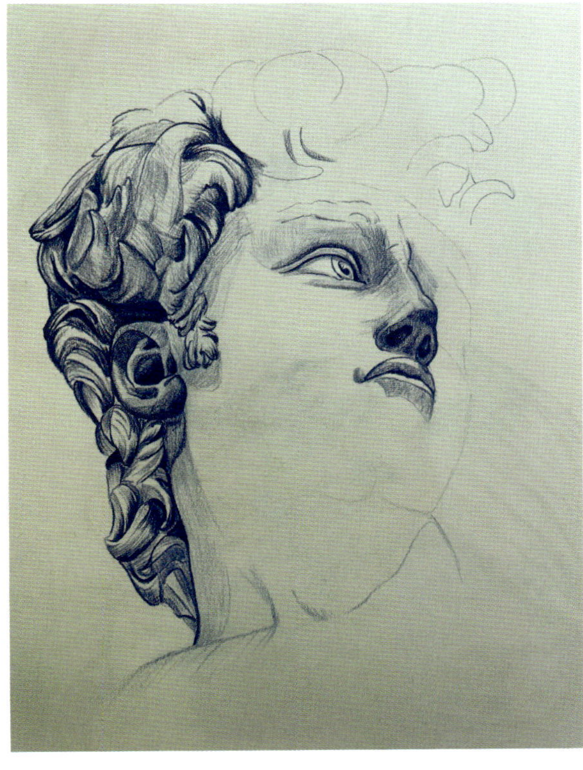

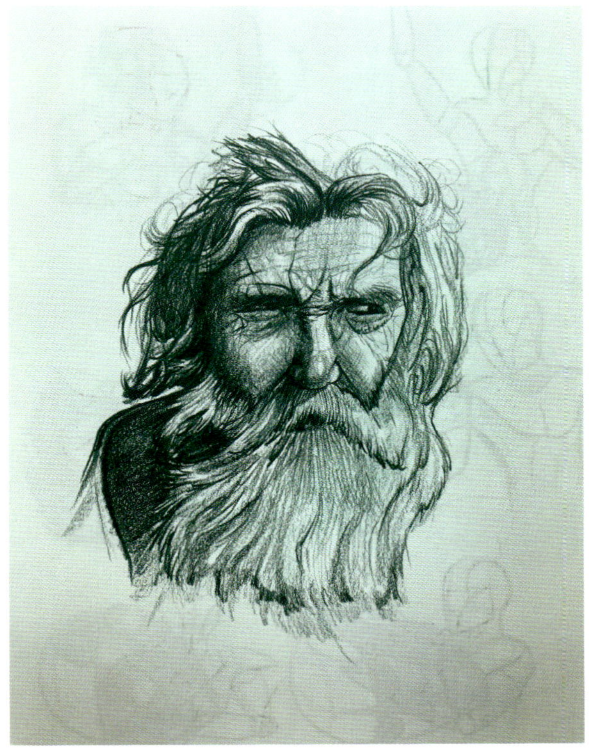

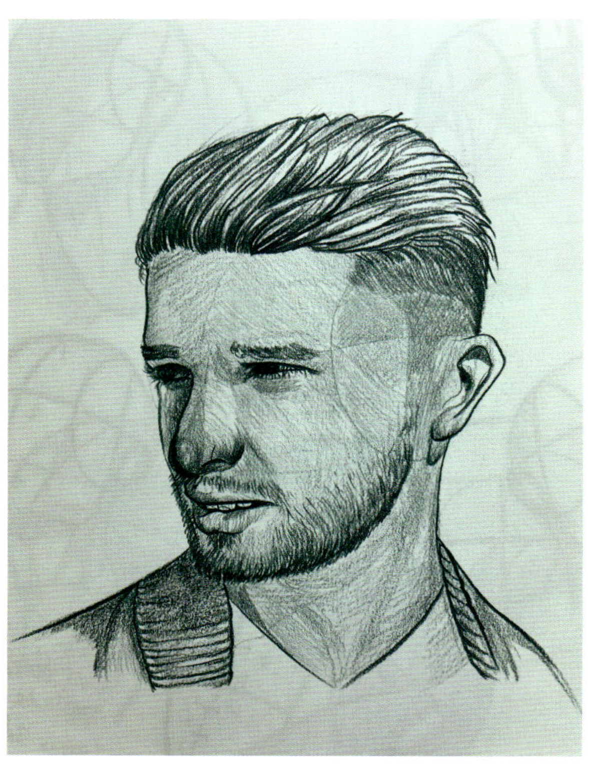

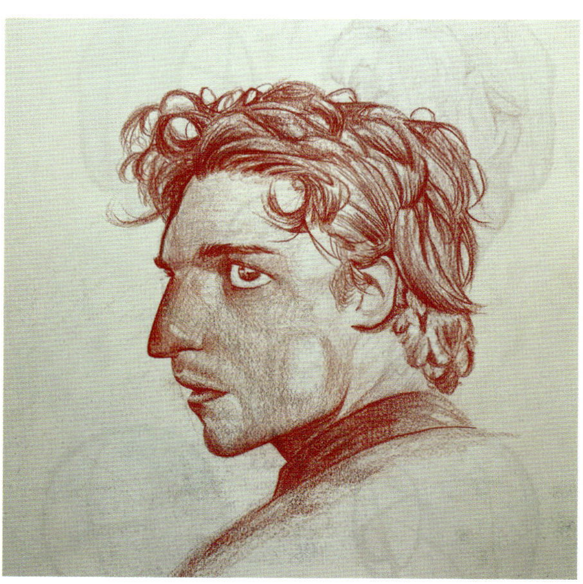

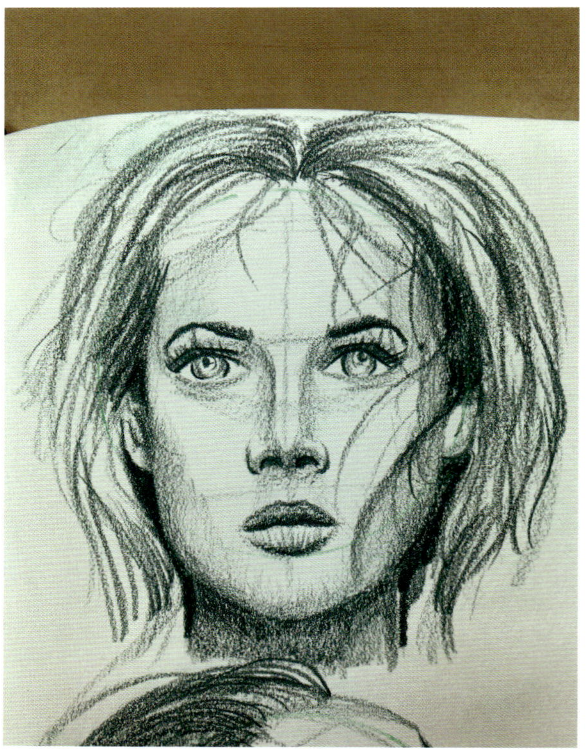

Acknowledgments

If you want to go fast, go alone. If you want to go far, go together.
—African Proverb

I was always able to draw better than most. It was always in my back pocket, yet I never used it for anything. It wasn't until one cold November night when I was asked by my now wife to draw a white rose for her. So, I sketched her a white rose on some printer paper that I had. It didn't take much more than 15 minutes or so and I handed it to her. She gasped and said, "you can draw like this?" to which I replied, "Of course, but you can't make any money doing it though." The next thing I knew she bought me a sketch book, pencils, a drawing desk, and began asking me to draw this for her, and then that, and then this too. That is how the journey began for me and I can say with absolute certainty that if it wasn't for Chandra Messer asking me to draw her that white rose on that cold November night that this book would simply not exist.

Telling people what your plans are is an interesting venture because it is many things, but it is rarely what you expect. When we announced to the world that I was going to pursue art, we were promptly told "good luck." However, there were people along the way that showed their support for the dream. When you are a visual artist, commissions are your life blood, and I had a handful of people that commissioned me to create works for them and supported me in their own way throughout the years.

My Aunt Barbara: Thank you for commissioning me to draw your dogs' portraits and for being an early supporter of my art.

My Uncle Joe: Thank you for sharing your love of the finer things in life with me and commissioning me to draw some of your favorite dinosaurs.

My Grandma Gettings: Thank you for always smiling and asking me how the art is going. Thank you for always telling me to "not grow up" as this helped me to look at the world differently and eventually become an artist.

My art teacher Mr. Kincaid: Thank you for writing me your letter of recommendation when I was in high school. You were the first person to ever believe in my artistic abilities.

My friend Tad: You were one of my first commissions when I was struggling to make ends meet in Seattle and I thank you so much for having me draw your daughter's portrait for her birthday.

My friend Nic: I always thought it was funny that you called your cat "Ms. Pickles". Thank you for commissioning me to draw her for you because I know how much you love her.

My friends Emily & Roy: You guys remind me so much of Chandra and myself. Thank you for your elk commission and for sharing your friendship with us.

My mother Lori: Raising me must have been a challenge but you managed to pull it off. Thank you for being my loudest cheerleader throughout this entire journey. I also want to thank you for always asking me for more and more of my artwork. I love you very much.

My brothers Colton and Hunter: Colton, thank you for helping me with the legalities of life. I appreciate our talks about film, literature, and the arts more than you know. Hunter, thank you for always helping me navigate my art through my technology. It has helped me so very much.

My cousin Basil: I want to thank you for our long phone calls talking about the channel and about life. Your support has been unwavering throughout the years, and I wanted you to know how much I appreciate you.

My friend Jared Grubb and family: Thank you for always being so happy to see and talk to me. You were there for me through the hardest of times in my life, and you helped me in ways that are hard to explain. Thank you for your friendship and for being an extended part of my family. I hope your babies love their drawings and that they inspire them to draw throughout their adulthoods.

My Publisher (Rocky Nook) and Editor: Kelly, thank you so much for seeing the value in my artwork and reaching out to us in partnership for this book. It has been a wonderful and humbling experience and one that I hope that I am able to do again with you to some capacity.

Lastly, I wanted to acknowledge **my father**: Sometimes I wake up and I wonder what you would look like now. What you would be doing for work, or if you would still be wearing the same seven shirts that you would routinely wear throughout the week. I wonder if we would still go out to our favorite Mexican restaurant and order our same plates of delicious food. However, there is one thing that I do not wonder and that is how proud of me I know you would be. I wish I could tell you about the journey and how much fun I've had. I wish I could tell you about the hard knocks and the sweet victories throughout the process. I know we only had a limited amount of time together in this life, but I want you to know that even though you are not able to read this book, your influence helped to shape it into a reality. Thank you for showing me how there is a right way and a wrong way to do something. Thank you for taking me to the mountain top just to sit there in silence and listen to the universe as we felt the wind blow through our hair together. I wouldn't be the person that I am today if it hadn't been for you. I appreciate everything that you did and didn't do for me. Most of all I want to thank you for teaching me to actually stop and smell the roses. I love you dad.

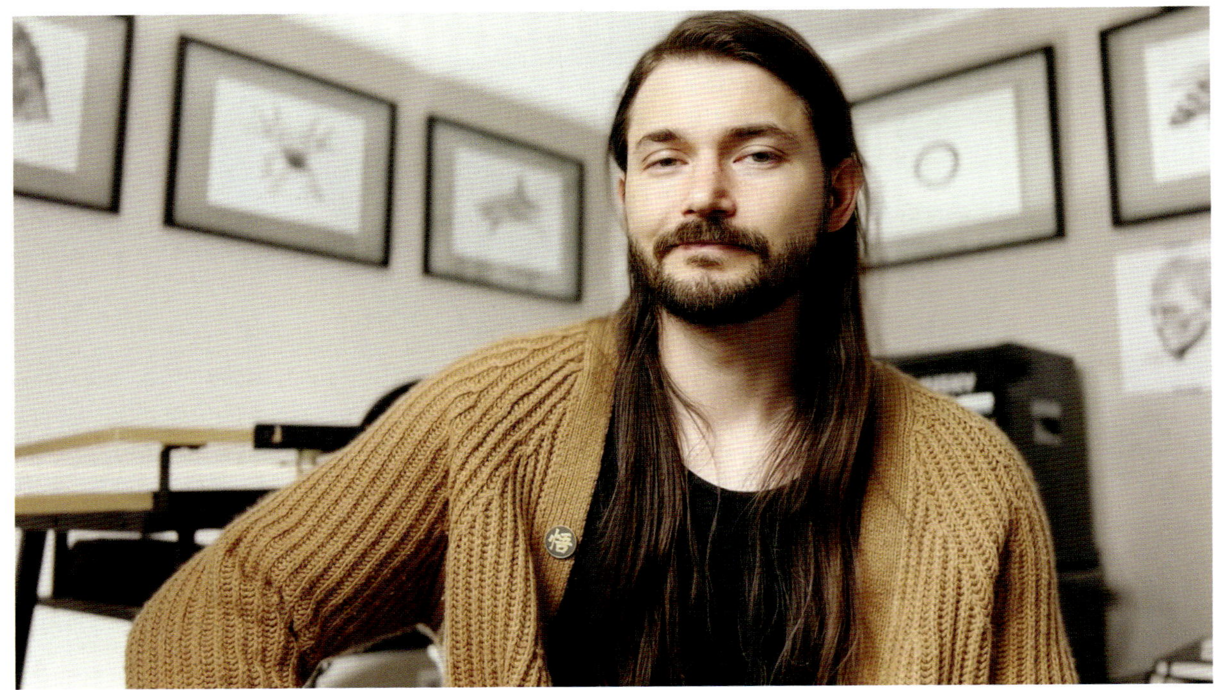

Author Bio

Braden Messer is a visual artist who specializes in teaching complex drawing concepts via simplified methods. He spent years honing his skills studying the works of names such as Andrew Loomis, John Asaro, and Leonardo Da Vinci. He co-founded Messer Creations where he creates drawing tutorial classes on platforms such as YouTube, Skillshare, and Instagram. He has spent the last 6 years making drawing concepts like the Loomis method easily accessible through his online videos so that everyone in the world with an internet connection can easily learn and express themselves through drawing.